how to be a BETA MALE

ROBERT CRAMPTON

how to be a BETA MALE

Brilliant bits and bobs about being a bloke

Doubleday

LONDON • TORONTO • SYDNEY • AUCKLAND • JOHANNESBURG

TRANSWORLD PUBLISHERS
61–63 Uxbridge Road, London W5 5SA
www.penguin.co.uk

Transworld is part of the Penguin Random House group of companies
whose addresses can be found at global.penguinrandomhouse.com

First published in Great Britain in 2017 by Doubleday
an imprint of Transworld Publishers

A CIP catalogue record for this book
is available from the British Library.

ISBN 9780857525024

Typeset in 11.25/14.25pt Minion by Falcon Oast Graphic Art Ltd.
Printed and bound by Clays Ltd, Bungay, Suffolk.

Penguin Random House is committed to a sustainable
future for our business, our readers and our planet. This book
is made from Forest Stewardship Council® certified paper.

1 3 5 7 9 10 8 6 4 2

To Nicola Almond, my darling wife

Introduction

New reader catch-up starts here. Urgent generic American accent suggested but not obligatory.

Previously on Beta Male . . .

I was born in August 1964 in Blackpool, Lancashire. Aged six, I moved to the western suburbs of Hull in what was then, and now is again, East Yorkshire. Unlike many (possibly most) of the people who get published in Britain (or indeed those who work for *The Times*), I attended my local comprehensive school. That doesn't mean, however (southerners take note), that my dad was a miner, docker, ship-builder or steelworker. He was in fact a college lecturer, while my mum was a teacher. I grew up in a four-bedroomed, mock-Tudor semi in the suburbs. Opposite a golf course, if you please. Contrary to the assumptions of most published writers in the UK, you can hail from north of Watford, not attend a private school and yet still not keep coal in the bath or race whippets. You can even – who knew? – be solidly middle class. As I am.

Indeed those of us (north, south, east and west) whose background includes a combination of a majority of the foregoing factors actually constitute a majority of the British population.

My school wasn't bad, yet neither was it much good, certainly not in terms of encouraging the ambitions of anyone who aspired to a career even slightly out of the ordinary. I'm guessing many readers had a similar experience. Hey-ho.

The best thing about my secondary education was, both of us aged eleven, meeting the girl who is now, years later (far too many years for my liking, I'd have been delighted to get it on there and then, pervy as that may sound), my wife. Having stayed friends in the interim, we started going out in 1990, aged twenty-five.

I left school in 1982 and then, in 1986, having mucked around travelling and protesting and generally making a damned nuisance of myself, I gained entrance to – and attended, and endured, and what's more even graduated from – Oxford University. There, thanks in large part to the urging of my more worldly peers (the esteemed commentators Jonny Freedland and Ian Katz foremost among them), I decided to pursue a career in the press. Shortly after leaving Oxford, moving to London and starting to work in newspapers, I also managed (to my enduring surprise) to persuade my old school chum Nicola that we should get together.

Double result! Becoming a journalist and shacking up with Nicola were, emphatically, the best two decisions I have ever made.

I started at *The Times* in 1991. Nicola and I moved to our home in Hackney, east London, where we still live, in 1995. Our son, Sam, was born in 1997; we got married in 1998; our daughter, Rachel, was born in 1999. When I began writing Beta Male, therefore, my children were aged four and two respectively. Nicola and I were both thirty-seven. As of this summer, 2017, Sam is twenty, Rachel eighteen, Nicola and I are fifty-two. So what follows is partly about Nicola and me moving from the last knockings of late youth into hardcore middle age, and more significantly about our children's journey from infancy to adulthood.

I should make clear that while my face, hair, brain, soul, midriff and most of all (oo-er, ouch) knees register every minute of my half (and a bit) century, my wife barely looks a day older than the day I first met her in the school youth club that autumn evening in 1975. We took on some other kids at table football. I'd played the game before, she hadn't. Even so, Nicola swiftly calculated the optimal approach and told me what to do. Obviously (because I fancied her rotten), I obeyed. Equally obviously, we won.

Not a great deal has changed since.

That, in essence, is what this book is about: timeless husband-and-wife comedy, in other words. I hope so, at any rate.

If I were to go a little deeper, which is to say be a bit more pretentious, I might claim that what follows also concerns – treated appropriately satirically and yet I trust sympathetically – the nature of modern masculinity. Or even, perhaps, the crisis – tragedy? absurdity? farce? – of same.

Whatevs. It's there if you want to find it. And if you can't be arsed, just enjoy the farting and knob jokes, no one will think any the less of you.

1 September 2001

The Mind, Body, Spirit section in the bookshop takes up twice the room allowed for Religion and Philosophy put together.

Shelf space does not lie. He who wishes to improve himself – or more often, I think the sales figures show, herself – turns to the convenience texts of the new prophets rather than the complicated texts of the old. If *The Little Book of Detox* and the like can sort you out, why bother with the very big book of Revelation?

Then again, why bother spending even £2.50 when you can read my reports from the front line of the struggle for self-improvement, each week, here on this page? I am like you! I too want to be better. I too want to improve my mind and my body. Most of all, I too want to improve, heal if you will, what the bookshelves call my spirit. And, like you, I too want to accomplish all of this in the easiest, most effort-free way possible.

I am the perfect patient; I will be the perfect guide. Neither cynic nor idiot, sceptic nor true believer, my mind is open, yet not so ajar that air is blowing through my head. Of course, my personality is unbalanced, sometimes dangerously so, yet I retain coherence almost all of the time. Of the Big Three, my mind is the one in the best shape. I can do sums and spell; I know a lot of facts, some of them not entirely useless; I'm a good listener; I can talk, think and write clearly enough to earn a living so doing; my imagination is active – indeed, in my more paranoid phases, I would rather it were less so.

On the other hand, my concentration is poor. I am intellectually lazy. I'm bad at carrying thoughts or action through to a conclusion. I have no world view. I have few creative or practical skills. I know no language other than English. I can't (or won't, we shall find out) make, cook, grow, draw or repair anything worth a damn. Blank deserts stretch where knowledge and appreciation of the classics, music and science should flower. I still have the desire, and perhaps the will, to turn this situation around.

My body stands in more urgent need of attention than my brain. Although I have recently accepted that I'll never be taller than 5 feet 10 (and a quarter) inches, the rest is up for grabs. I'm 13 stone 10 pounds – consult one of those weight charts and you'll see I'm borderline clinically obese. In my mid-thirties, maybe while I was asleep, someone strapped a wobbly, skin-coloured jelly around my waist, lashed it tight with those special 'fat bandages' and sneaked off without me noticing. Carry children's party food around under my shirt? No! The jelly must go. I also get headaches, exhaustion and mysterious twinges in the back.

I don't want to exaggerate. For a thirty-seven-year-old man, father of two small children, in a moderately stressful job in an extremely stressful city, I'm doing OK. I cycle to work and hardly ever get a cab home, even when it's raining. I'm clinging to the ledge of late youth rather than sliding down the slope of early middle age, though my fingertips are beginning to loosen their grip. I want to cling on a while longer.

I am watchful – last year, I realized that I was drinking too much, close to a bottle a night. ('Close to' as in drink one bottle, make inroads into the next.) This year, I've cut my alcohol intake to an average of twenty-three units a week. That's not bad for a journalist. I'd like to reduce it further. And I smoke. That's something I will deal with. But not yet. As any serious smoker knows, any programme of self-improvement means the immediate postponement of any plans to give up, thus allowing the self-improvement the chance to create the ideal conditions in which to give up at some point in the future. Soon.

What troubles me most is my spirit. My soul. It's not in good shape. In public, I'm fine: a good father, husband, friend and colleague. In private, I lose my temper more than I should. Sometimes, I smash things. Often, I struggle to contain the symptoms of a bad mood. The other day I got angry and my four-year-old son said: 'Is it a f****** hell time, Daddy?'

It was like a film. I ruffled his hair and said, 'No, Sam.' I thought: Bob, sort yourself out.

I harbour irrational hatreds for people I barely know. I harbour perfectly rational hatreds for people I do know, who wronged me years ago, yet I can find no sustainable way of alleviating the hatred. I have nightmares. Sometimes I have day-mares – unbidden visions of death and destruction. Sound bad? You don't know the half. I also chew my fingernails and have very bad wind.

So now I cup a hand to my ear. What's that I can hear you saying? 'Get some help, you lazy fat nutter.' Well, that's exactly what this column is about. I've tried lots of -isms, -erapies and -ologies already. I'm open-minded. In the coming months, I will seek out treatments and advice – New Age, old age, middle age – to solve all my problems, of mind, body and spirit, large, medium and small. I shall report as fairly as I can on the efficacy of what I do. By the end of this tour of duty, I hope to take my place as an amazingly erudite, finely tuned, perfectly balanced guru of personal happiness. If not, at least I shall be better informed. And so shall you.

15 September 2001

I am struck by how much so-called New Age advice is remarkably similar to what many people might call good, old-fashioned common sense. Take away the long words, and much of the red-hot, life-changing insight for the twenty-first century can be recast thus: eat your greens; make sure you have an early night; get some fresh air; go for a nice long walk; sit down and have a glass of water/cup of tea/proper think/good cry; sit up straight; take a deep breath; an apple a day keeps the dentist away; make a list; cross that bridge when you come to it; smile and the world smiles with you. Whole chapters of the old protocol are, defiantly, back. Some books even advocate haircuts and cold showers.

Fashions were beginning to change, but still, most people of my generation probably received some or all of this instruction as children. These nostrums, like the Lord's Prayer and Beatles and Abba songs, are buried in our psyche. We do not live by all of them all of the time . . . yet, deep down, with the possible exceptions of the haircut and the shower, we know that we *should*.

(Personally, I am convinced of the therapeutic value of a haircut, though I don't hold with cold showers. They leave me feeling lonely, vulnerable and angry, the victim of some alien temperature dial I have failed to understand.)

I'm not sure about younger generations – but those of us most likely to be seeking personal refurbishment have a good grounding. The walls may be sagging, the furniture threadbare, but the house stands on solid rock. However dilapidated the external structure, however tatty the interior decor, our familiarity with these exhortations gives us an excellent foundation on which to begin repairs. Reconnect with all that fresh air and vegetables stuff – ridiculed for so long but, as it turns out, absolutely *correct* – and we are well on our way.

4

Then it gets difficult. Not all of the New Age commandments can be translated into a handy old age platitude. Proper breathing, yes. Imagining little spaces in your head where you can seek refuge in times of anger or fear, where you can dress up and climb mountains, fly with eagles and swim with dolphins . . . no. Nothing I was told as a child equates to any of that. I don't recall Mr Akers, my headmaster at primary school, lovely man that he was, ever starting an assembly with the words: 'Now, children. I know life is hard sometimes, but I've always found it helps if you pretend you're wearing a big orange cloak . . .'

So when I see Jo Smith-Oliver, reflexologist, and when I'm lying on her couch and she asks me to think of a place where I can feel alone and calm (this technique is called visualization, much mentioned in most self-help books), then I feel the ground beneath the couch start to wobble a little. But I want help so I do as I am told – not because I trust reflexology in particular, but because I trust Jo Smith-Oliver.

Jo asked me what was most bothering me at the moment. I said: the tendency to lose my temper. She asked when this happened. I said: usually, at the end of the weekend. Why, she asked, because you know you've got work the next day? I said: no, the opposite. Much as I love them, I find spending long periods with my small children difficult – much more difficult than doing this job. My bad mood on a Sunday evening is not caused by the imminent resumption of work, but rather the accumulated frustrations of forty-eight hours' domesticity. (I can't believe I am alone in experiencing Monday morning as Friday night, and vice versa, especially among other men. Please, chaps, feel free to reassure me. I'm out on a limb here.)

Anyway, I said to Jo: when I was a little boy, we lived opposite a golf course. Between our road and the course was a belt of trees, ten yards across. We used to go over there, my brother and I, and we'd wait as the golfers hit their tee shots from away down the slope to our left. If they were any good, the ball landed on the fairway right in front of us. A few seconds, half a minute maybe: you could crawl out of the trees, snatch the ball, crawl back and listen. 'Where the bloody hell's my ball? I'm sure it went straight down the middle,' and so on. Most amusing.

As I got older, I progressed from this peculiarly middle-class, and yet satisfying, form of delinquency. I'd go into the trees alone, and sit ten feet up, on a summer evening, warm, shaded and hidden by the leaves, feeling a bit daring, but safe and in control. Twenty-five years later, I find I can still climb that tree. The trick is to be able to climb it with the world's naughtiest four-year-old at bath time, and not just when I'm lying, eyes closed, on a couch. Jo Smith-Oliver can't hold my feet all the time.

I see it this way: we have all these memories, bits of video if you like, all jumbled up. The task is to sort all the tapes we still want for ease of access, like putting all your CDs in alphabetical order on a rainy afternoon. You do a bit of editing, focusing, labelling. Put another way, you have a jolly good tidy-up. A clear-out. A spring clean even. You choose that bit of calming-down video that you need, that tree in the summer of '76, and you get it ready to press play the instant that next wave of aggravation breaks over your head.

I'm going to give it a try.

17 November 2001

You wouldn't believe the week I've had! Busy, busy, busy. Monday morning: Alexander technique off Oxford Street. Monday afternoon: manicure in Wapping, false nails sculpted on to my own ragged stumps. Tuesday: more Alexander technique. Wednesday: acupuncture, near Waterloo. Thursday: across to St John's Wood for palm-reading, then metamorphics (like reflexology, but tickles more). Friday: back to WC1 for yet more Alexander technique. All this and I'm also wearing a shiny magnetic bracelet and (so far this is known only to those I trust with my life, but, hey, I'm in the business of reaching out to strangers) a dinky little magnetic ankle chain under my right sock. Quite a week, no?

What's more, I'm sticking fast to the no-wheat, no-dairy policy – no problem. Must be about eight weeks now. I consult my records . . . yes, indeed: eight weeks as I write this. I've said it before but I'll say it again: this diet is a *revelation*! I'm eating more than I've ever eaten in my life, yet the weight is still coming off – a pound a week, regular as clockwork. More energy, fewer aches and pains, heroic bowel movements. Walking tall, chi fair pulsing through my meridians, pressure points clear as a bell . . . could anyone ask for more out of life? Could they? I don't think so.

Be all that as it may, I have a failure to report, I'm afraid. A setback! My fingernails, briefly (albeit falsely) perfect on Monday afternoon, are now back to how they looked on Monday morning. The falsies were not a success.

I held my hands together in front of my chest for inspection: fingers straight, palms down, like a child impersonating a rabbit. The nail technician – *not* a manicurist, actually, manicurists don't do false nails – pursed her lips. 'Shortest I've seen in four years,' she said. 'Very bad. A challenge. They should call me Anneka.' In fact, I think I *will* call my nail technician Anneka – the nail failure was all about me, not her. She's very good at her job, Anneka. She won a prize once, at the Nail Show at Earls Court, and she's about to open her own salon.

She continued her inspection. Overgrown cuticles, 'like a piece of cling film creeping up your nail'. Lots of dead cells. And, 'You bite the skin as well, don't you?' I nodded in shame. We sat in silence for a while. 'Ever had your nails done before?'

she asked, knowing the answer. I said, truth is, Anneka, I've never paid any attention to my fingernails *whatsoever*, no way, no how – apart, of course, from viciously biting them for twenty-odd years. Another silence followed. I asked whether anyone's fingernails could actually be in a worse state than mine. Anneka mulled this over for quite some time. 'If they'd trapped them in a car door,' she replied, and got to work.

She quickly determined that tips – plastic falsies – were not an option. 'There's nothing to attach them to.' Instead, she would have to clip a bendy metal bridge, called a form, to each finger, align it just so, then carefully paint a fingernail-coloured acrylic mix, which looks like a blob of wax, over my nail and out on to the form. Make sense? The mix sets; she buffs it (no filing, potentially damaging) into shape, moves on to the next one. Your own fingernail then grows unmolested underneath the false one. Can you bite them? I asked. 'You'd break your teeth and it'd taste horrible,' she replied. No biting then.

After two months – during which Anneka would regularly have to 'backfill' the false nail as your own nail grew – you would have achieved, in nail technician shorthand, 'length'. Then, you can do what you want: colour, or natural, or 'French' – that is, a white 'free edge' (the end bit), pink over your nail base. 'There's a lot more involved in it than most people realize,' said Anneka, crouched low with her brushes and her nippers, her pens and pushers, her 600-grit buffer and her bottle of tea tree and fish oil conditioner. Readily, I agreed. 'It's quite an art, really,' she said. 'I like arty things.'

The reason I now know so much about fingernails is that the whole painstaking business took two hours, or about twelve minutes per finger. I can't remember when I began to feel sick – around about the ring finger of my right hand, I reckon. Not long. At first, I thought it was the acrylic mix. 'Yes, the smell can get to you,' said Anneka. 'Guess that's why I'm mad!'

But it wasn't the mix, it was the filing – sorry, buffing. 'I actually do feel a bit nauseous,' I said.

'It's funny what things make people go funny,' said Anneka. 'I hate ice cream. It's too soft and . . . *cold*.'

I prayed for it to be over. Eventually, somehow, it was – and, after many years, I had fingernails again. They looked natural, they looked good – and I *hated* them. Hated the feel of them, hated the way when they touched anything a bolt of nausea shot up my arm, down my throat and into my stomach, hated the *falseness* of them. Anneka packed up her box of tricks.

'Your wife's going to be *so* jealous!' she said.

Is there any way, I asked, trying to sound all casual, that I could get these off by myself?

'No,' she said sternly. 'They must be soaked off in acetone.'

Huh! Not true! Pair of pliers did the job in no time. Ah well: you win some, you lose some.

1 December 2001

To Waterloo for acupuncture, and a bright, down-to-earth lady called Helen Fielding. Helen lives in Bristol, unofficial capital of the New Age, travels to London once a week. She grew up, an engineer's daughter, in Halifax. I thought: here's a woman I can do business with.

I quizzed her about meridians and chi energy, not needling her, just trying to pin down what these things actually are. She sympathized, quoting her own father's exasperation: 'But, love, if you can't see it, smell it, touch it, taste it, hear it or weld it, it doesn't exist!' I thought: well said, Helen Fielding's dad! Then I thought: hold on a second, Mr Fielding, what about electricity? You can *touch* electricity, if you stick a knife in a toaster, but you can't sense it any other way, and I don't think you can weld it.

Maybe chi energy is like electricity, you know it's there, and you can best judge its presence by its effects, rather than inherent qualities. Helen agreed. The point, she said, is to access it, harness it. Cut someone open, you won't find any chi. But stick a needle a quarter-inch into them and, undeniably, good things happen.

Sceptics beware, because acupuncture has two big points in its favour. First, for many conditions, enough evidence suggests that it works. A child has eczema, the parents try everything, then acupuncture cures the eczema. A lady has spondylitis, the needles go in, her pain is alleviated. A smoker wants to stop, acupuncture helps. The puncturer says it's all to do with the five elements and ying and yang and the shady side of the mountain and the twelve channels. The patient says: maybe, maybe not – truth is, I'm not fussed, I've got what I wanted. Most people have much the same attitude to penicillin.

Second, acupuncture is alternative only in the West. The Chinese have practised it for centuries. Most hospitals in China have dual wings – Western and traditional – and they cross-refer. Maybe here, with our yoga, diets, supplements and gyms, we're closer to that situation than we imagine, albeit without official sanction. I asked Helen the burning question: are the Chinese really healthy then?

'Some are. Most are like anybody else. The biggest factors are sanitation, food, shelter and rest.'

Helen asked a lot of questions. Headaches? Sometimes. Stiffness? Ditto. Memory? Not what it was. Circulation? Bad. Diet? Spectacular. Alcohol? Virtually stopped. Coffee? Trying to cut down. Smoke? Likewise. Energy? Improving, but not nearly good enough, not when I can sleep for seven hours and still feel tired.

Other problems? Since you ask, yes: mood swings, anger, short fuse, regrets, hatreds, frustration, paranoia, anxiety, obsessive need to follow routines. In short: physical health, not bad and getting better; mental health, suspect.

Helen looked up from her notes.

'You fit a pattern,' she said. 'We'll work on your liver. You're a livery person.'

I said: come again?

'It's written all over your face,' she said. 'Skin tone, demeanour, that frown mark, your need for structure, that's classic livery stuff.' She paused. 'Do you make lists?'

Yes, I said, all the time; people make fun of my list-making.

'Tell 'em to eff off,' she said.

OK, I said, dammit, I *will*.

She took my pulse. 'Hmnnn . . . big pulse. Lots of energy, but you're not accessing it.'

I removed my shoes and socks, clambered on to the inevitable couch. Helen swabbed my toes, wrists and shoulders. She said she would insert six needles. Deep breath in, prick, barely felt a thing. Ten minutes of that, and it was over.

I went back a week later. This time, Helen put ten needles in my back. 'One of the best unstressing treatments we've got in the armoury.'

She asked how I'd been, I said fine, still had the mood swings, though.

'They won't magically go away,' she said.

We talked more about alternative medicine, agreed that much confusion arises from language, rather than reality. A Western doctor would never say 'chi', not if her life depended on it, but would happily describe a patient as having a 'strong constitution', 'fighting spirit', 'the will to live' and so forth.

I asked Helen if she would ever see a conventional doctor.

'I'm not daft. Penicillin is a miracle drug. Neurosurgery, heart bypasses, hip replacements, they're wonderful. I'd defend the NHS to my dying breath.'

She says budgets and drug companies are the main problems with the NHS, 'the idea there is a pill for every ill'. Her GP 'goes green' when Helen describes the amount of time she is able to spend with her clients.

'I broke my toe falling over the back of the sofa,' said Helen. I raised an eyebrow. 'Don't ask! Went out at an angle, started swelling, hurt like hell. I thought: Casualty? On a Saturday night in south London? Nah! If I can just get a needle in there . . .'

She did, and the pain subsided enough for her to strap the broken toe to the next one.

'That's all they'd have done in hospital.'

And, you know, with my personality, years ago, when I was a child, I saw all sorts of 'mainstream' people. Different names – child guidance this, educational the other – and I'm not convinced they helped me any more, and some helped a lot less, than the various 'alternative' people I've seen over these past few months. So I think I'll stick with these alternatives for a good while yet, to see what happens.

8 December 2001

Peculiar, isn't it, what life throws at you? After all the hoo-ha I've been making about my no-wheat, no-dairy diet (ten weeks and going strong), I've been inundated with requests for more information. Well, all right, not an inundation . . . but certainly more than a trickle. A steady stream, perhaps. In any event, I'm now a diet guru. Never would have imagined it, but there you go. Manfully, I shoulder the responsibility.

The requests boil down to this simple equation: zero wheat + zero dairy = zero sandwiches + zero pasta + zero cheese = y, where y = what, exactly, do you live on? I sympathize: ten weeks ago I would have formulated the same equation. (Interestingly, no one asks about living without milk – and indeed, milk is the easiest thing to give up.) Stand by to learn the value of y.

When I get up, I have two large glasses of warm water with

the juice of one lemon. For the first few days, I could hardly keep this down. Now it's second nature. Eight o'clock, breakfast: an apple, sliced up, covered in sheep yoghurt, mixed with ground-up sesame, pumpkin, sunflower and linseeds. 'Hold on,' you say, 'yoghurt!?' Yes, but *sheep's* yoghurt. Sheep. I am avoiding cows' milk, not sheep or goats. Not sure why, but it works. Of the three, sheep is the nicest anyway. Tastes like Greek yoghurt. Possibly addictive. I'm up to a tub a day. The seeds, I know, sound hardcore and probably unpleasant. Really, they're not. You've just gotta look your prejudices square in the eye, and say, 'I will eat seeds for breakfast! I *will!*'

I then have a cup of very strong black coffee, with honey. Ought to give up the coffee: can't. Repair to the lavatory and read the sports sections. Too much information? Sorry, won't happen again. At about 10.30, I have a few almonds and dried apricots. And another coffee.

By noon, I'm hungry again. I can now go one of two ways. At home or the office, I visit either the fridge or the canteen and assemble a large, rice-based salad, including some or all of the following: tomatoes, carrot, cucumber, beetroot, chick peas, lentils, raw mushrooms, raw spinach, houmous, plus either tuna, mackerel or herring. If I find myself with a friend in a restaurant, having what we laughably describe as a 'working lunch', but actually indulging in what we all know, I think, is best called 'idle gossip', I'll have chicken or salmon, do that whole chargrilled thang.

If I'm out alone, going about my business, I've got a problem. What I should do – what I probably *will* do as my zealotry wanes – is have a sandwich. No harm in a sandwich once in a while, surely? At the moment, my commitment still burns bright. I ought to find a decent café and have a proper meal. Yet (is this just me?), I am self-conscious about eating sit-down food alone in public. (Don't know why – some deep character flaw presumably. Better find a therapy to treat it.) So I sneak more almonds and apricots, become irascible, scuttle back to the office. Got to solve this.

Usually, the big salad option is available. ('But it's almost winter,' you say, 'what about hot food?' I say: doesn't bother me. The hot-food obsession is a hangover from the days of hard, manual work, no central heating and poor clothing. If I worked on a building site, then I might need hot food. I once worked in a factory and ate chips every day for six months.) By 4 p.m., I'm hungry again. I have an apple and, something I've got into recently, a tin of sardines. Eccentric? Don't care: sardines are invigorating and, if you eat them quickly, your office won't smell of cat food for too long.

Home about 6.30 p.m. I have a few rice cakes with slices of mushroom, or beetroot. Do bath time and bedtime. Eight thirty: dinner. I have pretty much what I had for lunch. Boring? Yeah, but life *can* be boring. Got to embrace that boredom! Ten thirty: have breakfast again, except grapes rather than apple. Midnight: to bed. What have I missed? Oh, yeah: in among all this, two litres of water. Follow this diet and I predict you will lose weight, about eleven pounds a week in my experience.

But. Always a but.

You will have noticed that, quite apart from some obvious no-nos (including, sorry to be the bearer of bad news to both genders in turn, chocolate and beer), this diet does not include several other staple foods. No red meat, or not much. No crisps. And, I'm afraid, not much Chardonnay, amusing or otherwise. Or, hardly any. Here comes the sting in the tail. Sadly, I have to report that, in tandem with no wheat, no dairy, I have cut my wine intake by about three quarters, from four bottles a week to a derisory one. For all I know, alcohol being full of sugar, this might be entirely responsible for my weight loss.

Because – remember O-level biology – what is excess weight?

Stored fat, that's all. To use up the store, you first stop adding any more. I'm not saying no wheat, no dairy is a con, I'm saying it works because it is a useful structure to follow to achieve a low-fat, low-sugar diet.

There's another sting too, I'm afraid: exercise. The guru shall return to this next week.

22 December 2001

My editor tells me I'm turning into a New Age bore, a health fascist and, very possibly, a sad git. She says I've got to lighten up. Says it's Christmas, and nobody wants to read me . . . how did she put it, ah yes, 'boring on about sardines and walking everywhere'. Says people want something jolly at this time of year. Says the stuff last week about recording each mile I walk was the last straw, that some things are best kept to yourself.

B-b-b-but, b-b-b-boss, I stammered, I was going to write about my wallchart! She yawned and rolled her eyes. I said: the wallchart, fascinating actually, I've got all these lines representing weight loss, alcohol consumption, miles walked . . . She looked at me as if to say: what is this monster I have created?

'Just try to be funny,' she said.

I trailed off home (two and three-quarter miles, including an unnecessary deviation) and sulked for a bit. Moodily, heart not in it, I entered the mileage on my chart. I haven't walked further than the shops since (quarter-of-a-mile round trip, derisory). Extremism, that's the problem. All or nothing, excess or abstinence. Moderation, that's what I need to learn. I cast around for something jolly to write about, something in my life that wasn't about self-denial, something funny. There were just me and the cat in the house. He is an extraordinarily fat cat – British Blue, a big breed – quite the greediest creature I've ever come across, and I once interviewed Robert Maxwell. I stroked the cat, laughing at how fat he is. The vet treats me like some mad old woman, implores me to regulate the cat's food. But he's almost ten (the cat, not the vet. The vet's about forty-four. Medium build). He's having a good life. So the cat eats what he likes, which is a lot.

Being funny . . . hard, isn't it? I remember a time I was remonstrating with my son, last Christmas I think, when he was about three and a half. He'd been watching the TV, and had just wee'd in his trousers yet again, even though the lavatory was just twenty feet away.

'But why, Sam? Come on, tell your daddy, *why*?' I whispered, going for the man-to-man approach.

He wrenched his gaze briefly from *Wallace and Gromit* and looked me right in the eye. 'Am lazy,' he said, drawing out the word 'lay-zee' like a Mexican baddie in a western, bags of attitude.

I burst out laughing, and so did he. Does anyone else find that funny, though?

Then I thought about George Bush Senior, and that time he was sick in the Japanese prime minister's lap at a big state dinner, one of the funniest things I've ever seen. Remember when the Japanese prime minister was called Takeshita? Remember how the BBC had to pretend he didn't have this hilarious name? I laughed some more. The cat opened a fat eye to see what was going on. I thought about Frank Bough in his pullover, snorting cocaine with rubber-clad prostitutes (surely the best tabloid exposé of the twentieth century) and laughed about that.

Tell you what I'm going to do this Christmas. Going to get a bottle of my favourite whisky. (I know it sounds a bit bufferish at my age to have a favourite whisky, but, as it happens, I do.) Springbank, twelve-year-old. Going to get a bottle of that. Going to set a limit each day, a fairly high limit, without getting silly.

Going to start the whisky about mid-afternoon today, the Saturday before Christmas. Going to work my way steadily through it, three or four large ones each day up to and including New Year's Eve. All right, it's not exactly rock 'n' roll, but it's a start. Something funny should turn up after a while.

Springbank: I've always had that word on my conscience. In the mid-nineties, before we had children, we used to rent a cottage for the week before Christmas, up on a beautiful beach in Kintyre; a long, long drive, but worth every gallon. One year, I rang the Springbank distillery, which is just down the road in Campbeltown. I mentioned, so help me, *The Times* and all that stuff, and asked if we could come for a tour.

They were hospitality itself. A nice man – to my shame I can't remember his name – showed us round. Afterwards, he took us into the front office, where he'd lined up six large glasses, each one a different age. I drained them all – that's how I know I prefer the twelve-year-old. We drove back to the cottage, me singing 'Mull Of Kintyre' very loudly. Say what you like about that song: I love it. There's a promontory just outside Campbeltown called Island Davaar. At high tide, from a certain angle, it looks a little like a breast. I remember shouting: 'There's tit island! Look! Tit island!' in between bursts of bagpipe impersonation.

Anyway, I hadn't exactly promised to write about the visit in the paper, but it was sort of understood that I would. I didn't. Not a word. Just drank that whisky, thank you very much, good-bye. This has troubled me for six years. Not constantly, you understand, but every so often I'll think of it and shudder, like you do at certain memories. It feels good to have offloaded this one. Not funny, but good all the same.

Merry Christmas.

29 December 2001

So, resolutions. Before I start, though, I've remembered some-thing else that I find very handy for cheering myself up. Thought I'd pass it on. Remember that chap who was governor of the Falklands when the Argentinians invaded? Rex Hunt, he was called. Probably Sir Rex Hunt, come to think of it. Remember when he was getting off that little boat, wearing his Ruritanian uniform with that ridiculous plumed hat? Remember how, just at the moment that he stepped off the boat to the jetty, the boat bobbed back and he plunged right into the sea? One second he's going about his official business, looking a bit daft, the next he's gone down like a stone into the drink, looking a million times dafter. My word, that was funny.

Anyway, resolution number one: drink more. Not a lot more, but a bit. More than I did in the second half of 2001, less than I did in the first half. Unusual I know, to resolve to drink *more*, but, since the midpoint of the year, I have taken abstention to unacceptable levels. Deadlines prevent me from updating you on my progress through the whisky bottle this Christmas – I am, however, quietly confident that I'll be managing OK, build-ing up my match fitness, staying focused, like Michael Owen when he's through on goal.

I'm thinking, as an experiment, I might stick to whisky all year. It's mixing that does you in, isn't it? And great big glasses of Chardonnay at lunchtime, you know those huge ones that you kid yourself are only one unit, but are more like half a bottle, the ones that blow away the whole afternoon? Familiar? Or is that just a journalist thing? Anyway, whisky is the way forward.

Number two: control the temper. I wrote about my temper months ago, and haven't really returned to it since, because I'm ashamed that I still lose it. I've tried a few strategies – they don't work for long. Now, I'm out of ideas. Need some help. If there is anyone out there who has been on, or runs, one of those anger-management courses, and feels they can advise a hardened tantrumic recidivist, please get in touch. Seriously.

Number three: acquire some sort of new skill. I'm desperately unskilled: can't cook; can't mend or make anything; can't draw; can't play an instrument; can't do any party pieces such as juggling or magic or handstands or wiggling my ears independently of the rest of my head (though that's genetic, isn't it?); can't speak a foreign language; can't do impressions (except David Mellor, and people tire of him, understandably, and anyway, I'm not fat enough any more to be convincing); can't dance; can't sing. Can't, in short, do any of those extra, fantastic things that impress your children, endear you to others and generally make life worthwhile. Reading, writing, arithmetic, swimming, riding a bike, minor domestic chores, driving (after a fashion) . . . I've just about got the basics sorted, but that's it. Dammit, I'm thirty-seven years old, it's time to branch out!

That's a wishlist though, isn't it? I'm never going to get through all that new-skill acquisition in a year, probably not in a lifetime. As we all should know, long lists of general desires mean achieving none of them. So I should be specific, try to choose just one. What would I really, *really* like to be able to do? (*Pause, thinking.*) OK, I've got it (bit embarrassed, but here goes anyway): I'd like to learn to sing. Not wonderfully (a forlorn hope in any case), not so it sounds like I've been taught, just tolerably well will do, so family and friends might think I have an all-right voice that they could bear to listen to. I love singing, especially at this time of year ('Once In Royal David's City', 'In The Bleak Midwinter', 'O Little Town Of Bethlehem', 'Silent Night', cracking tunes), but I'm abysmal. Anyone out there prepared to take on the challenge?

So that's three resolutions. What else? Oh yeah, number four: lock myself in a quiet room, put a cold towel on my head, and try to come to a firm, considered opinion on European monetary union, the Middle East, health service reform and the other great issues of the day. At the moment, I'm twisting in the wind, depending on what newspaper I read that morning. If nothing else, I am determined to memorize those tricky Madrid conditions. Don't worry, I won't write about this.

And the last one? Tradition demands, doesn't it, that this should be smoking . . . but I'm not ready, not quite yet, not to quit. What I will do – and it sounds like a cop-out, because it *is* a cop-out, but it's better than nothing – is cut down. I'll monitor the fags like I've monitored the alcohol and the walking, set targets, maybe even dust down my wallchart, see if that makes any impact.

My aim is to become a social smoker, one of those maddening people that can smoke after a nice dinner on a Friday night and then forget about it for the rest of the week, those people who are able to treat tobacco in the same way most of us treat, say, apple crumble – as an occasional luxury. I always think such people must be profoundly happy, settled in their own skin, fully grown up. So, it's moderation for me in 2002 – moderation pursued with an iron resolve.

Happy New Year.

5 January 2002

Travel, as I get older, is less and less about destination, more and more about the journey. I don't mean this metaphorically, in some cod-philosophical New-Agey way. Well, maybe I do, a bit, but mostly, I mean it literally. The journey – specifically the mode of transport employed – is more important than where I end up.

As I like to travel with a lot of kit, while avoiding queues, security guards, dehydration and moments of gut-wrenching fear, then naturally the mode of transport I like least is the aeroplane. I would like, in theory, to go to all of the places covered elsewhere in this issue (except Blackpool, where I've already spent enough time, having been born there). But do I, in practice, want to go to the Maldives, the Himalayas (or The HiMAHlia as the old hands pronounce it) or the Cape so much that I would spend ten or twelve hours on an aeroplane to get there? No, not any more, not even if money were no object. I'd rather go to Wales.

I first flew when I was eleven, a journey from Birmingham to Corsica that involved a change in Paris. My cousin, then ten, and I travelled as 'Unaccompanied Minors'. Very exciting. We wore plastic folders – stamped 'UM' – around our necks for our tickets and passports. Even better, we were allowed to sit in the VIP lounge at Charles de Gaulle airport. I saw cashew nuts for the first time in my life. And – I think I was about twenty-two before I finally stopped talking about this – *they were free*! This was at a time when the average English child lived on a diet of bubble and squeak, tinned mandarins and Curly Wurlys, all of which you had to pay for, though admittedly not very much.

There were three other people in the lounge: Sacha Distel, the absurdly handsome French singer, and with him, one on each knee, Sacha's two outstandingly attractive female companions. Even at the age of eleven and still naive enough to be impressed by free snacks, my gut instinct told me that Sacha had done very well for himself.

That image of Sacha Distel in the VIP lounge, as you can well imagine, forged for me an association between glamour and air travel that lasted many years. By my late twenties, however, the link was growing weaker, corroded by the accumulated bitterness of a couple of dozen rubbishy charter flights. Just as aeroplanes suck every last drop of moisture from your body, so my desire to fly anywhere for leisure had all but evaporated.

Then I started to fly a lot for work – scheduled, sometimes *not in economy* – and I believed anew that flying was the absolute business. Any sniff of some long-haul, I was waving my passport.

For several years, when strangers at parties said, 'So, you must travel a lot,' I'd reply smugly, in my best Roger Moore voice, well, yes I do, actually. I'd be thinking: aren't I just the coolest little globetrotting journalist that ever was? Now I say: 'Never further than Newcastle, not if I can help it.' Anyone whose job involves some air travel probably goes through this phase. You start off thinking the planes are the best part. Then, unless you're daft, you realize they're to be avoided if possible, endured if not. I have taken this attitude to an extreme. Faced with a choice of, say, a megastar in Miami or something murky in Manchester, I'm itching to get myself down to Euston.

Now, I think my changing attitude to air travel encapsulates – rather neatly, if I may say so – a paradox at the heart of the self-improvement ethic. On the one hand, we believe we should embrace the new, overcome old fears, live our dreams, jump on aeroplanes and fly to distant lands. On the other hand, we believe we should value the old, look within rather than without for fulfilment, stop the striving after new things and new experiences, stay at home and tend our gardens – or, at most, toddle a little way down the M4 to a nice cottage in the West Country.

I'd love to be able to resolve this paradox. In terms of flying, I suppose a resolution would mean doing a bit, but not much. I'm in stay-at-home mode at the moment, happy, but conscious that some of the most formative and pleasurable times of my life have taken place in faraway countries at the end of long aeroplane journeys. Much as I love Blighty – and, joking aside, I *adore* Blighty, God's Own Country and no mistake – not even the most zealous patriot can deny that other people's countries do sun and sensuality better than ours does. Plus, there's a limit to how many motte-and-bailey castles my children can stand.

They complicate the issue further: I just can't face taking two small children on an aeroplane. Not my two small children anyway, and it hardly seems right to leave them behind and borrow someone else's just because they're better behaved. What's more, since I became a father, what was nothing more than a mild anxiety about being airborne has developed into a near phobia. Should I succumb to the fear and say to myself, well, that's OK, you're learning the value of acceptance? Or should I try to overcome the fear? My instinct is that I will do the latter . . . but not yet. Meanwhile, succumbing to fear provides an excellent holding position.

16 March 2002

This word 'depression' gets bandied about: I don't know whether I'm depressive or not. I've read books about hardcore depressives, plunging from peaks to troughs, people whose mood graph is all close zigzags, like a heart monitor gone haywire in *Casualty*. I'm not one of those, but I don't tick along low and level either. Softcore depressive, that's me. My graph is gentler, more curvaceous, more English – like a rollercoaster for cowards, or for elderly people with a touch of angina. Up we go, slowly, slowly, along we go, on the flat for a while, everything fine, nice and sunny, a few days, a week or two even, isn't this nice, lovely view up here, then, oh dear me, down we go, trundling back into the gloom for a while.

But not this time! This week, I looked down into the dip, and I saw those old familiars Lethargy and Anger, Self-Hatred and Paranoia lurking there, and instead of chugging on down the track to say hello chaps, how've you been, I thought: No! Not yet! I swung myself smartly on to the last few feet of level, sunlit ground, and thought: I'll stay up here for a while.

Now, how did I manage that? From where did I gather up the energy? That's hard to answer, really hard. Maybe it started with a short trip I had to make, a flight to Belfast. Usually, that would be bad. (Belfast isn't bad. In fact, Belfast is great. Belfast is full of fine, impressive people.) Bad because of the flying part. I try to avoid flying. I woke up that morning worried sick about the flight. But it came, and it went, and I sat with my friend John, and I only asked him once, or maybe twice, when the engine note altered, to peep out of his window to check that the wing was still attached to the fuselage.

So that was progress. Having to do something you don't want to do is a useful way of bolstering self-worth. So is not doing something which you sort of want to do, but which you know is bad for you. From the airport, we went to the hotel. In a hotel, of course, things that are bad for you centre on the listless consumption of cooked breakfasts, or pornography, or both. I don't usually hanker after either – but in a hotel, there they are: available, easy, dangerously corrosive. John and me, though, we screwed up our resolve, and we said: No! And again: No! I felt better for it. I think John did, too.

Small victories, right? You score a few of them, you form a winning habit. You stay up on that sunny plateau a while longer. You start to see what's important. You start to value what you previously took for granted. I built a Lego spaceship for my son. It wasn't much of a spaceship – in fact, it was rubbish – but I stuck a lot of thin blocks on thicker blocks, at right angles, and said they were missiles. He loved it! I thought: that's the main thing.

I went to a party and someone I hadn't seen for years snubbed me. I thought: never mind, and went to talk to someone else, someone I've always thought I'd like if we had a proper chat.

And I *did* like them! My daughter announced that trees that keep their leaves are called evergreen trees and trees when the leaves go away, they're called sidwass trees. She's only two! I thought: is it a sin to feel this much pride?

My friend Alan and I got talking about that horse that used to be on the showjumping years ago, the one called Sanyo Music Centre. We laughed ourselves silly at the sheer cheek, the *outrage*, of naming an animal after such a specific piece of hi-fi equipment. I thought: how lucky I am to have a friend like Alan. We might never have met – and no one else I've asked watched the Horse of the Year Show avidly or often enough to remember Sanyo Music Centre, or to find it in the least bit funny.

I suppose what I'm doing is Being Positive. Being Positive is the big daddy of the extended family of New Age dictums, a close cousin to Visualize Success, What Goes Around Comes Around, Follow Your Dreams and Take Time Out to Smell the Roses. (I think Don't Sweat the Small Stuff might be related to Being Positive too, but I've never fully satisfied myself that I know what Don't Sweat the Small Stuff actually *means*, and I can't face reading the book.)

I'm usually bad at Being Positive. To me, Duracell Triple-As can be positive. Mathematical symbols can be positive. Certain sorts of proof can be positive. But I've never believed that a person could be – nor should be – positive, because positive means absolute, unquestionable, definite. The language of science as applied to people does not have a very happy history, does it? But I've performed a little linguistic trick on myself. I've retranslated this banal language of the battery into a language that means something to me, a language I like, a language with a proper human application: the language of religion. Being Positive I leave to others. Me, I'm Counting My Blessings. For the moment, it seems to be working.

23 March 2002

To north-west London again, for metamorphics with Amanda Goldman. Another agreeable treatment, another lovely woman, keen to talk and to listen, not taking it all too seriously. There was what looked like a deeply symbolic and serious sculpture in the corner of Amanda's room. I asked her what it was.

'Don't know, darling,' she said airily. 'Some sort of watery thing to make people feel relaxed.' I knew I'd like her when she said that.

When she said, 'I see myself a bit like Patsy and Edina, still twenty-two, still going down the King's Road in a short skirt,' I knew I'd like her even more.

I've been at this six months now. A pattern is emerging, is it not? I go to some clinic or centre, I sit – or, more usually, lie – down, then an admirable, calm, sorted-out woman does her thang. We get on well, we have a laugh, a talk, a listen, and I leave.

When I leave, I think: that was great. Then I ask myself: what made it great? The treatment? Or the woman? The answer is always: the woman. Colonic irrigation with Jane, the food test with Amanda (or Mandy as I now call her in our emails, ever since she started calling me Bobbi), reflexology with Jo, acupuncture with Helen, getting me chakras balanced by Brenda, the mind-blowing facial from Hanan, the palm-reading from Diana, and now metamorphics with this new Amanda: I get something out of each treatment, if only a nice lie-down, but the deeper satisfaction comes from the quality of the connection with the women. If I'd had all the talk without any of the treatment, I'd still be a very happy little fellow indeed.

Metamorphics is a case in point. In metamorphics, unblocking, or re-routing, energy is the goal – as usual. As usual, it's about overcoming stuck-ness. As usual, it's about discovering the real you, the you you can be. As usual, you have no idea whether it works or not.

The metamorphic technique, according to the leaflet, 'uses light touch on points known as the spinal reflexes on the feet, hands and head'. A 'light touch' is right. Metamorphics is so laid-back, so minimalist that you aren't aware of much being done to you at all. Yet something went on. After an hour of it, I walked all the way home: seven miles, three boroughs, four postcodes. I felt happy. I felt I had made another small but valuable connection with another person: not a connection for use in the future, necessarily, but a connection of use and pleasure in this present, for this hour, now.

Whether or not metamorphics metamorphoses me long term, it has certainly metamorphosed Amanda. Or rather, she believes it has – and belief is what is important. She has, she says, 'boundless energy' and has become 'aware and alert to the opportunities and excitement each day holds'. She is fifty-five and looks ten years younger. Her daughter is thirty years old.

Sounding like the cheesiest kind of flatterer imaginable, I heard myself saying, 'My word, Amanda, you don't look *nearly* old enough!'

Amanda ignored my lapse into Leslie Phillips with good grace. Up until a few years ago, she said, she obsessed about relationships. 'I had that terrible fear that if I wasn't with X then I wasn't complete or whole.' She also worried about eating the right food, taking the right supplements and going to the lavatory at the right time. She'd jump on each passing New Age bandwagon, thinking, Fantastic! This is the one! only to be disappointed.

Now, she has gained perspective.

'For the past four days I've been living on takeaways – but I'm thinking: don't worry. My body's saying: that's OK.'

Amanda told me her father had died four days previously (hence her takeaway diet).

'I have the sadness at losing someone delightful, this lovely, lovely man. But I don't have a fear of how I'm going to manage.' She says she can 'honestly say that I'm not fearful of anything'. That's an enviable thing to be able to say, isn't it? It takes a big leap of faith to believe that having your feet, head and hands lightly massaged can lead to the acquisition of such life-affirming, world-beating confidence, but . . . who knows? Amanda says it's worked for her.

But what about me? Is any of this working for me? I simply don't know. But I do know – and here's a secret – that throughout these six months, all these women listening – or, in Amanda's case, talking – I've stayed pretty much inside my comfort zone. And very comfortable the zone has been too. I've learnt a lot, but I can't say that I've confronted my fears as Amanda has confronted hers. Why not? Because what I've been doing, gushing and gossiping with women, is really, truth be told, just a more intense version of what I've always done, as long as I can remember, since I was knee-high. Women? Emotions? Don't scare me, never have.

Men, though . . . men are a different story. Men don't talk much, do they? At least, not to other men. If they do talk, they don't say much. I'm fine with individual men . . . but men together, doing their men things, that has always unsettled me. But it's good to be unsettled once in a while, isn't it? So tonight, I'm going to a kung fu class. This, I am not looking forward to.

27 April 2002

An unfortunate chain of events has ensnared me in an awful domestic blunder. I went for some hypnosis. Or rather, hypno-*therapy*: an important distinction. Hypnosis, we know, is people with central European accents swinging pocket watches across your eyes, saying, 'You are now feeling very sleepy. Ven I click my fingers you vill do *exactly* as I say.' If not that, then hypnosis is shiny dinner jackets at seaside venues getting girls to run around the stage in their underwear. Hypnotherapy is . . . well, I'm not sure what hypnotherapy is. Neither the hypno nor the therapy got very far.

I was tired when I went into the session at 1 p.m. on the Saturday. I'd been travelling again that morning, enduring an endless jolting journey back to Paddington after a shoddy night's non-sleep in a Welsh hotel – the sort of hotel where the heating pumps out like Reactor Number Four and they still have sheets and blankets; thermostats and duvets being new-fangled non-senses that'll never catch on. I was also resentful that I'd been handed a customer satisfaction survey as soon as I'd got on the train and completed it in complimentary fashion long before the diversions and delays had unfolded. (That's a really low-down tactic, don't you agree?)

I'd said to my wife that although this hypnotherapy session on top of the morning on the train was taking a big chunk out of the weekend, it might help with my smoking. She was under-standing: after a decade of pressurizing me unsuccessfully to stop, she's willing for anyone else to have a go. Try to be back by two, she said, I've got to go out in the car.

My wife is always going out in the car, whereas I go every-where by bicycle or train. I'm not sure what she does when she goes out in the car. Sometimes I suspect she just gets on the M11 and drives up and down it, very fast. She loves cars, does Nicola. And mending things. We once did a survey in a magazine. You had to rate yourself for so-called feminine and masculine qualities. My totals veered towards Julian Clary. She was Steve McQueen meets Jeremy Clarkson.

From the moment I went in for the appointment, events

developed with the iron predictability of a seventies sitcom plot. Indeed, that Saturday afternoon turned into a sort of *Terry and June* for the early twenty-first century. Instead of June wants Terry to mow the lawn but, arf arf, he went off to play golf with the boss and got stuck up a tree, it was Nicola needs Robert to look after the children while she races around in the car, but guess what!? He's down at the yoga centre having hypnotherapy! And, oh no, he's fallen fast asleep!

I went into the centre, past the stairs which lead to kung fu and yoga and into the treatment room at the back where I go for reflexology, osteopathy and, now, hypnotherapy. The room was exceptionally warm. The blinds were down. A candle burned in the corner. All in all, it was extraordinarily soporific. I sat in my usual chair and in came Linda, the latest in the ever-lengthening line of women to ask me a long list of personal questions in this room, and rooms like it. I love the personal questions, just as I can't resist filling in surveys about trains or whether I'm a man or a woman. The other day the osteopath asked if I ever had trouble going to the lavatory and was forced to start discreetly stifling yawns when I was still boring on ten minutes later.

Anyway, Linda and I had an amicable conversation about the benefits of giving up smoking, all of which I entirely accept. She maintained eye contact, and spoke in a slow, measured, reasonable way, but other than that I detected no hint of hypno. After a while of batting the smoking thing back and forth, she said we'd start the therapy. I lay down on the couch, now so familiar that I swear it's begun to assume the shape of my body. I settled down under my favourite little crocheted blanket and closed my eyes. Linda began to speak in a very soft, very slow voice, telling me to relax my toes . . . my feet . . . my ankles . . .

Next thing I knew, I woke, as Ian Fleming might have written, with a start. My body felt like lead, my mouth like sand. I knew that something had gone terribly wrong, knew that I'd been asleep far longer than I ought to have been, knew that, as Terry might have said, gurning to camera behind June's back, that I was deep in the doghouse. The whole centre seemed unnaturally quiet. For one ghastly moment, I thought all the ologists might have gone home and locked me in till Monday morning. I suppose that's what would have happened to Terry Scott, in the unlikely event of him finding himself in a yoga centre in 1977.

But this is real life, and everything I write here is true. It was 3 p.m.; the receptionist was still there. (Linda, however, was nowhere to be seen, so I did not get the chance to ask her what on earth she thought she was playing at, and why she placed so little value on another human life.) I struggled into semi-consciousness, paid my £35, and staggered home, thoroughly unhypnotized and smoking like a condemned man, grateful to receive what turned out to be only a medium-sized bollocking.

11 May 2002

I've never had much luck with cars. It took me dozens of lessons and four attempts to pass my driving test. Why so long? My instructor looked like a walrus – an *actual* walrus – so that probably put me off. But it's not much of an answer, is it? Maybe I just wasn't very good at driving.

Within days of finally passing my test in the winter of '82, I was in my dad's Hillman (Imp? Hunter? Avenger?), tearing round the deceptively cambered north-west corner of Pearson Park in Hull. As you probably know, that's a dangerous corner in any conditions, the more so when it's dark and icy. I ploughed into this Triumph Herald at about . . . oooh, at least 22 mph. Felt a lot faster, though. Gave me quite a jolt – didn't do the Hillman or the Triumph much good either. Smashed headlights all over the road. Once I'd gathered myself, I drove off. I was eighteen:

what was I supposed to do? Act responsibly? I believe there were seven other people in the car at the time.

Naturally my dad wanted to know why his car no longer had any headlights. Naturally, I told him that when it was parked some selfish so-and-so had driven into it and cleared off. Naturally, he believed me. Naturally, the next night, two policemen knocked on the door: Good evening. Mr Crampton, are you the owner of a gold-coloured Hillman blah, licence number blah blah? And naturally, they knew that he was, because there behind them stood the very car, minus both its headlights. I can still picture my dad turning from policemen to me, raising his eyebrows and cocking his head in inquiring fashion.

Unfortunately, the Triumph Herald belonged to the wife of the Bishop of Hull. She was a determined woman, this bishop's wife, blessed with lightning reactions, devilish eyesight and – really bad luck this – an encyclopedic knowledge of cars. She'd got to her window just in time to catch a fragment of my registration and the distinctive silhouette of what she, *unbelievably*, knew to be a Hillman whatever. Armed with the further forensic evidence of all the gold paint on her car's bumper, it wasn't long before the wife of the Bishop of Hull drew me inexorably into her ever-tightening net. I got Driving without Due Care, Failure to Stop and Failure to Report. Seven points on my brand-new licence, £100 fine, not a good start to my career at the wheel.

Or maybe it was. Maybe it was a useful warning. Maybe the Good Lord sent me the Bishop of Hull's wife and her lifelong subscription to *Autocar* and *Motor* as a sign, a message to calm down, motoristically-wise. I've never had another accident. From that night on, I became a cautious and infrequent driver, clocking up an annual total of around a thousand carefully negotiated miles.

So it was with some trepidation that I took delivery last Friday night of a bright red, bucket-seated, tarmac-hugging Lotus Elise. My friend Michael is doing some publicity for Lotus. He had nagged me to do a test drive. Eventually, anxiously, because I owe him a million favours, and because self-improvement should sometimes mean doing something mindless and materialistic, I said OK, I'll have one for the weekend. I know that makes me sound ungrateful, a bit 'Oh, it's simply too too much bother, darling' – but long experience has taught me the truth of the ancient rule that there is no such thing as a free Lotus. I knew that my penance would be to spend the whole weekend worrying about this damned car parked outside. Worrying about driving it, worrying about it being stolen. Frankly, I was surprised – and somewhat disappointed in the local youth – when it was still there each morning.

Anyway, I psyched myself up for the test drive. Saturday night, we went to dinner. It was a pantomime just getting into the thing. (I *knew* I should have gone to finishing school. I do believe my *pants* were showing at one stage.) Luckily, as I wrote a fortnight ago, my wife loves driving and knows loads about cars – possibly more even than the wife of whoever was Bishop of Hull in 1982. Nicola knew, for instance, that the Lotus had a hard suspension and a 'positive gearbox'. Impressive, eh? On one corner, she told me to 'watch the understeer'. I swear I glanced down under the steering wheel to check for a problem.

'I'm sorry,' I said, 'I don't know what you're talking about.'

So we drove the one and a quarter miles to dinner with Nicola issuing directions and gear changes like we were a rally driver and his navigator in the forests of Finland, if you can imagine a very slow rally driver who doesn't much like to get out of second. Junctions took ages. London drivers seem to turn even more unforgiving than usual at the sight of a flash sports-car, especially one with its headlights on full beam and its windscreen wiper flailing at top speed. Nicola told me I should be more assertive.

'You can't drive this like a Ford Fiesta,' she said.

Honestly, we could have walked it quicker.

Next day, having put all of two and a half miles on that baby's clock, oh yeah, I sat in the Lotus in front of our house and pretended to drive it really fast. My three-year-old daughter was very impressed.

15 June 2002

I was going to write this week about a machine I've borrowed that helps you sing in tune. But the instruction manual is the usual nightmare and I haven't been able to get the thing working yet. Anyway, I have a dramatic story to tell instead. I'm not sure what this story has to do with self-improvement, still less enlightenment, but I'm going to tell it anyway. It's not every day you get into a fight.

The Sunday evening of the Jubilee weekend, the Crampton family goes to a charming old-fashioned steam fair in the local park. The children enjoy a miniature railway, a swing boat and a merry-go-round. They acquire two inflatable aliens. We have a hot dog and chips in the late-afternoon sunshine. The mood of the crowd is good. The mood of my children is excellent. It is all very pleasant. We decide on another ride, an aeroplane device that spins round and round and up and down. There isn't a proper queue, so when it should be your turn, it's a bit of a free-for-all to secure one of the planes. We miss one go and wait.

The ride stops and I go on to the wooden decking and lift my daughter, Rachel, three, and her prized pink inflatable alien into an aeroplane. I'm about to get in beside her when I hear my wife calling my name. Turning, I see that she is grappling with a man. He is trying to barge her out of the way so he can put his own child in her aeroplane. Sammy, my son, five, is crying. Nicola, my wife, eight stone, is resisting. She tells me later that the man, in contravention of all shared parental etiquette, not to mention the law, had bundled Sammy out of the way just as she was lifting him on to the ride.

My first action, mostly from outrage, partly from a desire to distract this bully's attention from my wife and son, is to bellow an expletive. This seems to work. The man, presumably unaware until this point that my wife has any adult company, looks up from his continued manhandling in surprise. I start to close the gap between my aeroplane and the one under such aggravated dispute.

Then I remember Rachel. Genetically and culturally pro-grammed never to leave my children alone in public, I turn to collect her. Scooping a puzzled Rachel, still clutching her pink alien, out of her aeroplane, I resume my dash towards the man, insofar as you can dash anywhere with thirty-five pounds wriggling under your arm. So it is that me, my daughter and our alien charge into battle. Reaching the man, whom Nicola is still gamely wrestling, I barge into him with my child-free arm.

Turning to meet this new threat, he barges me back. We are evenly matched in age, size and street-fighting know-how (which is to say, he, like me, doesn't seem to have any. Although I tried to think of some really nasty head or elbow tactic I couldn't for the life of me come up with one. On reflection I think it is probably a good thing that my level of violence remained only commensurate with his). My aggressive intent is, I think, the greater, but then I am handicapped by having to carry my daughter under one arm. In any event, the result is stalemate. We stand and shove each other at close quarters for what seems like ages but is probably just a few seconds.

I can smell his sweat. I try to get a grip on his jumper, but my fingers keep sliding off the taut, scratchy material. I am amazed, later that evening, to see two or three livid bruises on my right arm. I see fear and anger in the man's face, and he probably sees much the same in mine. I become aware of Nicola shouting at me to desist. She is, understandably, anxious about Rachel, although judging by Rachel's expression – a calm, mildly interested smile – she is enjoying the drama from her ringside seat, although her alien is starting to look a little deflated.

Obeying my wife, I stop pushing. The man stops too. His wife arrives. So too do two young men manning the ride. For a moment or two, all is confusion. Then the would-be queue-jumping bully and his family depart, sulking but silent. I watch them drift off through the fair as Nicola lifts Sammy into his aeroplane. Thanks partly to me, and mostly to my wife's tenacity in the first place, Sammy gets his ride.

Here, I suppose, is the relevance of this story to this column. Very occasionally, it is not just understandable to lose your temper: losing your temper is absolutely what is required. Here, I was presented with a horrible bully pushing my wife and son around, attempting to prise from them by force this small pleasure for which we had patiently waited our turn. A detached, non-temperamental, civilized, dare I say middle-class response would not just have been futile, it would have been a dereliction of duty.

One of the young men from the ride asked me Rachel's age. 'I'm sorry,' he said, shaking his head. 'She's too young. You've got to be five.'

My daughter swivelled round to me, her lip and her alien trembling in equal measure at the sheer unfairness of what the man had just said. She burst out crying.

6 July 2002

A fortnight ago, I wrote: 'If I wake up in the morning and remember I'm supposed to be going out that evening, my heart sinks, and I spend a good deal of the day hoping whatever it is will be cancelled.' I said that this sinking feeling struck even when the arrangement involved people that I like. I then posed the question: 'Do other people feel this way, too, I wonder?'

Well, the answer comes back, emphatically, yes, they – *you* – do. I've had more letters and emails on this subject – all from people saying yes, that's exactly how they feel, too – than for anything since colonic irrigation (inquiries about that continue to arrive, almost a year later, usually from women wanting to book a treatment for their husband's birthday, which I find very sweet, and very fascinating).

Here is a selection of your comments (not wanting to hurt your friends' feelings, I've kept them anonymous): 'I accept invitations in the belief that I will enjoy what's on offer, but as the date draws near the doubts set in.' 'I spend a great deal of the day secretly hoping [the event] will be cancelled and I can spend the night watching television or reading instead.' 'I've had a dread of social engagements all my life (I'm now in my sixties).' 'I look in my diary on the due day and shudder. The very mention of a pint or, heaven forfend, a *party*, is generally met with a heavy heart. Even with my closest friends, when the day dawns, my first thought is often: How can I wriggle out of meeting them?'

One emailer asks: 'Is this a male thing?' Before I wrote the column, I would have said, yes, definitely. But then several women in the office read it and they all felt the same way, too. And almost half of the responses have come from female readers. So this vein of misanthropy I've tapped into is not running solely through men. I can't just put it down to the I-want-to-be-a-hermit, now-please-get-out-of-my-shed syndrome that many men, me included, fall victim to in our thirties, especially if we're married with children. (Though, truth be told, I was like this when I was twenty-two.)

Another emailer (presumably from my home town) says he feels the way I do and then asks: 'Is it a Hull thing?' Good question but, no, I don't think it is. Two reasons: first, many people in Hull – as you will all know, familiar as you are with Ferensway, seething on a Friday night – do still go out, and at least some of them usually look as if they're enjoying themselves. Second, while I accept that my readership is proportionately higher in Hull than elsewhere (extended family, parents' friends, mothers of people I was at school with), I can't believe all these emails have come from just the one medium-sized northern city. No, I think I have uncovered a nationwide phenomenomenom. (That is a deliberate error, by the way. Spellcheck didn't like it, but me, I *hate* spellcheck. I *spit in the face* of spellcheck.)

Now, from the self-improvement standpoint, I ask myself two questions. First: why do so many of us dread social engagements? Second: accepting that, on any given day, thousands of us are making our way to these social engagements wishing profoundly that we weren't, does this matter? (I'm assuming that most people, like me, don't *always* cancel. When you do blow someone out, though, my advice is that the big lie is less insulting than the small one – or, much worse, the truth. 'I had to go into hospital' is better than 'I feel a bit under the weather'; 'The car has been stolen' beats 'It's half an hour's drive and I can't be bothered'; 'I will be sacked if I don't work tonight' is superior to 'I was too lazy to finish off properly at the office'; etc.)

Back to the first question: why the dread? Well, lots of reasons, mostly prosaic, some existential. I dislike the travelling. I resent not being able to wear pyjama trousers and a vest all evening. I despair of other people's coffee-making abilities. I worry that I'll have to make an effort not to be bored or boring or both. I hate having to stand, or sit in a hard chair, rather than being able to lie on the sofa scratching my crotch.

I fear the pressure of 'we're all having a great time' when, quite often, and it's nobody's fault, we're just having an OK time. I don't like having to go into the garden to smoke and break wind. I suppose, in summary, socializing for me brings with it the fear of enjoying less freedom than I would have in not socializing.

Which brings me to the second question: does it matter that so many of us, when we socialize, do so against our will? Hardcore self-improvers must say yes, of course it matters! They must say, 'Be true to yourself. Go if you want to, but only if you want to, and if you don't want to, tell the truth.' I say: rubbish. If we acted selfishly and honestly all the time, society would fall apart. What matters is that we go, rather than that we *want* to go. This, I suppose, is called duty. My correspondents know this, I suspect, as well as I do. They moan and grumble, and hope for a cancellation, as do I, but in the end, more often than not, they go, as do I. And occasionally, sometimes, quite often in fact, they have a good time, as do I.

5 October 2002

Saturday night in east London and I'm finding out how much pressure I can take. Not much, is the answer. The tonsillitis is back. A doctor at the hospital has just confirmed it. The antibiotics I got the previous evening from another doctor have failed to impress the infection in my throat, as I had told him they would. The pain has now spread along the left side of my tongue and into my ear. The second doctor, the one I have just seen, has said that I need to go to another hospital, three or four miles distant, which has a specialist ENT department. He shows me a freephone in the reception area. I call and the cab company says they will be fifteen minutes.

I haven't eaten all day. I go to the hospital shop and buy a sandwich. Forcing it down, looking out for the cab, a woman in slippers tries to beg a cigarette off me. I say I haven't got any. She indicates the sandwich instead. I say, no, you can't have my sandwich either. She mumbles something at me. Groups of people arrive to visit relatives or friends. Several of them are so raucous, I think they may be drunk. My throat, tongue and ear throb abominably. Each swallow is agony.

The cab doesn't come. Darkness falls. After half an hour, I go back to the phone and call again. The woman says the cab is on its way, and it's an S-reg Escort. I wait once more. The begging woman comes up again. It troubles me, in a confused sort of way, that someone should beg off a sick person in a hospital. A car pulls up and the driver calls to me. I think it might be my cab but no, he wants me to move a wheelchair round to the passenger side for his wife, or girlfriend, to get into. It isn't at all obvious why he can't do this himself. He stays put while I move the chair. The woman then says something to him – so I can confirm she is able to speak – but what she doesn't say is thank you to me.

Back inside I go. I call the cab company again. The woman says isn't he there yet? I say no, and I'm ill, and I really don't believe that he's just around the corner, and neither the make, nor the colour nor the registration of the car are of any interest to me, only its location. There's a crackle of static, and then the woman explains that the driver must have misheard her original brief because he's gone off somewhere else. He will, she says, be at least another fifteen minutes. I hang up while she is still apologizing and walk out of the hospital on to the street. My ear feels like it might explode.

At the first junction, a scruffy middle-aged man with hardly any teeth leans in front of me and holds out his hands in supplication. Assuming he is another beggar (I shall never know, he might have been in genuine distress) I dismiss him with a vicious expletive, and he's gone. I've never done anything so publicly cruel to a stranger before. I feel ashamed of myself. I see a group of men and women about my own age queuing for a Gary Numan comeback concert. Although I have nothing against Gary Numan or his many fans, my lip curls.

I phone my wife. I can hear my daughter screaming in the background. My wife explains, over the din, that Rachel is upset because I am not there. In time-honoured fashion, I vent my hatred of minicab firms (longstanding) and Gary Numan fans (hitherto undiscovered) on my wife. She says that she will find a babysitter and pick me up. Over the next half an hour, in the course of several mobile phone calls, I am savagely rude to my wife about the slow pace of her arrival.

We get to the other hospital. The lift is broken. I swear and storm up the stairs. We arrive on the ward. To my shame, I am rude to a young nurse on the desk. She says I should wait in the TV room and I say I don't want to. We wait in the corridor. A man passes carrying what looks like – what in fact is – a bag of blood. After a while, the specialist arrives and, for what must be the twentieth time in two months, I describe the lengthening history of my throat. The specialist says she thinks I should stay in overnight and go on an intravenous antibiotic drip.

A nurse gives me a painkiller and the doctor puts a catheter in my hand. The sight and stab of the needle turn my stomach. Usually, I'm all right about needles. I want the antibiotic; the doctor says she first wants to put a little camera down my throat. I say: if you must. She fiddles with the machine and begins feeding a tube up my nose.

And that's it. That's me done. That's my pressure threshold – higher than some, I suppose, lower than many others – reached and breached. As the tube goes down my throat, I start crying.

Proper crying: shoulders shaking; sobs; chin quivering; skin all smeared and tenderized. Is it me? Is it me? asks the doctor. No, I say, no, Doctor, it's me, it's me, it's me. After a minute or so, I'm OK once more: in pain, but at least not in tears, and life goes on.

2 November 2002

This is getting silly. After a year devoted to getting healthy, I keep getting ill. I never used to get ill – not proper, going-to-the-doctor ill. But at the moment, after all these treatments, all this pampering, I'm averaging an ailment a week. First, second and third came the tonsillitis. Then I got an infected finger, requiring the application of a hot poultice, something I thought had gone out with smelling salts and cavalry charges, but no, it seems not. Then I developed a series of extremely recalcitrant pustules on my neck. (Excellent word, *pustules*. Rather revolting, I know, but this rare opportunity to use it in print has proved irresistible.)

And then, two Saturdays ago, I woke up (in Hull as it happens, to attend Hull Fair, for which a sort of tacit three-line whip commands the Hull diaspora to return each year) and I realized there was something funny going on with the right-hand side of my mouth. It wasn't working properly. I'd have a swig of tea, a big *northern* swig, and some of it would come straight back out again. Also, my right eye felt strange: it kept flickering. And my right ear hurt. And the right-hand side of my jaw was a little numb. And I had a headache stretching from behind my right ear up and over the right-hand side of my head.

Over the course of the day, I came to accept that I didn't have full control over my face. The right-hand side was, though I hesitated to use the word, even to myself, partially *paralysed*. The paralysis left my face feeling crooked, though it turned out the crookedness was nigh-on invisible, in the way that what feels to you like a massive blemish goes unnoticed by others. Coming under no external (i.e. female) pressure to act, I did what I always do with a problem I don't want to address: I ignored it in the hope that it would go away. Classic male response, I realize, but then it wasn't all bad news: the left-hand side of my face was working normally.

Hull Fair, one of the enduring, unadulterated pleasures of the past thirty-odd years, passed off well, though both my father and father-in-law won prizes for my children on the rifle range, while my marksmanship failed to win anything. (An irritation, naturally, but you must take these reverses like a man.) Back in London on Sunday, half my face still immobilized, I spat Diet Coke all over the host's kitchen floor at a children's party. Alone at the time, mounting a shameful early raid on the buffet, I got away with it.

Sunday turned into Monday and Monday turned into Tuesday. Nothing changed. If I ate and drank carefully, I was OK. My balance was slightly out, but I found that if I planned each leg and foot movement in advance, I was serviceably mobile. Each night, I'd go to sleep wondering in a curious, third-person kind of way whether I ought to be putting my affairs in order, but then I woke up . . . still partially paralysed, but still alive, so still I took no action of any kind.

Then, Tuesday evening, I'm walking home from work with my friend James. James and I have just crossed the Whitechapel Road. Suddenly, my vision jerks, jumps, as sometimes happens at the cinema when they change the reel. For a split second, my head convulses. My whole body is flooded with fear.

Oooo James, I say: I've just had a funny turn.

'Is this a ploy to get a taxi?' he asks. (We have an exercise pact to walk rather than cab home.)

No, I say, it isn't. And I tell James about the weird goings-on in my face.

After that, things move quickly. James informs on me to my wife. Nicola badgers me to go to the doctor. Of course, I continue to prevaricate. She rings the doctor's anyway, describes my symptoms, says the doctor wants to see me straight away, like now. And, after much light-shining and face-prodding, the doctor says that I have as clear a case of Bell's palsy as she's seen outside of a textbook.

'Ever heard of it?' she asks. Sort of, I say, and I don't like the word 'palsy', not one bit. (Don't much like the word 'Bell's' either: only drink the stuff in an absolute emergency.) She then tells me that Bell's palsy – paralysis following damage, usually viral, to the seventh cranial nerve – is not a grave condition, nor do I have a bad case of it. It usually goes away of its own accord within a short time, leaving no lasting damage. (The internet says that George Clooney once had it, and he's turned out all right, hasn't he?)

I say: 'So, Doctor, I definitely haven't had a stroke?'

'You definitely haven't had a stroke,' she says.

'Not even a small one?'

'Not even a small one.'

Walking to the chemist's, I reflected thus: even though I was, obviously, immensely relieved not to have had a stroke, I had been quite prepared to believe, from Saturday morning to Tuesday evening, that I *had* had one, albeit minor, and my preference had been to allow that (as it turned out, imaginary, though not so far-fetched) condition to go untreated, possibly to worsen, rather than to make any sort of fuss. I wondered, handing over my prescription, how many people, how many *men*, go to an early grave each year because they share that same preference.

14 December 2002

In pursuit of some pre-Christmas laughs at absolute rock-bottom prices, my editor orders me to send off for a chest wig – £4.95 inc. p&p on the internet – and it duly arrives. It's a really dismal specimen: cone-shaped, maybe six inches along each side, the brown hair all sad and sparse and moulting even as it comes out of the envelope. Remember when carpet tiles first came in? Was it about 1975? I seem to remember my school being plastered with them overnight around that time anyway. When I see the chest wig, it reminds me of one of those tiles after about five years' use. It looks like the type of thing you might find in a derelict office block. It's disgusting.

On the back are three strips of tape to peel off and, under them, the glue that attaches the wig to your body. The idea is that I'm supposed to wear this wig on my entirely smooth chest to see if it makes me feel more Brosnan, more Burt, more Magnum PI, more *manly* than I otherwise do, and also to see if anyone laughs at me. The whole project is an obvious ploy by my superiors to humiliate me. I've never coveted a hairy chest. I've always regarded both Burt Reynolds and Tom Selleck (though not Pierce Brosnan, I admit) as being in that category of man who is reckoned by someone, somewhere, to be really gorgeous but who just, obviously, isn't. (David Gower is another one. The best current example, though I know I'm out on a limb here, is Prince William.)

Still, got a mortgage, gotta do what I'm told. I try to think of a suitable occasion on which to christen the wig. The problem is, aside from my natural reluctance to be seen by strangers wearing a really shoddy chest wig, I just don't go out that much. Day after day, I come home, put the children to bed, have dinner (I stopped calling it tea after about ten years in the South, but still refuse to call it supper), watch the television, go to bed.

Opportunities for bare-torsoed public hairy-chestedness, especially at this time of year, when I like to wrap up warm, are few and far between.

Turning the thermostat right up, I decide to test the wig on my children. I nip into my so-called office, strip to the waist, peel off the strips of tape, jam the wig in place, and lurch out at my children as they are going about their business one Sunday afternoon. Sam (almost six) looks concerned, points and shouts: 'What's that there? How did it get there?' Rachel (almost four) looks delighted, points and shouts: 'He's joking you up, Sammy! He hasn't growed it!' They then both simultaneously recognize the potential for assault this new situation provides. 'Let's ouch him up, Sammy!' shouts Rachel. Sam signals his agreement with a growl. They take it in turns to rip off the wig while I have to pretend to yell in pain.

This all seems so futile. I'm perfectly happy to be hairless. There was a time, it's true, when I hankered for more *facial* hair – around 1984, when George Michael was ruling the golden age of designer stubble. I always rather liked George Michael, and his stubble, and for a while there, with my inability to grow so much as a goatee, I felt left out. But it was a phase, it passed, I'm over it. As for body hair, I never even had the phase. For instance, I liked Freddie Mercury too – especially his vest – but I had no strong feelings about his hairiness. I sit in my room and think that I might have to refuse the chest-wig assignment, and take the consequences.

But then, a social event presents itself! There is to be an open evening at the children's school – glass of wine, bit of a nacho, quite possibly a dip. It's not twenty-four-hour party people, but it's something, it's an outing, it'll do. The other parents at the school are not exactly hairy-chest-type people – it's a Montessori, you get funny looks if you *don't* bring your kids by bicycle – but even so, I calculate that the fact I am wearing a very cheap carpet tile on my chest will at least give us something to talk about apart from the usual.

I scuttle into the lavatory on arrival, pull up my T-shirt, jam it under my chin, slap the rubbish wig on to my chest, tease a few strands out over my collar, watch as they come away in my hands, start again, adjust the strands ever so gently in the mirror . . . and venture forth into the throng of pleasant, Merlot-clutching people, people who all say supper I'm sure. I do wonder, I must say, as I try, and as per usual fail, to mingle, what on earth it says about me that I can treat my children's place of education merely as a venue for my own shoddy experiment in cheap chest-wig-wearing reaction studies?

Seeing my wife, I start to cross the room. The wig, its glue exhausted scandalously early, drops plumb down my shirt front and sticks in the waistband of my jeans. I contemplate a quick dash back to the lavatory, but the principal of the school starts her talk, and we sit on tiny chairs and listen. So I have to spend the next hour wearing this really shoddy stomach wig which nobody can see and which, after a while, starts to itch. This, we can all agree, is pointless. The next day, I march into the office and tell them: look here, I'm a serious journalist, there's no way I'm writing a column about wearing a chest wig.

1 February 2003

I am fond of filling in forms. I enjoyed, for instance, filling in the census form a couple of years ago, and recently I spent a pleasant afternoon on the internet scrolling through the first published results of the census. I like data. I like *Wisden* and *Whitaker's*. I like election results and school league tables and no doubt when I get older I shall like examining railway time-tables too. I make no apology. There are millions of people, well, all right, millions of *men*, like me, and we're not *weird*, or *sad*, or – awful word – *anoraks*, we're just set up this way.

I often hope that I will be stopped in the street by an opinion pollster, whom I can then bore to death . . . but so far, no luck. In the meantime, one of the few other pleasures I take from the internet is the number of tests, surveys and questionnaires it generates. Saves me having to buy women's magazines. This week has brought a glut of such surveys, with three pinging around the office on successive days. Naturally, I dropped everything and gave each survey my fullest attention.

The first one claimed to be able to predict your gender through your answers to such questions as 'Would you rather be hungry or cold?' (the women said hungry, the men said cold) and 'In a certain light, would nuclear war be exciting?' (all the women plus those men who hadn't taken leave of their senses said er, no, it would *not* be exciting at all) and 'Do you sleep on your back or your stomach?' (Rubbish question, because almost everyone sleeps on their *side*. If I sleep on my back I always – as far as I'm able to know – have nightmares, usually about having murdered someone.)

The gender test was not, as it claimed, 100 per cent accurate, but it got almost all of us right, which isn't at all bad. My test result predicted (with '86 per cent confidence!') that I was, in fact, a man. 'Yeeees!' I growled, jumping up and delivering a couple of swift, short uppercuts to an imaginary opponent, presumably someone I suspected of casting doubt over my potential result. Then I went off into the main bit of the office to laugh at the one man who'd been told he was definitely a woman. Nothing against men who think like women, you understand, it's just that tests in any form grip me with a primitive, surging machismo to which I am not, usually, prey. I can't help it.

The second test was psychometric. I've been hearing about psychometric tests for years, so I was tremendously excited. But what disappointment! I understand that in some industries more credulous than my own these tests are taken seriously, that careers can rise and fall according to whether you strongly agree or merely agree with statements such as 'I am always careful to double-check my work.' If true, this is grotesque.

Having done this test, I was sent an interminable 'assessment profile', one windy, flatulent page after another. Much of this sludge was flagrant repackaging of my own answers. For instance, I'd been asked whether I preferred to work on my own. I strongly agreed. The profile said: 'Robert Crampton will prefer to work by himself.' Genius, eh? The test asked if I was bored by abstract theoretical debates. I said no, I wasn't. The profile said: 'He will enjoy working with abstract ideas and concepts.' (That does not necessarily follow. Abstractions don't bore me as such, but they are still hard going, and intellectually, as in so many other ways, I am very lazy.)

When it tried to branch out on its own the profile was almost always wrong. Probably because I'd said I was methodical and organized, which I am, the profiler had deduced I must also be terribly decisive, that 'in preparing a project, [Robert Crampton] will set out a detailed plan of action without delay'. This, hilariously, about a man quite capable of putting off decisions for oh, twenty years, a man who hasn't made a 'detailed plan of action' about *anything* since drawing up his O-level revision timetable. It is perfectly possible, I have found, to be perfectly methodical, perfectly organized . . . and perfectly inactive. The profile also kept referring to my 'subordinates' when, as is well known, I don't have any. All told, a let-down.

Not to worry, back to the serious stuff. The Office Flirt Test was much more on the money. They might as well give people this to fill in at job interviews as all that psychometric palaver. 'Do you notice if people are wearing a wedding ring?' (Yes.) 'Do you enjoy talking on the phone?' (Of course not.) 'Do you know the relationship status of most of your colleagues?' (We talk of little else.) After plenty of this, you are sent your result, which takes the form of a comparison to an animal: cat, vulture, etc. I was – this made me *so* happy – a *lion!*

Once again, I roared triumphantly and bounded out to make fun of the colleague who'd been told he was a lizard – the same man, as it happened, who'd been told the day before he was a woman. It's strange, I've always seen this guy as a straight-forward male human being. Turns out I've been working with a small female reptile. I dunno: you want to think the world is made up of these facts, these hard observable facts, but then you test even what seem to be the most glaringly *obvious* facts about a person . . . and they fall apart in your hands. You never can tell, can you?

22 February 2003

Huge news, at least for me, in this little life that I live: I am moving. This is the seventy-eighth and final column on this page. From next week, it's the back page for me. Even though nothing much will be different, I'm still anxious. I don't like deviations from the routine. Don't like changing the car, or the furniture, or my current position on the sofa. Don't like chan-ging my clothes (though I do change my pants every day, twice a day if I've got a hot date with a new therapist) and I especially do not like changing my address.

I didn't like moving from Solihull to Hull when I was six. I didn't like my parents moving from the suburbs into the town centre when I was eighteen. (They're talking about moving again at the moment, twenty years later. I don't like it.) I didn't like moving to university when I was twenty-two (late, I know. I needed the extra four years to assemble the necessary A levels). And I didn't like all the moving I had to do once I was there, that endless shuttle from college to Hull to my girlfriend's flat in

Camden and then back to college and into a load of hassle over the Blu-tack craters on the walls of my room. (Hey, listen to me whinge: middle-class life is so hard, isn't it?)

When I moved to London full time, I didn't want to move to Hackney because I was used to Camden, and then I didn't want to move to Islington because I was used to Hackney, and then I didn't want to move back to Hackney because by then I'd got used to Islington. We've been in this house eight years now. Sometimes, I reckon we should move: somewhere greener, with fewer murders might be nice. My wife agrees. It's only bricks and mortar, she says. I'm not so sure, I reply. I get attached to places.

When the vendor was showing us around in 1995, I asked him three times what he did for a living. Twice, he ignored me. The third time, through gritted teeth, he said: 'I'm an *actor*.' (I later found out he was in *The Bill*. Which – sadly, because he'd have probably knocked a couple of thousand off – I don't watch.) He must have forgiven me because, the day we completed, sitting at what had that very minute become my kitchen table, he cracked open a bottle of champagne. As he talked about the great times he'd had in the house, the tears were rolling down his cheeks. He wasn't acting. Turned out he didn't want to leave the house any more than I wanted to move into it. A year or two later he tried to buy it back, but I was well dug in by then.

This stick-in-the-mudness has always applied, even to the shocking dump of a bedsit I had after I first came to the capital. I lived in the attic. The landlord, Stan, lived in the basement, with numerous other tenants in between. He liked a drink a bit too much, did Stan, and he knew it, so he had this rule: one G&T per night, that was the limit. Technically, Stan stuck to his rule – except his G&T glass was more like a goldfish bowl than a glass. A goldfish bowl on a stand. A goldfish bowl on a stand with half a bottle of gin in it. Once he'd drained that, he wanted company, and I'd hear him staggering up the stairs, knocking on doors as he went, giving me plenty of time to turn off the light and lie on the floor holding my breath until he went away.

Hard-hearted, I know, but that bedsit year provided the best television of my life. There was no time to waste! I watched solidly from the fall of the Berlin Wall in '89 through Mandela's release, the poll tax riots and Italia '90, right up to Maggie Thatcher's last moments of power that autumn. It was extraordinary viewing. As a young journalist, I thought maybe I ought to go and see some of this stuff happening first hand, so I got myself down to Brixton for a poll tax demo and got a half-brick on my head for my trouble. As I was being stitched up in casualty, I thought: I'll not move too far from the telly from now on.

My future wife and I got together that summer, 1990. She thought: Christ, he watches a lot of football, but consoled herself that the World Cup was only once every four years. She didn't know I was *always* like that: same frequency, different teams, far less excitement. Nicola had me out of that attic and into a nice flat by Christmas. Nice, but small. I clung on there by my fingernails for over four years, long after we'd outgrown the place. By the end, before we did the deal with the lachrymose actor, we were living like Ellen MacArthur, utilizing every spare six inches of space.

Speaking of which, I don't know if this new slot will be bigger or smaller. I hope neither: I kind of like it the size it is. As for the name, I know that columns at the end of magazines are generally called, in the wonderfully inventive wordplay of my trade, Rear View or The Last Word or And Finally. I think this will still be called Age of Enlightenment, though the deputy editor did suggest Robert Crampton's Back Passage, above the strapline

'He's so up himself'. A bit harsh, don't you think? Or maybe not, considering that the now familiar mix of humiliatingly invasive therapies, total self-obsession and engaging lavatorial humour will remain the same.*

15 March 2003

Somewhere not far below the topsoil of our national personality lies the urge to garden. This urge may lie dormant in your youth, but as you get older, mark my words, up it comes. My own horticultural cravings grow stronger with each passing year. As I close in on forty, I find that dead-heading geraniums and watering the rubber plant just don't satisfy me any longer. Visits to my parents' house, where latterly I have tended to spend a lot of time scratching around under soft-fruit bushes, provide some relief. But not enough.

There is a city farm not far from where I live. My wife noticed that this farm wanted volunteers to help in the garden. Anxious, I suspect, to preserve her iron grip on the decision-making power in our own garden, she suggested I go along. So I did. The people at the farm, in their cosy kitchen-cum-potting-shed, seemed happy to see me, in a vague kind of a way. The place glowed with a sort of dishevelled benevolence, reminding me powerfully of the peace camp in High Wycombe where, twenty years ago this winter, I lived for several months. I was given a mug of tea and a form to fill out. Under Criminal Convictions, Relevant Skills and Previous Experience I wrote 'none', 'none' and once more 'none'. Then I went outside and got stuck in.

I've often referred in this column to my laziness. Maybe I have given a false impression. Confronted by something new and challenging, then I do indeed usually take refuge in idleness

* As you'll know, the column was renamed Beta Male. For obvious reasons.

and inaction. But faced with a familiar, open-air, repetitive and (most important) *totally unskilled* manual task, my work ethic is unimpeachable. Sweeping up leaves, for instance, I'm very good at that. And cleaning out gutters: no problem at all, always see that through. So, presented, as I was at the city farm, with an ancient fork, a wheelbarrow full of manure and a dusty patch of earth to fertilize, I knew I could cope.

Before long, I was joined at the neighbouring patch by Julia, a fellow volunteer, a veteran of the area. I asked Julia why she'd come. 'It's better than sitting around at home smoking fags,' she said. 'And I don't have a garden at home.' Julia weeded, I dug, and we bitched matily about the shortcomings of Hackney council for quite a while (not difficult). She asked what I did for a living. 'You here undercover, then?' she wanted to know. Yeah, sort of, I replied, wondering if the Age of Enlightenment – or indeed Beta Male (old habits die hard) – counts as proper investigative journalism.

I used my boot to smear a recalcitrant clod off my fork, a fork which seemed to weigh as much as a small child. Julia suggested I swap it for the modern, lighter one she'd seen back in the potting shed. Of course, that was out of the question.

'No, I'll manage,' I said, and Julia chuckled.

We exchanged desultory opinions about United Nations resolutions and the like, the strange geopolitical small talk that people make these days.

A third helper arrived. This was Ritchie, a nine-(or thereabouts)year-old girl, full of bundles of spirit-lifting self-confidence. Ritchie chatted away, making Julia and me laugh, keeping up an endless series of questions: 'What's your name? Are you two married? Why not? Why are you here? What job do you do? Do you like Tatu? Are you famous? Do you like opera? Is that a worm?' and, more than once, 'Have you met Kylie?'

The sun came out, the wind fell away. It felt like the first day of spring. I dug on. Muck-spreading may be simple, but you still have to evolve a method, get yourself a bit organized. Ultra-low-level forward planning – as in 'first I'll do that bit, then I'll do that bit' – is one of my strengths. So that was good. Ritchie asked Julia why she was weeding while the man (me) was digging.

'Because he's a man,' said Julia.

I straightened from my toil, exhaled in a manly fashion, wiped my hands on the seat of my jeans, revelled in this ancient division of labour. It is entirely possible I rubbed my forearm across my brow at this juncture, too.

Then Ritchie started telling Julia, in a serious woman-to-woman kind of way, about her boyfriend, so I diplomatically went off to fetch another load of compacted poultry crap from the main supply. Through the yard I went, empty barrow bumping over the cobbles, dodging the chickens, geese, ducks and turkeys, quite the Farmer Bob, happy as a lark. Out beyond the farmyard, two or three early lambs were soaking up the weakening sunshine. An Irishman in a boiler suit advised me on the correct way of transferring manure from a big pile into a wheelbarrow. Thanking him, I trundled back to the garden.

Ritchie had gone and, a little while later, Julia disappeared too, not to return. I worked on, spreading the muck, raking the muck, digging the dirt . . . not so different from a normal afternoon in the office, really. A blister came up where my wedding ring chafed against the fork. And my feet started to ache too. Plus, the sun called it a day and the wind got up. I didn't much enjoy the last half-hour, truth be told, but I plugged away, rubbing my back, work ethic kicking in, getting the forking job done. Afterwards, at the sink, the soap and water ran black from my hands.

12 April 2003

Before I met Jennie Crewdson, I admit I wasn't taking Rolfing entirely seriously. To be honest, I wanted to do it because Rolfing, just the actual word, *Rolfing*, sounded funny. I was going to make jokes about people who followed the teachings of Rolf Harris as a form of therapy: singing 'Two Little Boys', drawing mediocre sketches very rapidly with marker pens, wearing large spectacles, that kind of thing. But now that I've been Rolfed, all is changed. Now I think that Rolfing is one of the best treatments I've had, up there with the Alexander technique and osteopathy, to both of which it bears some relation.

Put at its crudest, Rolfing is a superior, exquisitely painful massage from someone who really knows what they're doing. It is more complicated than that, of course, as anyone who has tried to read *Rolfing* by Hans Georg Brecklinghaus will know. Developed in the middle of the last century by Ida Rolf, an American biochemist, Rolfing is, Jennie Crewdson explained, 'a method of structural integration working in the connective tissue [of the body] to separate it where it is stuck and to lengthen it where it is shortened so that the body is realigned within the pull of gravity'. I liked this definition. I liked the fact that Jennie spoke in proper sentences about things that are known to exist. In this game, that is a rare bonus.

In fact, I liked everything about Jennie. Never has my rule that the therapist is more important than the treatment been more applicable. She was, like all the best teachers, or doctors, or parents come to that, sympathetic but no-nonsense, demonstrably in charge. She seemed to be a woman at ease with herself: grounded, as a Rolfer might put it. When she uttered those familiar words 'start getting your clothes off', I jumped to it. Having trained originally as a physiotherapist in the sixties, Jennie has since qualified in reflexology, reiki,

NLP, Bowen technique and something called spinal touch.

'I'm very passionate about what I do,' she said.

I came back from the lavatory in my pants.

'Oh my goodness! Haven't you got anything else other than those?'

I looked down at my underwear, an elderly pair of blue shorts.

'They're no good to me at all,' said Jennie. She fetched a pair of white Y-fronts, the kind I haven't worn since I was sixteen and the boxer revolution arrived on these shores. 'I'll put them through the machine later,' Jennie assured me. She saw my clothes dumped on the floor. 'Look at you, what are you like?' she sighed. 'You're a man,' she added, answering her own question.

'We need to talk about pain,' she announced. 'Rolfing is famous for its pain. The rule is the pain should never be what is unacceptable to the individual. Too much pain and the body closes. At the most it should be "ouch, ouch, don't stop".'

I said OK, I can handle that. (Truth is, I quite like a bit of pain. I suppose I subscribe to that belief that pain and pleasure are two sides of the same coin.) Jennie asked me if I'd had much work done on my body before. Yeah, over the past eighteen months, I said, quite a lot.

Next, she asked if I'd ever been bullied and I said yes, because I'd been fat when I was a kid.

'You stand now as if you still have the weight,' she said.

Have you been reading my column? I asked.

'No, I've never seen it,' she said. 'I'm sorry.'

Don't apologize, I said, it makes what you just said much more credible.

She said I lean back too much, that I hold myself up with my shoulders, that the high arches of my feet are 'usually a sign of anxiety in childhood', that 'the body is a history book of significant events in our lives', and then, 'I can't help it, you're not going to like it, but I'm drawn to your feet, I'm going to do them.'

I shrugged: always been a martyr to me feet, I said.

Then it was on to the couch and into an hour of some of the most considerable pain I have ever endured/enjoyed. On the tape, you can hear me catching my breath. Jennie was gouging the underside of my foot with what felt like a digging tool of some sort.

'It's just my fingers, sweetheart,' she said. 'Let me know if it gets too much.'

I looked out of the window at the blue London skies and tried to leave my body behind, having read in *Bravo Two Zero* that this is what SAS men do under torture.

'Stay in your body!' ordered Jennie. 'Come into the pain! Breathe! Go through it.'

Jennie worked her way up to my shin. She said she was trying to release the interosseous membrane, which connects the tibia and fibula. Her tone softened, reminding me of the way the midwives spoke to my wife during childbirth.

'You're doing really well, Robert, *really* well.'

The pain was just about bearable.

'Sometimes people can go into emotional release,' she said, and indeed as she started on my thigh I suddenly felt tearful. 'Give yourself a minute,' said Jennie.

I breathed hard and said: 'That was . . . mental.'

And so it went on. Left foot, left shin, left thigh. It all hurt, but in a *good* way, if you know what I mean.

'When I had my feet done,' admitted Jennie, 'I nearly passed out.'

She didn't bang on too much, but as she worked, she made a few observations, and everything she said about my life was accurate. I'm going to go to see her again. There are only eight Rolfers in this country: Jennie, Giovanni, Russell, Alan and

Matteo in London; Anna and Simon in Bristol; and Prue down in Lewes. There ought to be more.

17 May 2003

In the thirteen years we've been together, I've cooked my wife three proper meals. That's three more than some men, but it's not a record to be proud of, all the same. I've made her hundreds, maybe thousands, of salads and sandwiches, brewed up buckets, no, *barrels* of tea and coffee. (I was going to write 'innumerable cups' but let's see: average of two cups a day, say seven hundred a year, multiplied by thirteen, that's 9,100.) I've put quite a few things in the microwave and I've damned sure ordered a lot of takeaways. But proper meals, the ones that involve hobs, herbs, heat and recipes: three.

The first was in 1991. Trout. I wrote about it in the newspaper. The second was in 1999. Monkfish. I wrote about it in the newspaper. The third was last week. Salmon. For our fifth wedding anniversary. (Except my parents were staying, so it wasn't really your classic romantic set-up.) Anyway, in keeping with tradition, I'm writing about it in the newspaper. Do you see a pattern emerging? I'm a fish specialist, aren't I? Like that man down in Padstow, Rick Stein. I ate at his restaurant once.

Fish, that's my thing, yes, except my loyalties don't lie in Cornwall. No disrespect to Rick, but in the kitchen I'm a Hugh Fearnley-Whittingstall man. Several years ago, I interviewed Hugh, down on his smallholding in Dorset. I'd always liked him on the telly – his manner, his dishevelled appearance, his extremely long surname, twenty-one letters plus a hyphen – and I liked him in the flesh, too. He cooked me lunch. It was the first time he had cooked for a journalist, and he was a bit nervous. I wasn't very well, and it was a hot day in a low-ceilinged room. Hugh had talked very graphically about what you can do with a pig's testicles . . . to cut a long story short, I was sick in his upstairs lavatory. He had taken it very well.

I decided to phone Hugh to get some advice. Hugh cleared the air early on by saying he didn't hold my throwing up in his home against me. Then we moved on to my menu, Hugh coming good under pressure with a seasonally spot-on six-course meal. When I began to flap about getting the ingredients in deepest Hackney, he said he was coming up to London anyway and he'd bring a box of stuff from his garden. That night, a dispatch rider arrived at my house bearing rhubarb, radishes, four lettuces and half a dozen eggs on the back of his motorbike. I cannot deny that this felt tremendously exciting, like getting Beluga flown in from the Caspian by Learjet, only maybe not quite as decadent. My wife bought the rest of the gear from Sainsbury's.

On the big day, under instructions from my mentor, I cycled to the fishmonger's to buy some sea trout. I found a very long queue in a very small, very busy shop. The only trout I could see on the slab were rainbow trout and to be honest I'd no idea whether they live in the sea, or rivers, ponds or wherever. Hugh had been vehement on the subject of farmed trout: total no-no, in his book. As the queue shuffled forward, I girded myself to have one of those conversations most Englishmen will go a long way to avoid.

Er, I whispered to the man when it was my turn, have you got any sea trout?

'Sorry?' he said.

Have you got any sea trout, I repeated, a little louder, advancing just over the borders of audibility.

'None left,' he said, as I knew he would, 'only rainbow trout.'

Oh, I said, sensing the press of shoppers behind me, where are they from?

'Hampshire,' he replied.

Oh, I said again, wishing I were anywhere else, wishing I'd

never met Fearnley-Verylongname, are they from, er, a *farm*?

He made a face and consulted a colleague. This man shrugged. Other men were called in. A conference ensued. Some giggling took place, I'm sure of it.

After a lifetime, the first man came back. 'Yes,' he said, 'they're from a farm in Hampshire.'

I'll have the salmon, I said, thus blowing my main course out of the water.

It's so *time-consuming*, isn't it, cooking? Do some people really do this every weekend? Every *day*? Surely not. I'd put in several hours before I even began to prepare anything, let alone cook. I actually started weighing, washing, peeling and chopping in earnest about 7 p.m., and nothing became edible before 10 p.m., and that was with my dad acting as plongeur-cum-commis-chef-cum-extraneous-stewed-rhubarb-disposal-unit while my mum occupied a more general supervisory role, coming into her own during a particularly fraught half-hour of custard-induced trifle anxiety. I'll be thirty-nine years old this summer, but when you're with your parents, 90 per cent of the time, you don't get much beyond the age of nine, do you? Ten, maybe, at a push, if you're acting very grown-up.

People who can cook say it's not hard, it's logistics. That's not right, though. You need experience as well, and three meals in thirteen years just isn't enough. I found myself having to do everything in super-slow motion so as not to cock it up. As it was, even over three hours, I had to ditch two of Hugh's suggested six courses, two and a half if you count the croutons that were supposed to go with the sea trout (which was actually four bits of salmon). By that late stage I simply couldn't be bothered with croutons, much as I like them. I can't believe people regularly work as hard in their kitchens on a Saturday night as I had to do in mine. Or do they? I don't think I'm lazy, not really . . . but maybe I am. It's a worry.

7 June 2003

Over the years, I've tended to avoid all-male company. It's not them, it's me. I don't mind the banter. In fact, I like the banter. I also like talking about women, football and obscure trivia. It's the beer, that's the problem. I like beer but I'm no good at drinking it. After (often, in fact, during) the second pint, I must begin a succession of visits to the lavatory. These visits become so frequent as to render my contribution to the group peripheral. It's frustrating. The whole edifice of adult behaviour, I sometimes think, may well be built upon small physical frailties and idiosyncrasies, in this case, a bladder the size of a ping-pong ball.

Last Tuesday evening, however, I made an exception. The four of us left the office at 5 p.m., climbed manfully into Tony's Saab, wound the windows all the way down, yeah, and crossed the river. On that particular day in London, four white men in their late thirties heading south while wearing significant amounts of denim could only mean one thing: Bruce Springsteen at Crystal Palace. Women will not be remotely surprised to know that on the way to see the Boss we talked about football, bands and where we might get a burger. We also fussed a lot about the best route to take through the heavy traffic, without much reference to a map.

Chris pointed out a restaurant in West Norwood where a girlfriend had once thrown her dinner in his face.

'As we sat down for the meal,' he told us, 'she said, "Look, that wedding I went to at the weekend, I'm sorry, but I got drunk and ended up sleeping with this guy in the band."'

'That's all right,' Chris had replied, 'because three weeks ago, at that wedding I went to, I ended up in bed with a friend of the bride.'

'Did you really?' asked the girlfriend.

'Yeah, sorry, I did,' said Chris, assuming they were quits.

'About that guy in the band,' the girlfriend said, 'I was making it up.'

She then stood up, frisbeed her plate into his forehead and stormed out. Chris had to pay the bill with blood and chicken dripping down his face. The relationship had kind of tailed off after that.

We'd been building up to this Bruce trip for six months. Since buying the tickets, we'd taken to gathering once a week or so at Christian's desk to discuss the following: choice of clothing; transport arrangements; what time we should leave work; how many days' stubble we should cultivate; whether we could hire a Chevy somewhere (in the event we couldn't be bothered to even try, hence Tony's Saab); likely catering facilities at the venue; number of Bruce albums owned; number of Bruce gigs attended; whether Tony should even be allowed to come, Saab notwithstanding, given he'd admitted he hadn't actually bought a Bruce album since *The River* came out in 1980. I threw myself into the planning and tried not to worry about the lavatory.

The day dawned. I arrived at work to see that Christian had made the schoolboy error of teaming a blue denim jacket with jeans of exactly the same shade: the classic Shakin' Stevens mistake. People kept asking him to sing 'This Ole House', so I said he could wear my cord jacket and I'd wear his blue denim one, because I had black jeans on so that would be OK. Good idea, said Christian, proving that it's not just girls who can casually swap their outfits about. That unfamiliar jacket made me feel not quite my usual self all evening. That was a good thing, because when I'm my usual self at live shows it means backache, self-consciousness and raging bouts of envy directed at whoever is up on stage.

We found a pub just outside the venue. It was packed and potentially hostile, but we managed to get served without breaching etiquette. Two of us had Guinness, two had Stella. I struggled with the last third of mine but I was thirsty, I got it down.

'Time for another?' said someone.

'Yeah, why not,' said someone else.

I knew this was the night's defining moment. Obviously, ordering a half was out of the question. Summoning up my years of self-improvement slog, reminding myself that I'd known these men for ages and their good opinion of me really ought not to be compromised by whether I immediately drank a further pint of beer or not, I took a deep breath and said: 'I don't *want* another one.' There was a silence . . . then someone said: 'Fair enough, let's get one in the stadium.' In my elation, I forgot to go to the lavatory in the pub. I felt like I had won a small but important victory: not over the three of them, but over the large part of me that lacks the courage to set my face against the prevailing wind.

That large part soon reasserted itself, of course. We had two more pints each, the second of which I knew would cause me problems during Bruce's legendarily lengthy encores. But I had it anyway, because that's what the others were doing, and because I'd already had two so my judgement was impaired, and because at some level I just plain wanted it.

Sure enough, even though I'm a big Springsteen fan, I spent the final forty-five minutes of the performance asking Christian how much more of this stuff he thought there might be. Shuffling finally to the exit, searching wildly for a discreet hedge, struggling to focus on the post-Bruce analysis, I was in a world beyond pain. But sometimes, I suppose, hey, you've just got to live a little, haven't you, and take the consequences.

14 June 2003

Been getting down recently, getting in a bit of a trough. No specific reason, except I can't seem to shift this extra weight, and summer is now upon us. Weekend before last I took my shirt off to play some football.

'What's all this?' said my father-in-law, in his winsome Yorkshire way. 'You look like you're pregnant.'

Yesterday I put a pair of last year's shorts on and it was a real squeeze. I just about got them fastened, but fit anything so much as a fiver, let alone a bunch of keys or, say, a flapjack with chocolate topping, in the pockets? No way.

Also, I'm underslept, thanks to three consecutive nightmares. On Sunday, I was talking to a very senior executive on this newspaper, who insisted on holding the conversation by the side of a busy road, which meant I could hardly hear anything he said, except the last bit, when he sacked me. That was clear enough.

On Monday I suffered a lengthy humiliation at the hands of an old enemy, who dissected, with perfect clarity and in front of a large audience, every weakness in my character. He also lived in an absolutely massive house. Then on Tuesday I was shot in the head. Each nightmare woke me up at 6 a.m. on the nail, sweating, frightened and angry. That's not a good way to start the day, is it?

Later on the Tuesday I was sitting at work, yawning, slapping my paunch and feeling sorry for myself when what should land on my desk but a copy of *Wearing the Ruby Slippers: Nine Steps to Happiness* by Dr Kristina Downing-Orr. Synchronicity, eh? Usually I regard the self-help books that arrive in the post as a sort of reverse perk of the job. They bore me to tears, with their daft titles and the way they always suggest that life is about the seventeen circles of truth, or the six ways of being, or indeed the nine steps to happiness. Last Tuesday, however, feeling too tired, fat and lazy even to walk the ten yards to the unwanted books box, I started flicking through.

I came across something called 'The Happiness Questionnaire'. That's good for fifteen minutes, I said to myself, reaching for my pen. You had to register your degree of agreement with such statements as 'I am nearly always cheerful' and 'I very rarely experience frustration and anger'. Huh. The scoring was complicated, but I roused my brain, worked out the system, and was delighted to realize that I had achieved a very low mark indeed. For instance, on one section, the highest possible mark was twenty-seven. The average score, said the book, was 19.8, 'so if your total is below seventeen, then you may be excessively pessimistic in your views'. I scored three. As with any test, if I can't do really well, I like to do *really badly*. I cheered up.

I turned to the next exercise, 'Assessing Your Self Esteem'. Dr Downing-Orr invited the reader to imagine themselves on a boat with the Queen, the Pope, Nelson Mandela, Stephen Hawking, Madonna, a brilliant young scientist who has just discovered the cure for cancer and a woman who is going to have a baby. Naturally, the boat is about to sink and naturally, there is only one life jacket. You have sixty seconds to convince the ship's captain (I pictured him as a sort of Bernard Hill figure, with a beard and an old-fashioned naval uniform) that the life jacket should be given to you.

I set to work. Straightforward ageism meant that Elizabeth (77), John-Paul (83) and Nelson (almost 85) did not detain me long. Maybe ten years ago, holding his country together by sheer force of personality, Mandela would have had a case. Not any more. Glug, glug, glug. Stephen Hawking is younger, but, in theoretical physics, you do your best work before you're forty, and he's well past that. Also, I interviewed him once and didn't much like the man. Down he goes. Madonna gave me momentary pause for thought. She's the mother of two young children and the provider of innocent pleasure to millions, including me. On the other hand, I didn't rate her last album, and, for no particular reason, her husband irritates me. She's pretty fit, she can swim for it.

The brilliant scientist and the expectant mother were the hard cases. On strict utilitarian grounds, the scientist should get the life jacket. But I'm not a strict utilitarian, and, I reckon, the way science works, if he'd *really* found the cure for cancer then someone else in his lab, or in some other competing research institute, would know all about it too, or it will be on his hard disk or somewhere. Either that or he's exaggerating the whole thing. If he's so brilliant he can build a raft, can't he? So it came down to me versus the mother-to-be. We're like Kate and Leo on that one flimsy piece of wood bobbing about in the freezing north Atlantic, except I'm so fat it wouldn't bear my weight, so that's a bad analogy, but anyway, which one of us should survive?

Of course the book says that 'the person who deserves the life jacket most is you'. It would say that, it's a *self*-help book after all, and this is an exercise about *self*-esteem. But saying it doesn't make it so. I found myself pondering the answer far more seriously than I had anticipated. And, what do you know, I surprised myself by not being able to get round (in theory, at least) that business of women (except the Queen and Madonna) and children first. It's a *self*ish business at bottom, this one that I find myself in, but it shouldn't always have to be me, me, me.

28 June 2003

Ever since I was about eighteen, I've been thinking about growing a moustache, just to see what happened, just because I could (kind of, anyway). Possibly this desire was a vestige of reaching adolescence during the seventies, a decade in which Burt Reynolds was considered to be the sexiest man alive. Thinking about it, then yeah, that *was* the reason. I felt a moustache would make women fancy me like they used to fancy Burt Reynolds.

Every so often over the past twenty years, I've started down the moustache route. I've given the growth maybe ten days, then chickened out. Last month, May, I decided to try again. Some part of me, even at thirty-eight, maybe *especially* at thirty-eight, still needed to be a man who could grow a moustache, even though I now knew it wouldn't make me look any more like Burt Reynolds used to look, even though I don't, any longer, actually *want* to look more like Burt Reynolds used to look. Yet I thought: I'm going to lay this moustache business to rest once and for all.

One Sunday, I did what I usually do. I shaved the whole beardy area, including the moustache bit. This process takes about three minutes, every fourth or fifth day, more often if I have to interview someone who I think might give a damn about even my minimal stubble, like a politician, for instance, or Sir Alex Ferguson. I went out to a fortieth birthday party, the only sort of party, along with those for six-, five- and four-year-olds, that I go to these days. Over the next week, nobody said a thing. As I have written before, not that it's an issue for me or anything, I really am a very unhairy person.

The following Sunday, I shaved again, this time leaving the moustache area untouched. My dad, who was staying, noticed instantly.

'What on earth have you done that for?' he said.

I thought about giving my father a whole spiel about how a moustache-capability signifies the transition to full adult maleness and so forth. Instead I sort of muttered, all surly, 'Because I felt like it.'

He sighed.

As I have also written before, not that it's an issue for me or anything, your parents can turn you back into a teenager remarkably swiftly.

The next day I drew some comments at work, mostly because I stood very close to people while pointing at the area immediately below my nose. The men were supportive. I got one Clark Gable, one Terry-Thomas, and quite a lot of generalized facial hair anecdotage. That wasn't bad. The women, on the other hand, were less forgiving.

'Och no, that's *terrible*,' said Kate, the words somehow carrying extra opprobrium in her Scottish accent.

'How long are you going to do this for?' asked the editor.

'Look: I just don't like moustaches, OK?' said Lucy.

Later, Nicola, my wife, registered the growth for the first time. 'That's awful,' she said. 'Can you please get rid of it.'

The next weekend brought another birthday party. This one had an extra element: it was a joint father–daughter sixtieth and fortieth. My moustache was now two weeks old. Growth had stalled. I was spending most of my time in front of a mirror, vigorously stroking the little hair that had accumulated, something I suspect Burt did not have to bother with very much. I realized that I could, in theory at least, time permitting, count the individual hairs.

When we got to the party, before we were even through the door, Nicola told anyone who would listen that she hated my moustache. The women nodded sympathetically. But the sixty-year-old birthday boy went out on a limb. 'Well. I *like* it,' he said. 'It's sort of *piratical*. It makes you look more, I don't know, *dangerous*, somehow.'

Hmmm, dangerous, I said, I like that. Then I worried that nobody thought I looked dangerous before I had a moustache.

Back to work and back to earth.

'Oh, you're not still doing that, are you?' said Kate. 'It's not really *grown* very much, has it? It's kind of . . .' She searched for the right word.

Stupid? I suggested. Pathetic? Juvenile? Pubescent? Inadequate?

'Yes, yes,' she said, 'all of them . . . but also *sparse*, that's the word. It's *sparse*, isn't it?'

I could not disagree.

'I'm thinking,' she went on, 'I'm thinking someone who's worked at Microsoft for too long.'

Other women suggested Colombian drug barons, Peter Bowles, backbench Tory MPs. Someone did mention Che Guevara . . . who was it? Oh yeah, that's right, it was me.

The moustache straggled along for another fortnight, shipping ever more virulent abuse to my face and God knows what behind my back. The killer blow was eventually delivered by my four-year-old daughter. I asked her what she thought of my moustache. She laughed wildly, then, seeing I was serious, gave the matter due attention.

'Here needs to be more hair, Daddy,' she said at length, 'in between the other hair.'

I knew then that it had to go.

And in the end I'm none the wiser, am I? On the one hand, throughout the whole experiment, my moustache did not engender one single favourable female comment. This made me wonder whether, although there are an awful lot of moustaches in the world, there are in fact any women at all who find them attractive. On the other hand, my moustache was a very poor one indeed. Had it been all thick and luxuriant and Burt-ish, would women have had a different reaction? Who knows? In a few years I'll give it another go.

20 September 2003

I've had one or two emails from younger readers who don't understand what Beta Male is about. Fair dos, I didn't come across the word, or rather letter, 'beta' for a long time either, not until it started appearing, usually followed by a minus sign, on my essays at university. I had to ask my tutor what it meant. He was so shocked at my ignorance of this squiggle that he made sure I became thoroughly familiar with it over the ensuing three years.

I still haven't forgiven that tutor, a grudge which in itself is a perfect example of beta male behaviour. An alpha male would either a) not get second-rate marks in the first place or b) if he did, be man enough to blame himself rather than imagine it was somebody else's fault or c) if he did harbour a desire for revenge, do something about it. What he would not do, this alpha, is what I have done: fester along resentfully, but inactively, for a decade and a half.

This concept of the alpha male eluded me for a long time, too. Maybe I should have paid closer attention to David Attenborough, one of those cultural presences who have, like the Queen and George Best, simply always been there for my generation. Much as I admire the great man now, as a youth I never actually got round to watching any of his fantastically informative and exciting programmes. I had decided they were a bit . . . well, *boring*. This is one of many small misjudgements that have impoverished my life.

I think I eventually met the term 'alpha male' in *Brazzaville Beach*, William Boyd's novel about monkeys, or maybe apes. The alpha male is the lead monkey, the top banana, in the pack (pride? herd? group?). As such, he gets first dibs on everything: food, females, decision-making, the lot. The alpha male is, if not always the biggest one, then certainly the most violent, or potentially the most violent. The personae inhabited so successfully by, say, Roy Keane, or Michael Caine, or Alastair Campbell, with whom I seem to have become mildly obsessed, prove that an ability to project at least the possibility of violence forms a big part of the blueprint for human alpha males, too.

This may be a handicap for me in my quest to move from beta to alpha. While I am as fond as the next man of pretend violence (with cafetière plungers, for example, I still find it amusing to impersonate Hardy Krüger trying to blow up the bridge at Nijmegen), I am not much of one for the real thing, notwithstanding that (admittedly rather frivolous) fight I managed to get into last year, which some of you may remember. An aberration. I come from a verbally rather than a physically aggressive tradition. My father is a pacific chap and so, for all his chop-your-head-off bluster, is my son. He's not keen on football, for instance, because he doesn't much like the way people bump into you and tread on your toes. I was the same at his age. Still am, really.

I've made spasmodic efforts to toughen up, but they always come to nought. As a younger man, I was drawn to boxing for a while, sparring a few rounds with a man half my size. Within the opening seconds, he punched me in the chest (the *chest!*) and it really hurt. Afterwards, my trainer said if it had been a proper contest, I'd have been disqualified for lack of effort, if I hadn't been booed out of the ring for cowardice first.

So I'm going to have to work on the violence-projection. Either that or give up on it and learn to find acceptable surrogates, like the time Giles Coren came into the office and we fenced around for a bit then competed over who could eat the most mustard-coated cherries on the deputy editor's desk. (Honours were shared, and we're much less wary of each other now, so these rituals do have a positive function.)

Even given that boxing experience, it has taken me quite a while to realize that I didn't measure up as an alpha male. In fact, I still hadn't realized this when my editor said she had thought of a great title for the new column she wanted me to write. That's the way journalism works, like the time she dispatched me to the Orkneys to write about some young seals who had been mysteriously shot by persons unknown. It was a riveting read, if I say so myself, but the main reason I was sent in the first place was because she dreamt up a headline and was desperate to use it: Pup Fiction.

Anyway, what this column is about is me trying, even at this late stage, on the final run-in to my fortieth birthday next summer, to turn myself into a better man. So it's a bit like the old column, in that it's about self-improvement, but the territory is more . . . hairy-chested. Facials, manicures and, I hope and trust, colonic irrigations are a thing of the past. From here on in it's all Masculinity, crisis of, personal and global.

So Beta Male is about 'And then you'll be a man, my son.' It's about learning to do the stuff your dad can do. It's about learning to do the stuff your *wife* can do. It's about skilling up and smartening up. It's about making the transition that men used to have to negotiate when they were about thirteen, and then until fairly recently when they were about eighteen, but that now many of us in the West at least manage to defer until our fifth decade. It's about achieving a state of advanced masculinity and then deciding what elements of that you want to keep or reject. Basically, Beta Male is about learning to eat really hot curries, and then realizing why this maybe isn't that important. Or indeed, why it is. That kind of thing.

25 October 2003

I'm not allowed to do any proper DIY in our house, and I can understand that. Usually, I do my menial jobs, scooping handfuls of soggy leaves out of gutters and so forth, and I go about my other business, and the fact that I don't get to use the tiny amount of dexterity I do possess for anything more ambitious doesn't bother me. But there is a vestigial urge somewhere in there, a belief that it is important, however seldom, to at least try to add value, utility or adornment to your surroundings through your own labours, rather than your ability to buy someone else's.

And when I explained this to my wife, she took a little pity. No, there was nothing I could do in our house, but, instead, maybe I could help out her friend Tom by putting up his new blind. She had been going to do it, on account of Tom being even more useless than me, but perhaps I would like to give it a go. He has a sort of raised sleeping platform, Tom, and the idea was that this new blind would screen the bed from the rest of the room, making it all cosy for the winter, like Heidi in her Alpine loft.

'Blinds are quite difficult,' said my wife, 'but this isn't a *tension* blind, so that's not so bad.' She collected the various tools I might need from the places she keeps them, gave me some advice, and sent me on my way. Tom was out at work. I had keys, but even so, getting into his place can be like those heist movies where robbers in boiler suits have to disable several locks before opening the strongroom full of gold bars, or bundles of money, or bearer bonds as it often is these days. The key obstacle is a big metal grille, a barrier which ideally requires the use of a thermic lance, popular with criminals in the eighties but now, it seems, out of fashion, because you don't hear much about them any more. This grille wasn't in place, though, which was lucky because my wife's toolkit doesn't run to a thermic lance.

Once inside, I pulled the gear from my bag. Trying to go all efficient, I called out the objects one by one: 'Hammer, check. Pencil, check. Tape measure, check. Banana, check.' And so forth. Then I opened the little sachet of screws and brackets and stuff and tipped them into a bowl, so as not to lose any. 'I am tipping the bits and pieces and stuff into a bowl,' I said to the empty room, 'so as not to lose any.' Then I looked at the bed platform itself, and I couldn't help noticing that Tom was half-way through a Wilbur Smith novel called *Monsoon*. 'Shame on you, Tommy!' I announced, flicking through to see if there were any dirty bits. I tried to vault the four feet or so up on to the platform by facing away from it and hoisting myself up backwards, but my bottom jammed on the edge and I fell over.

Undeterred, I got a chair and climbed up that way. The platform was maybe five feet below the ceiling, so I had to inspect the top of the wooden frame, where I wanted to fix the blind, in a sort of quarter crouch, because I am in fact more than four and a half feet tall. I saw where the metal brackets, Full Metal Brackets as I called them, because I thought it was funny, were to go. I also saw that two existing hooks were in the way. They were only silly little picture hooks, but I twisted them for ages, wedged in this painful bendy position, and they wouldn't budge. So I got my hammer and smashed both hooks to oblivion. 'Take five, Bob,' I panted, 'and eat the banana.'

Back at work, I did a bit of measuring, shouted, 'Ooooh, it's going to be close,' and started to screw in the brackets. It took a long time and I lack DIY fitness, so my neck, shoulders and back all ached intolerably, like Orwell when he went down that coal mine in Wigan in 1936. Eventually, after an hour or more, stripped to the waist, picturing myself as a sort of older, fatter, more hideous version of that builder in the Diet Coke advert, it came down to what my DIY efforts always come down to: a sweaty wrestling match in a confined space with a bit of metal, a bit of plastic or a bit of wood, or in this case all three.

Straining and swearing, writhing and riving, simultaneously supporting the weight of a six-foot blind while trying to prise a bracket an eighth of an inch further open with a screwdriver, I surprised myself by beginning, *in extremis*, to recite the Lord's Prayer. 'Our Father, which art in heaven, Hallowed be thy

Name . . .' (I'm a *Book of Common Prayer* man, the milk-and-water modern version doesn't have nearly the same muscle) . . . 'Thy kingdom come. Thy will be done in earth, As it is in . . .' And at that point I surprised myself a great deal more, and it turns out there is a God, because the blind popped into what I believe may very well be called its locating spigot without any further ado. How about that?

It didn't go up and down, of course, this blind. I'd put the plunger on the wrong end, but my wife fixed that later on when she took the whole thing down and put it up again. Tom seems happy, and so am I.

8 November 2003

Still up north this week, but the action moves a few miles west of Hull, out into the picturesque villages of East Yorkshire, an area recently named in some survey or other as the best place to live in the whole country, just as Hull itself was selected as Britain's 'crappest town' in a new book. Out there in the rolling Wolds, where you can still pick up your dream Georgian farm-house for thruppence ha'penny, my brother-in-law owns a garage. He specializes in the four-wheel drives favoured by the local quality, most of whom have an amazing amount of disposable cash.

I asked Colin, that's his name, if I could spend a morning working for him. When he'd finished laughing, he said yeah, that'd be handy, because his usual Saturday lad had gone off on a shoot, and if I came instead he'd still not have to make his own coffee. (When they say 'shoot' in East Yorkshire, incidentally, they mean *killing* things, as opposed to filming them.) My wife dropped me off at 9 a.m. Our car stayed, too: I was to help perform its service, an endeavour which greatly amused my brother-in-law and greatly worried my wife.

Colin is my wife's baby brother. As I met my wife when we were eleven (my *future* wife, I should say, because although Hull lags behind the modern world in many respects, as detailed in the crap towns book, marriages between eleven-year-olds, even back in 1975, were in fact prohibited, as they still are), I must therefore have first met Colin when he was about six. Given that, you'd think he'd treat me with a bit of respect, wouldn't you? But he doesn't. In fact, it is I, in my craven way, who requires his good opinion, rather than the other way around.

This is partly because I admire his talent for mechanics, and partly because he has the gift of making me laugh at inappropriate moments during family gatherings. But mostly I defer to Colin because I once saw him walk full tilt into a lamp post, and not even flinch. Not even *comment*. I always wail and whinge if I so much as stub my toe, yet it wasn't Colin's grace under fire I liked, more the world-weariness of his reaction, the refusal to be intimidated by a lamp post, the instant acceptance that bad things sometimes happen and you must deal with them and move forward. That, rather than a high pain threshold, is a gift worth having, and I don't have it. Had it been my nose connecting with that unyielding metal, I'd have been depressed for days.

The standard course that this column should now follow is to chart some humiliating failure on my part. But, in truth, I've had enough of running myself down (and so, she has let it be known, has my mother, which is the clincher). Needless to say, I'm not much good with cars. But then I don't need to be, because my wife loves them. My family covers a normal ten thousand miles or so a year: I doubt that I drive even five hundred of them, preferring to slump against my seatbelt, tongue lolling, while my wife burns off BMWs at traffic lights.

Besides, there is no humiliating failure to report. Mike, the mechanic, who pretended to let me help him, rapidly got the measure of his pupil. He asked me if I had the service book for our car.

'The what?' I said.

'The service book,' he said.

'I'm sorry, I don't know what you mean,' I said.

He asked where the locking wheel nut was kept.

'I don't know.'

He asked me about the condition of the spare tyre.

'I don't know anything about the spare tyre.'

After that, he got the idea. When he later asked me to press the brake pedal so he could check the lights, he added: 'It's the one in the middle.'

That's the kind of guidance I like.

I did OK. I changed the oil without getting any in my face, as Colin predicted I would. I began to use the word 'sump', one of my all-time favourites, with genuine confidence. I had some fun with a thing called an impact gun and then some more with another machine called a TFR spray. I made lots of coffee, which I've always been good at. I nonchalantly picked a few trapped leaves out of the engine while Mike changed the spark plugs. Borrowing some overalls, I strutted around a bit, hoping we might all do a couple of verses of 'Uptown Girl', waving our spanners around in front of Christie Brinkley and so forth, but sadly my brother-in-law doesn't run that sort of operation.

Still, Colin indicated that I'd done 'OK', which in northern-speak equates roughly to a 'fantastic' or an 'amazing' in the inflated linguistic currency of the South. Our car hasn't fallen to pieces. Do I feel more manly? Nah, not really, no. But I do feel reassured. It's always bothered me that if things go belly up here, I haven't got a lot to fall back on. Now, my new scenario goes like this: get sacked; sell house in London; buy pile in pretty East

Yorkshire village; get job as world's oldest apprentice mechanic. Makes me feel a lot better.

22 November 2003

A rare night out last Friday. During the afternoon, my wife rang to see if I'd done anything about booking a restaurant. Of course I hadn't, so I suggested we go where we always go, hoping she'd agree. But no, she didn't. I sensed that she was in that mood where a woman wants you to *make something exciting happen*. She asked me to book a new place in Islington that she'd read about. I phoned them up. The guy on the other end told me they were full. I said, oh, OK, thanks anyway, and rang my wife back.

Naturally, she was disappointed. But here's the thing: I could tell by her tone that *I was being held responsible* for the lack of availability at the new restaurant, as if I should somehow have divined that here was where she would want to go and booked it sooner, or else found some way around the brute fact of it being full. It was now incumbent on me to find somewhere else, somewhere nice, somewhere we hadn't been before. From out of a clear blue sky, cruising towards the weekend, suddenly I had a problem. Such is the eternally perilous nature of male–female relations. You can't drop your guard for a moment, you really can't.

I asked around at work. Someone suggested a place: 'Giles Coren says it's the best restaurant in north London,' they said. 'That'll do,' I replied. Got the number, booked it, job done. A few hours later, we walked in. Straight away, I wished we hadn't. You get in a panic, you make a mistake.

When I walk into a smart restaurant, I'm intimidated. Those nagging anxieties about cutlery and such like, they don't go away, not fully. I don't trust my own behaviour. I never know whether to wipe the plate because it's the gourmandy, rustic French thing to do, or *not* to wipe the plate because wiping the plate is still, in fact, disgusting. I also struggle with the language. Of the 137 words on the menu, I counted eight I didn't understand (I did this arithmetic later. My wife and I have been together a long time, but we can still sustain a conversation over dinner, though we do repeat ourselves): butternut, rémoulade, charlotte, darne, harissa, boudin, délice, griottine. Not a clue. Quite a few others, e.g., parfait, boulangère, galette, confit, I sort of grasp, but would be hard pushed to describe in any detail. Then come those words (artisan, for instance, or pied bleu, which means blue foot, doesn't it?) that I understand perfectly but not in the context of a restaurant menu. I asked for duck.

The waiter gave me a little bow and the wine list. Being handed a wine list always sends a surge of panic through my abdomen. This thick leather volume went on for ever. I flicked back and forth, the words swimming, realizing that it wasn't arranged in the normal way. Finding the second-cheapest wine, my usual tactic, proved impossible. Flustered, still conscious that my wife wanted me to behave in a way other than the way I usually do, I ordered something called the Flight of Tiresias.

A 'flight' turned out to be a selection of different wines by the glass. The thing about Tiresias, having just looked him up in *The Penguin Dictionary of Classical Mythology*, is that he was blind, possibly because of seeing Athene naked or possibly, opinions differ, because of something he said to Hera about sex. Three glasses arrived, numbered one, two and three, along with a form to fill in. I had to guess the grape type and country of origin of each of the three. Get three out of the six questions right and I'd win a bottle of wine.

As a teenager, my dad and I used to make wine from those Boots kits. We had some demijohns, bungs and those little U-shaped pipes that went in the top and bubbled. We'd empty a

can of hock-type concentrate (or claret, or whatever, my favourite was Moselle) into the demijohn and add the yeast and sugar.
Two months later: eight bottles of wine. It wasn't bad, that stuff.
I used to like drawing the labels in felt pen. But my wine
education never progressed from knowing that Boots Burgundy
was darker and gloopier than Boots Beaujolais. I don't think I've
got the palate. Words like 'oaky', 'grassy', 'fruity', 'spicy' and
'apricoty' mean nothing to me, they're just normal words with a
Y on the end. Twenty years of smoking can't have helped.

After a lot of crossings-out, half-remembered holidays and
mind-changing, I submitted my form. The waiter seemed
embarrassed when he brought it back, along with another form
containing the right answers. In fact, I think he was sniggering.
I scored a big, fat, full-bodied, oaky zero. I wasn't even close: my
country was always ten thousand miles away and something I'd
always thought of as a grape turned out to be a region. If
I'd written any old answer, without even tasting the stuff, I'd
have had a better chance. Saying every wine was an Australian
Riesling, for instance, would have got me three points and the
freebie. So it was really quite hard to score nothing.

My wife was, I think, rather impressed.

29 November 2003

In a last-gasp attempt to turn myself into the man I always
thought I would become but haven't, I've been reading the
papers very attentively, so as to start the day all well briefed and
go-getting. This is in conjunction with my autumn suit-wearing
offensive, which has had a tremendous impact. Senior executives
have said hello to me in corridors, asked me to write for their
sections, even favoured me (the male ones at least, the female
ones tend to call Security) with manly nods in the lavatory.
Jeans never got this respect. Those dot.com businesses in Seattle,

where employees wear vests and play ping-pong all day? *The Times* isn't like that. Money well spent, that suit.

Now, I realized, I must tailor the words to match the clothes. Self-obsessed, anecdotal whimsy would have to go. I decided to reinvent this column as a *tour d'horizon* of *les sujets de nos jours*, using lots of French phrases to impress readers while hectoring them about how they should live their lives. So I've been reading the papers, and my eye has been caught by lots of articles about how the birthrate is falling because people are delaying having children. I thought: I know, I'll pontificate about that. I read on, and discovered the most common reason for the delay is that people are increasingly reluctant to give up the liberated, free-wheeling lifestyle of the child-free.

I started staring out of the window, thinking about myself. The new grown-up objective commentator had lasted two paragraphs. I was thinking (proof that self-centredness can survive parenthood if you put the effort in) about my life, with no reference to anybody else, let alone wider social trends. I tried to remember what my own so-called 'lifestyle' was like during those distant, fading years before I became a father. What exactly was it that I sacrificed when my first child was born almost seven years ago? What did I actually do with all that spare time? I thought for quite a while.

I used to laze around in bed for longer, that's for certain, especially in the mornings. I distinctly remember lying there listening to Gary Richardson doing the sports round-up. Now I throw off the duvet just in time to miss the whole of 'Thought for the Day', unless it's Anne Atkins, who's great. If I get it right, I can race into the bathroom, out of platitude range, get dressed, collect the children, cajole them downstairs, organize the Weetabix and put the kitchen radio on just as the vicar finishes his final sentence and Jim Norrchhh-tee comes back on. Do I envy all those people without children who can listen to the weather forecast while horizontal? A bit, I suppose. So that's one thing.

What else? Oh yeah, I used to go to the gym, albeit sporadically, and now I don't go at all, though I probably could go at lunchtime if I weren't so busy reading newspapers and wearing my suit. My friend Joe, whom I saw last weekend, he makes time for the gym, and he's got more children than me, *and* an idiotic dog called Begel to worry about as well. Mind you, Fiona, his wife, she does a lot of baking, so he needs to exercise more than I do. Do I miss the gym? Not remotely. It was all a bit pointless and narcissistic. Anyway, I'm not in appreciably worse shape at thirty-nine than I was at thirty-two, other than the inevitable ravages of time. I do a sit-up now and again, if I'm in the mood.

There were a few other things, now that I remember. Before we had children, we'd go to the theatre occasionally, taking it in turns to fall asleep during the second act. I watched more television, rarely missing an episode of *Brookside* from its earliest days up until it went silly with one siege too many. So that was useful. I'd also watch a lot more sport on the TV. If I hadn't watched any of it, it wouldn't bother me now, except for Benn–McClellan in '95, that was exciting. I paid the cat a lot more attention. And I definitely spent more time, even more than I do now, writing in my diary, introspecting, raking over the past and generally moping about. Dr Feelgood says all that is very bad for you, so it's just as well I cut down.

That was it, that was the lifestyle so abruptly curtailed in a delivery room at University College Hospital one beautiful sunny day in the early spring of 1997. Obviously I should have made more of the freedom I'm supposed to have had (though the truth is, I still had to go to work, and fulfil numerous other obligations, wipe the surfaces in the kitchen, put the rubbish out next to the bins and so forth). But obviously too a lot of that freedom was only the freedom to waste time. I didn't do any good works then that I don't do now, or socialize any more, or read more, or nurture my career, or learn Russian or anything like that. I travelled a bit, and I should have done more, it isn't easy now.

Ten, twelve years ago, my wife was always badgering me to fly off on city breaks with her to European capitals, or go skiing, she was really keen on that kind of thing. She probably knew her life would soon change a lot more than mine.

21 February 2004

I thought it would be really funny, or at least a little bit funny, and also instructive, to see what would happen if I did what women do and phoned my friends to talk about interior design. I have never done this before. Indeed, being a man, I phone my friends as rarely as possible. I decided that should change: I would ask for my friends' advice about the kitchen, which is too small, and therefore domestically provocative. Aside from flatulence and the whole driving/navigation minefield, the smallness of our kitchen probably gives rise to more marital friction than anything else. My wife talks to *her* friends about the kitchen. I thought I'd give mine a go. First, I phoned my friend Michael.

Er, hello Michael, I said, I need some advice.

'Go on,' he said.

About the, er, the, um, the *kitchen*, actually, I said.

'Yeah, your *kitchen*,' he began, sounding anything but surprised, but rather like a man given a chance to vent a long-standing grudge. 'There's that bit above the microwave, isn't there? Where the glasses are? That little corner? Sort of round the side of the cooker? That's very *cluttered*, isn't it? Admit it. I've always thought you should get one of those stacking step things from Ikea. Stack everything on that. Be a lot better, I think.'

I said fine, I'll look into it, I'd no idea you felt so strongly. Anything else?

'Yeah,' he said. 'Smeg fridges are good, but don't get pink, my ex had one.'

Next, I dialled my colleague Alan.

'Bob, that's amazing! I've just had a new boiler put in. Barry the Plumber. Ariston, £2,000.'

I like to think I know Alan very well, but I wasn't aware of his encyclopedic knowledge of kitchen appliances, appliances which he discussed as if he had memorized dozens of sales brochures.

'I like the reassuring presence of an Aga in the heart of a kitchen,' he said. And, 'I did a deal with Neff through Möben Kitchens, conveniently twinned with Dolphin Bathrooms,' and, 'I love my Alessi cafetière, an extravagance at £60, but it's given distinguished service.'

Excellent information, Al, I said, what do you feel about colour?

Here, I feel Alan lost his way a little. 'I like glass and steel, shiny black units, stone sink, slate draining board, tiled areas with a motif, though not every tile, maybe every fourth one, possibly a mandala motif within a lozenge.'

What's a mandala? I asked.

'A sort of Indian starburst,' he said.

Next, I called Andy in Bristol, the cleverest person I know. We usually talk about politics. Or at least *he* does, while I try to remember what he's saying so I can pass it off as my opinion to impress others. Surely, I thought, Andy wouldn't want to talk about my kitchen. I was wrong.

'Hmmm,' he said, lasering in on the crux of the problem, 'basic breakfast-bar approach, right? Good for leaning on and pontificating, but hampering expansion, right?'

That's about the size of it, I admitted.

'Well,' he went on, 'either you retain the bar and stick with that contemporary open-plan dining style, that poncey idea that your guests sit sipping wine at the bar while you toss a plate of pasta together, which is very *London*. Or you could opt for a more classical configuration.'

And which would you recommend?

'Oh, I hate people coming round to eat, so I say f*** the open-plan and stick them in the dining room.' He added that he had recently read a history of fridge-freezers.

Finally, I phoned John. We've worked together for ages, John and I. We've spent weeks, months even, in each other's company: on motorways, on planes, in the echoing dining rooms of a hundred provincial hotels. We've never once talked about kitchens.

'Hey, Bobby Boy!' said John, adopting his tried and tested comedy Ulster accent, 'What's up?'

Well, John, I said, the thing is, I'm fed up with the kitchen and I wondered if you had any suggestions.

There was a pause. 'How do you mean?' he said guardedly.

I mean, you know, my kitchen's too small, have you got any ideas?

'What sort of ideas?' he asked.

Well, maybe you've seen something on a makeover show, or in a magazine, and you've thought, wow, that'd be just right in Robert's kitchen!

'No,' said John, puzzled, 'I haven't done that.'

Well, never mind, I said, tell me what you think anyway.

There was a very long pause. 'Eggshell,' he said, eventually, 'otherwise it comes off. Get a fine brush for the edges. And put masking tape on the bits you don't want painted.'

OK, I said, that's useful . . . what colour is *your* kitchen, John?

'Er . . . um . . . blue!' he said, with the air of someone who has just dredged up the answer to a tricky general-knowledge question.

What shade of blue?

'Er . . . not dark blue, not light blue, not navy . . .' John ran out of types of blue.

Royal? I suggested.

'No, not royal. Aqua maybe. Is there aqua blue? That colour you get in the sea? Is that aqua? Is that all right? Is that what you wanted?'

I said, John, that's fine, the hoary old caricature of the dopey male has been a long time coming, but I knew you wouldn't let me down.

10 April 2004

Just four months to go to my fortieth birthday, and so many failings to put right. I'm on a diet, lost eight pounds in a month, yet even so my target of regaining the 33 inch waist I haven't possessed for, ahem, quite a while, seems a long way off. Still, a start has been made. By way of a tip, incidentally, I've given up carbohydrates in the evening and gone easy on the cake-biscuit-crisp triumvirate the rest of the time. I've also stopped eating the children's leftovers, which was a fairly disgusting habit in any case. Following this regime has lost me two pounds a week, nice and steady.

I've combined the diet with more exercise, though not *that* much more, otherwise I know from experience hunger would overwhelm me and I'd stuff my face with whatever was to hand. My new bicycle computer is a massive help. I now end all journeys by cycling around in circles to bring the total distance up to a round number. Invaluable. I've also become very keen on the maximum-speed function. This week I clocked 25.7 mph, albeit wind-assisted, on the slope that leads west down to the river from the Tower of London. The magic 30 mph mark cannot be far away. After that I'm aiming to get flashed by a speed camera. What I need is a long hill in a thirty zone without too much traffic and certainly no potholes, speed bumps or those hidden tripwires with bombs on. If anyone knows of such a place, I'd be grateful to hear of it. I'm willing to travel.

Meanwhile, jigsaws. Not the cutting tool, nor the ever-popular women's outfitters, but the cosmically futile puzzles that I've never been any good at. By way of a joke (and because, in as much as I have hobbies, local geography is one of them) my wife gave me a jigsaw for Christmas, a 225-piece section of the *A to Z* centred on our house. This is a clever idea of someone's, isn't it, the personalized jigsaw map. Unless you live in the middle of a large field that is, or a lake, like a duck, in which case I imagine such a jigsaw would be exceptionally hard, not to mention suicidally boring. And indeed uninformative.

Anyway, one afternoon recently, around the deadly 4 p.m. mark when your blood sugar hits the floor and all you want is a doughnut or a Kit Kat or a longish lie-down, or all three, I decided I wasn't good for anything else so I'd give the jigsaw a go. I didn't want to. I have hated and feared jigsaws for as long as I can remember. Patience, clarity of thought, concentration, medium-term forward planning, fine motor skills: these are the qualities you need to do jigsaws, these are just some of the qualities I lack. But I reckoned if I could conquer my jigsaw-phobia, that'd be progress. I cleared a space on my desk and shook the nasty little bits of cardboard out into a pile.

It was an agonizingly slow business. You're supposed to do the edge pieces first, aren't you? My five-year-old daughter told me that when she was about two. Took me a good twenty minutes of listless picking up and putting back down before I recalled this advice. An hour later, perimeter in place, I turned my attention to the guts of the neighbourhood. Trying to stay all methodical, I pre-sorted all the light green of Victoria Park into one group, but then . . . then I got fed up, truth be told. So I abandoned any method and instead backed a hunch on two apparently compatible bits, wrestled with them for ages, gave up, got depressed, lost my way. Pretty soon I was trying to drive a railway through the middle of a church, re-routing canals into hospitals and the like. And so it went on. Around 6.30, going-home time, my colleague and room-mate Alan Franks suggested it might help to turn all the pieces face up. I said hey Al, you're right, I wouldn't have guessed you were any good at this sort of thing.

'Bob,' he said, 'I'm not.'

Alan got sucked in after that. Together, we pored over the whole sorry mess, Alan in my chair as the senior pro, me leaning over his shoulder, swearing. As the office slowly emptied around us, and the ache between my shoulder blades grew ever more rampant, and the clock ticked, we faffed on and on into the night, twisting random bits of real estate this way and that, occasionally celebrating, more often hanging our heads in dejection as whichever nodule under scrutiny proved recalcitrant. Alan was right: he wasn't any good at jigsaws either. We brought the thing in at a shade under four hours, shook hands, went off home. Later my wife knocked it off in fifty-eight minutes. She's got that sort of brain: enjoys maths, anagrams, packing the car boot for holidays, that sort of thing.

So, predictable humiliation. Indeed, the phrase 'stitched up like a kipper' comes to mind. And yet also, partial success. At least I saw it through to the end, and that's worth something, isn't it, though I can't say precisely what. With many tasks in life, I suppose, there comes a moment when you must confront and face down, face down quite ruthlessly, the essential futility of what you are doing. Jigsaws are excellent training for those moments. Not entirely a waste of time then, not entirely.

15 May 2004

I think I may have invented a new Olympic sport. Or at least refined an existing discipline. I'm calling it the dad triathlon. Like a normal triathlon, the dad triathlon involves a run, a swim and a cycle, with some extra dad tasks thrown in. It's late in the day, but maybe there's still time for me to compete against a lot of other dads from around the world in Athens this summer. By satellite link-up, perhaps.

The rules need some tightening up, though the first one is clear enough. This states that the competitor should force his family into a four-mile walk that his children, who plead to go by car, do not want to make. The walk could be along the white cliffs of Dover on a bank holiday Monday, for instance from, say, the village of Kingsdown to the Bluebird tearooms at St Margaret's at Cliffe, the village where Noël Coward lived in the forties before swanning off to Jamaica.

Wherever the venue, the family must set off in bright sunshine wearing shorts and sandals and within a few minutes be confronted by a vicious headwind and darkening skies. It is essential *both* that the dad's wife must have asked him beforehand if he thought the children had enough clothes on (to which he must have replied yes of course stop fussing, or words to that effect) *and* that early in the miserable trek the dad has dismissed any idea of turning back because deep down he believes plodding up a cold, steep slope in a vest is good for you. Under rule two the shivering, resentful children then refuse to make the return journey on foot. Their mother, employing the time-honoured rubric, will say don't worry, Dad Will Go Back To Get The Car.

So begins the first leg of the triathlon. The dad starts back in fine spirits, running, welcoming this tiny domestic crisis as a chance to do something traditionally paternal. He knows such opportunities to show that his core male virtues of physical fortitude and self-sacrifice are in full working order don't come around too often. He sets off at a fast pace, hoping his family are watching (they aren't). He looks at the sky and urges the rain to do its worst; saturation forming an excellent prelude to martyrdom. Then his kidneys start to hurt and he has to slow down.

And then Dad's shins ache, and he wonders who lit a fire in his lungs, and he is obliged to complete his journey at a sort of agonized jog/brisk walk. At the car park, thigh muscles screaming, he first stalls then over-revs his engine, and then confuses his wipers with his indicators. On the drive round to collect his family, the dad runs into an inexplicable traffic jam, and he may well pound the steering wheel and swear quite a bit as any hope of a time quick enough to impress his wife is eaten away.

Once safely back at the family's comical, and yet surely, if I mention it in *The Times* often enough, soon-to-be-fashionable triangular orange holiday chalet, Dad expects a cup of tea and a bit of a sit-down with the sports pages. But no, his wife now requires him to complete the second leg of the triathlon by taking his daughter swimming. Dad may protest, until his wife points out that his son has developed virulent diarrhoea while waiting in the tearoom and he's quite welcome to stay and deal with that instead if he wants. Dad gets his trunks and daughter and heads for the pool.

The dad triathlete has an ambivalent attitude towards swimming pools. On the one hand, even though he's lost some weight recently, he's self-conscious about exposing his body. He also gets cold and bored quite quickly in the water, and of course finds the whole changing-room tussle with small children very stressful. On the other hand, Dad used to be a bit of a swimmer in his youth, having attended a club for a while, the one at the East Hull baths on the Holderness Road run by former England international and butterfly specialist Terry Glenville, for instance. Even though that was all a long time ago, Dad still fancies himself quite useful in the aquatic department. So he'll probably want to spend most of his time badgering his five-year-old daughter to watch while he performs what he calls a 'racing dive', something that most neutral observers would find hard to distinguish from a bellyflop.

The final leg follows the drive back to Hackney, or wherever, during which Dad dozes in the passenger seat in a cloud of chlorine with his tongue lolling out. A late-night packed-lunch panic will send Dad off on his bicycle to the local mini-market, trying to find some nice middle-class tubes of yoghurt, plus some mini-tomatoes and cream cheese, returning instead with a loaf of flannel bread, a jar of Marmite and some blackening bananas swinging from his handlebars. He then has to knock these together into something his children might want to eat the next day. Stack the dishwasher, deputrefy the cat litter, do the bins, put the bolts on, and the dad triathlon is done. It's not easy, but no one said it would be.

What do you reckon? Would anyone want to watch?

7 August 2004

By the time you read this, I will, God willing, on a beach somewhere in Pembrokeshire, probably drunk, probably in the rain, probably with Abba in my ears, be about to turn forty years old. My first thought on the imminence of the fifth decade is: how did *that* happen? My second is: what *presents* will I get? (Actually, I already know my wife has got me a juicer. Great big thing, does cabbages and turnips and everything. Very happy with the juicer, too huge to take on holiday though, hence my going so childishly early on the unwrapping.) And my third thought is that the onrushing landmark provides a good excuse to compile a short personal inventory.

Where to start? Well, obviously, with my *hair*. It's all still there, and only a tiny bit grey, and I've finally come to terms with the way it irritatingly sticks up at the front. It's not great hair, but it's hanging in there, so that's fine. Overall, physically I'm feeling good, far far better off at forty than I was at, say, thirty-six, when for a few weeks in the summer of 2000 I nudged 15 stone 10 pounds, about the same weight Evander Holyfield used to fight at. Way too much for a man of 5 feet 10 who isn't heavyweight champion of the world.

Now I'm a very smug 12 stone 3 pounds. I went for a long cycle ride with one of my children's teachers the other week. I was giving away ten years and, worse, he's Australian, with one of those ultra-fit southern hemisphere faces. I was all ready to start guzzling amphetamines and injecting extra blood into my groin to keep up with him but no, I didn't have to. It helped that he'd been on lager tops until 3 a.m. the night before, but that's his lookout, isn't it?

On the other hand, I still smoke. Back in the days when it seemed like a long way off, as opposed to three days, I promised the children I'd give up on my fortieth birthday. I went to this hypnotherapist, and I'm hoping that'll help, especially as I fell asleep for half the session: £150 is a bit on the steep side for a siesta, don't you think?

And yesterday my osteopath said my wrists were showing signs of the dreaded RSI. She reckoned my typing technique (the frenzied two-finger stab) was probably to blame. So, after the shorthand, I've now got to learn to touch-type, another skill I wish I'd tucked away at school, so much more useful than being able to say, 'I have broken my leg, my dog is called Lumpi, do you have anything for a headache?"* in German, or trying to make a poker.

My mental health is, I think, improving, too. I'm learning to live in the moment, something I've never been good at. I had a few good moments last Sunday afternoon, for example, a couple of hours of them indeed, on the railway chugging down through Kent with a carriage all to myself. Socks off, sunglasses on (*love* sunglasses), reading about cricket and American politics in the papers, drinking tea, eating Brazil nuts . . . when you reach a certain age, you appreciate the finer things in life, it's true.

Intellectually, though, I do feel I'm treading water. I haven't got stuck into a heavy book in ages. I might have to take David Stevenson's *History of the First World War* on holiday. I might even have to read it. And technologically I'm still mired in the Stone Age, acutely aware, for example, of the 560 unanswered emails in my in-box, some of which are now two and a half years old.

What else? Oh yes, I'm becoming more sartorially confident, which is good. I bought a couple of new shirts recently. One pink, one stripy. Neither of which I would have worn five years ago. And I've had a stroke of luck in the ever-troublesome footwear department. My wife tells me Birkenstocks are now fashionable, which is gratifying after all these years of people sniggering at mine. Who knows, one day clumpy black £18 trainers from Asda might have their moment, too?

All in all, turning forty, I don't know what all the moaning and groaning is about. It's much better than thirty (burning up with frustrated ambition, prone to assassination fantasies) or twenty (see previous parentheses and multiply) or, God forbid, ten (fat, temperamental, underpants still made of nylon). Now, at forty minus three days, I can command a (limited) amount of

---

* 'Ich habe mein Bein gebrochen, mein Hund heist Lumpi, haben Sie etwas gegen Kopfschmerzen?'

respect from the younger members of staff here, which is great, although one did tell me yesterday that I stank of fish. Even so, I seem to have stumbled into that happy (and, I don't doubt, short) period after Young Man With Potential and before Clapped Out Old Fart. I intend to make the most of it. One thing I'm going to do, after three years and 154 columns on the bounce, is take a modest holiday from this slot. Back in three weeks.

11 September 2004

My wife, determined to spend as little time in Hackney as possible before the new term began, went away with the children at the end of the summer, up to Hull and, before that, to Nantwich to stay with her friend Karen. I joined the family for the intervening weekends, feeling like one of those Italian fathers who head out of Milan every Friday in August. A bit like that, anyway: chugging through Northampton on Midland Mainline isn't quite the same, I imagine, as sweeping up to Lake Maggiore on the autostrada. Mind you, Nantwich is nice, isn't it? I couldn't help noticing that a lot of people were wearing neck braces. Is there a problem with necks in south Cheshire? A local neck expert might like to respond.

During the week I was alone in London. And left to his own devices, it is surprising, or maybe it isn't surprising, how rapidly a man's domestic standards start to slide. The dishwasher was broken awaiting repair, so to cut down on washing-up, I instituted a bold new crockery policy: namely, to use the same Pyrex bowl for everything. That's tea, coffee, Ugly Breakfast – a sludgy paste of fruits, yoghurt and seeds – mackerel salad, everything, quick wipe round with kitchen roll in between. This worked well. I suppose it is *possible* the problems I had on the Thursday were indeed caused by food poisoning, but a dose of that's always useful for keeping the weight down in any case.

That veneer of civilization? Paper-thin, I'm telling you. The cat litter got pretty rank. And of course I made hay with lavatory seats, tinned food and extravagant displays of flatulence, setting myself challenges such as 'Come on, Bob, do you reckon you can make it from the fireplace to the front door in just the one fart?' (Answer: absolutely you can, with continuity maintained throughout.)

Up in the first-floor cupboard where it usually shakes and shudders out its span, the washing machine was also up the spout. At this time of year, for some reason, all useful appliances like to down tools. (The video is jammed, and the microwave's been protesting too.) The telly and the kettle, thank God, soldier on, though Sky Box Office has been unavailable since I was cutting down a plant and the secateurs went through the special cable as well.

'Take care not to cut that white flex,' said my wife.

'What, this one?' I replied, holding up the two ends.

I had been tasked with getting Hotpoint to repair the washing machine under our usurious warranty scheme. Naturally, I failed to make the call, and equally naturally, I lied to Nicola about it, insisting I'd been trying repeatedly and huh, bloody call centres, couldn't get through. She hadn't believed me, and meanwhile, I'd become reacquainted with underpants from the very bottom of the pile, underpants from a previous geological era. And I'd started wearing specialist socks too: woolly hiking socks, white sports socks, red and black Nicaragua Must Survive socks. And T-shirts I'd had my hair cut in, ones I'd normally avoid at all costs.

But where I really lost my way is with bedtime. Some truculent teenager deep within remains in rebellion against the very notion of a normal bedtime. Also, I have developed an addiction, I don't think that's too strong a word, to films, any films (except horror, detest horror films) that start at one in the morning. In the usual weekday set-up, I can resist my cravings. Free from uxorial constraint, I don't even try.

The first night Nicola was in Nantwich I settled down to a film called *Rapid Exchange* (tired old mid-air heist scenario, exceptionally poor, cinematic equivalent of junk food, watched it all the way through). The next night, I did *The Edge* (Anthony Hopkins battling a bear in the Alaskan wilderness, fabulous scenery, excellent bear-scoffs-minor-character scene, thoroughly recommend it). After that I was fighting fatigue and deadlines for the rest of the week.

So far, so predictable. But the other affliction of being alone always takes me more by surprise, even though it always happens, and even though I've felt it more strongly these past few years, since I had children, I suppose. By Wednesday morning, thirty-six hours in, I was so damned *lonely* I was talking to the cat. 'Hello, Flash, how about that bear, eh? Hey, imagine if *you* were a bear and not a cat, and imagine if *we* had a fight, who do you think would win?' By Thursday, the bonds of sanity slipping free, the cat was talking back. 'Just going back to your bear question, Bob, it'd have to be me, wouldn't it? Those bears are pretty big, eight hundred pounds or more, the grizzlies, ten feet tall on their hind legs,' miaow, purr purr, etc., etc.

It's not healthy, too much time alone. Not for me, anyway. By the time you read this, everything should be back to normal.

11 December 2004

Laid low by something nasty, hot and cold all over, off solids for days. I've not been properly ill since the triple tonsillitis hospitalization of 2002. I blame too much cycling around Victoria Park by moonlight, trying to get airborne, like in *ET*. Being slightly ill, that's fine, provided you're still well enough to potter about indoors, read, maybe shuffle two hundred yards to the shops and rent a DVD from the supercilious Finn who gives you a pitying look if you choose anything mainstream, anything that isn't Iranian or Turkish and with the words 'darkly comic masterpiece' on the box. You can lose weight, have a relax in the warm, get your strength up for the festive. But being *this* ill is not at all fine. You can't do anything worthwhile and your personal hygiene goes to pieces.

You also have to listen to the radio a lot. No hardship when it's Melvyn grappling with Carl Jung, or Tracey Emin on *Desert Island Discs*, but I draw the line at *Money Box* and the afternoon play, the same play I seem to have been switching off for twenty-five years. Fantastic taste in music, by the way, Tracey Emin: 'I Feel Love', 'Young Americans', 'Burning Love', every one a coconut, much appreciated by myself and also by Phil the Builder and his pal Jeff the Painter, who'd come round to do a little light labour on the endless project that is our bathroom. We discussed the excesses of modern art, Phil and Jeff and I, arriving at a trenchant consensus within seconds. Tracey told Sue Lawley she favoured the redistribution of wealth.

'You can give me a few bob,' Phil told the radio, and the three of us chuckled in a sceptical, man-of-the-world kind of way.

Soon afterwards, I went back to bed.

I have peculiar, overheated, dry-throated dreams if I sleep during the day. On this occasion, I dreamt I was having an affair with Viktor Yushchenko, the world's most popular Ukrainian. He was wearing a woolly hat with snow on it – very seasonal. I'd watched a documentary on George Michael the night before, and in the dream, Viktor and I were guests at a ski chalet, in the Alps I believe, like in the video for 'Last Christmas', only without the big hair and hoop earrings. He's not a bad-looking bloke, Viktor, at least he was until poisoned by persons unknown, but if I had to write out a list of candidates with whom to share an unconscious erotic moment, he wouldn't be on it, no disrespect. I woke feeling enfeebled and confused. A few days later I watched *The Beach* and dreamt my wife ran off to Thailand with a shark who looked like Leonardo DiCaprio.

I don't like not having any strength. Does any man? A colleague copied something to me off the net, one of those jokey lists that seem always to originate in some City bank and then do the rounds. This one was a series of definitions of true masculinity: having a scar, taking out £200 from the cashpoint, nodding at coppers, and so forth. The thing was, it was supposed to be ironic, yet I found myself agreeing with almost every proposition, except the ones to do with pubs and power tools, contact with which I keep to a minimum.

The first definition said: 'Opening jars: nnnng, she's struggling. You take it from her, open it effortlessly and pretend she loosened it for you. She didn't. Jars are men's work.' That's meant to be a joke, right? A send-up of traditional male virtues? I have to admit it represents my attitude to jar-opening in every particular. If, at least once every day, I could come across a woman trying to open a jar, and open it for her, I believe I'd be happy. Chutney, jam, mini-gherkins, I'm not bothered.

To prove you're a real man, you have to take your chances where you can. My son had a loose tooth. Family, I said, in a low voice, impressively croaky with infection, leave it to me, and took him off with some dental floss and a hankie, a bit like when the adult men took Kunta Kinte off into the bush in *Roots*. He agreed to let me hook the tooth out provided we could talk about guns afterwards. A lot of wiggling and out it came, plus just enough blood to swell Sam's seven-year-old chest with pride. Then we did the rate of fire of a Bren gun, a specialist subject of mine, *The Observer's Book of Firearms* being one of those comfort books I revisit when feeling low.

We amass these facts and fears and fantasies, we men, while

women, I find, are much better at seeing the world the way it actually is.

'Why is the tooth fairy real if other fairies aren't real?' asked Rachel, Sam's five-year-old sister, at bedtime. 'And,' she added, the cold light of rationalism in her eye, 'if she's small enough to fly under the door, how can she lift the tooth?'

'Look, Rachel,' said Sam. 'It's not me, and it's not you, and it's not Mummy or Daddy, so it *must* be the tooth fairy.'

She accepted that, reluctantly. Father Christmas, I sense, could be under threat, if not this year, certainly next. I need to get well and enjoy the whole ho-ho-ho rigmarole while it lasts.

29 January 2005

I have to say I do enjoy working in a preponderantly female office. Last week, for instance, I managed to finesse an all-female lunchtime ice-skating trip (all female, that is, except for me, who had arranged the whole thing hoping precisely for this gender imbalance to result). As it happened, this outing was only a moderate success from my point of view, as I was largely ignored in favour of an absurdly handsome ice marshal called Dwain (minuscule bottom, big smile, didn't fall over and get his jeans all soggy). Even so, the five-to-one ratio was gratifying.

And a couple of years ago, at an office hen party where I and the other chaps were granted honorary woman status, I infiltrated a conversation in which the bride-to-be discussed with an otherwise exclusively female group of our mutual friends and colleagues her choice of *underwear* for the big day. (Agent Provocateur, as it goes.) It was . . . *fabulous*. I sat there, hardly daring to breathe, thinking: if I stay *very* quiet and *very* still, perhaps they won't notice I'm not a woman. This must be one of the benefits of being a gay man, I imagine, in that you're privy to this sort of chat *all the time*, though I suppose if you *are* a gay man, this sort of chat doesn't carry quite the same frisson.

Less spectacularly, the relative lack of men here makes it a pleasant place to be. Generalization is a perilous business, yet as a rule I find that women are less competitive than men. (A caveat straight away: while my son spent his school sports day sprint sauntering along waving to acquaintances in the crowd and trying to engage his rival in the next lane in conversation, I caught my daughter crouching down at the start line after everything had finished, staring hard at the track ahead. What are you doing, Rachel? I asked.

'Practising for next year,' she replied, her five-year-old face a mask of concentration.

Professional athletes call this technique 'visualization', I believe.) I enjoy being able to move freely around the office, safe in the (almost) certain knowledge that a borderline psychopath in a suit isn't going to plunge a knife in my back while I'm bent over filling the kettle.

Sometimes, though, spurred by some atavistic longing, I hanker for a taste of aggro. Which I think explains why I ended up challenging Esther the researcher to a cake-baking contest last weekend. Someone said about four-ish on the Friday that what they really fancied was some *lemon drizzle cake*, and Esther volunteered to make one and bring it in on the Monday, and I said, hey, I'll make one, too. That was all fine, but then I got carried away and said *yeah*, Esther, we'll see whose is better, we'll have a *blind tasting*, award points for presentation, texture, drizzliness, etc., etc., nah nah ne nah nah. (Another caveat: if this sounds a bit *much*, a bit *male* maybe, a bit *macho*, think of the WI stall at the average village fête.)

Esther said, 'Are you serious?'

Deadly, I said, and then, even though she's only twenty-four, I gave her the thousand-yard stare, so help me, the ice-cold flat-eyed killer stare that I learnt partly off watching too many Clint films and partly off my friend Gavin, who is in the army and can be a little scary when he wants to be. And then I got a recipe from the net and went home to assemble my eggs and butter and flour and lemons and other drizzly paraphernalia, and also to work out what baking parchment was and whether we had any. And then, because I had also learnt from Gavin the admirable military motto that prior planning, preparation and practice prevents piss-poor performance, I got hold of *another* recipe and *another* load of ingredients and decided to make *two* cakes, one then the other, so the second one would be *better*. Nasty, eh? All's fair in love, war and baking.

Sunday afternoon, ably assisted by my competitive daughter, who has the same appetite for raw cake mix that I had at her age (and still have, truth be told), I did the dry run. It turned out OK, not a house brick or anything like that, nothing you could have used as the basis for a drystone wall, and it certainly got eaten that evening in fairly short order, but it wasn't as good as the cake Esther turned up with the following day. Not nearly as good. Too soggy. Thinking back, everything was fine until right at the death I got flustered by a tricky metric/imperial conversion for the syrup and used too much. In short: over-drizzle. A schoolboy error.

And the next one, the second one, the live one? Well, the children were in bed, I was calm, I was rehearsed, I was in the zone, that cakey bakey force was with me, yes indeed. Something clicked into place with your pulsing and your whisking and your folding, and the next one, I say so myself, the next one was pretty damn good, good enough to prompt one of those occasional workplace fantasies where we all say we should resign and go off to do something else, in this case, setting up a company to sell Bob's Lemon Drizzle Cake. A triumph. It's winner stays on. Next week, Lucy and I do battle over the Victoria sponge.

19 February 2005

So, after the Springsteen gig, after the Beat the Intro pop quiz, after the lunchtime bowls, another boys' outing, this time to play pool, that prince among pub games. The original idea came from Harry Hardie, twenty-five, on the picture desk. Harry, in that relaxed, inclusive, idealistic way of the young, thought it'd be cool if some of the guys went out for a beer, had a chat, maybe shot a few frames, that kind of thing. We said, sounds great, and then we (not Harry, the other five of us, the grizzled, battle-hardened hacks around the forty mark) started the entirely predictable business of winding each other up into a competitive frenzy.

By the time the day arrived, I had drawn up a complicated and, if I may say so, rather superior wallchart to log all the results, with space for a written commentary on each match, final standings, best break, pot of the night, dullest shot, etc., plus a section headed Other Useful Information. Nicknames had also been assigned. A quiet after-work drink had turned into the usual grim test of masculinity. I don't think it was what Harry had in mind.

'At least let me be Harry 'The Hedgehog' Hardie?' he said plaintively.

Nah, sorry Harry, we all said, you're fifteen years younger than us, you're Harry 'Boy' Hardie and that's that.

We got to the pool place at 7 p.m. to find we couldn't get a table until half eight.

'Oh no,' said Nigel, 'we're going to have to *talk* to each other for *an hour and a half.*'

We managed it OK, in the event, spending twenty minutes determining the rules for the night: one shot on the black, no nominations, no kicking, biting, gouging or punches below the belt please, gentlemen, etc. My favourite (and I continued to find this amusing even three hours later) was number four, use of nicknames compulsory at all times, as in: 'Drink, Interesting?' 'Guinness, please, The Grinder,' or 'So, who do you fancy at work then, Psycho?' 'How do you mean, Tornado, just on the *Magazine* or across the whole newspaper?' or 'Hey, Fast Bobby, what are you working on at the moment?' 'Well, Harry, sorry, I mean Boy, I'm doing this thing on Michael Owen,' and so forth.

Around about that point Harry tried to broaden the discussion out a bit, but we weren't having it. Instead we made our predictions. Harry, Nigel 'The Grinder' Gosden and Chris 'Psycho' Hitchcock (geddit?) all thought Mark 'Interesting' Davies would bore us into submission with his attritional, safety-first style. Interesting shrugged modestly and said he thought youth might prevail. 'Tornado' Tim Pozzi fancied The Grinder's chances. And in a shocking breach of etiquette 'Fast Bobby' Crampton said he reckoned that 'Fast Bobby' Crampton had it as good as won. After that The Grinder told a cracking joke about a bloke coming home drunk carrying some snails, and I trotted out the one that starts 'The M1 motorway walks into a pub . . .', surely the best opening line to a joke ever. Everyone contributed several others but, in the way of jokes, I can't remember what they were. After that we talked about women for an hour.

And so to the table, and the challenge of rendering a report on fifteen frames of pool between six highly average players in any way readable. I came (so much for predictions) joint last. It's not that I'm that *bad* at pool. In fact, I'm *good* at chalking the cue and posing around the table. I can even string a few shots together and act like I meant them when they work out, not the full Paul Newman, admittedly, but sufficient to fool a casual observer. I think my essential problem was, well, how can I put this . . . ? Oh yeah, this'll do: most of the other players were *better* than me.

Naturally, I didn't admit that at the time.

'The thing I can't understand about tonight, Psycho,' I said, sidling up to him as he prepared for his final, deciding, frame, 'is that you don't seem to be any more competent than I am.'

'I'm sorry, Fast Bobby,' he replied, 'but I've won four frames and you've won one, and that was only after you fluked a couple of pots. So I'm not going to sit here and say I'm crap just to make you feel better.'

At 11 p.m., after they'd turned the light out above our table, in an atmosphere of almost unbearable tension, Psycho beat Interesting on the black ball to become the overall winner.

Out in the street we all said how great it had been, nice one, Harry, we'll have to do it again soon. Someone suggested darts, someone else ten-pin bowling, someone else reckoned we should just have a fight and have done with it.

'Or maybe,' said Harry, 'we could go out and not compete at anything, just *talk*?'

Cue shocked silence.

'Steady on, Harry,' I said after a while, speaking, I know, for all five veterans, 'that's a bit radical, isn't it?'

Next day, Chris 'Psycho' Hitchcock got a pencil and whittled himself a little trophy in the shape of a miniature pool cue. It's on a plinth on top of his Apple Mac.

We're all trying our best to take it like men.

5 March 2005

Many years ago, when I first worked on this magazine, we carried a regular feature about celebrities' favourite games. One week, Jools Holland, possibly not taking the question as seriously as he ought, said that he liked Stobart-spotting. That is, every time you were on the road and saw an Eddie Stobart lorry, you scored a point. Like Jools Holland, I too take pleasure in haulage companies with amusing names: Norbert Dentressangle naturally comes to mind. And the big news is that last Friday, not far out of Lincoln on the A15, around about RAF Scampton, I found a new one: Zaccheus Hinchliffe & Sons Ltd. Getting pinned down at 45 mph on the A15 is normally a real pain, but the addition of Zaccheus Hinchliffe & Sons Ltd to my collection made it all worthwhile. You know you're back up north when you see a name like Zaccheus Hinchliffe.

But this is the fashion issue, so that's all by the by. An hour after Scampton, my wife and I had unceremoniously dumped the children in Hull (not just in the street, at their grandparents') and were on our way north again, heading for the McArthur Glen designer outlet just south of the York ring road. As we parked up (in the Magenta Zone as it happens, handy for Gap, Timberland, M&S and, if you like that type of thing, Mexx, bit of a hike to Paul Smith, Margaret Howell and Joseph, though), I realized, and this took me aback, I realized that I was *excited*. Excitement at the prospect of going clothes shopping is an incongruity strange enough to be worth examining.

Having stuck with the classic male attitude (hostile, truculent, mulish, indifferent, ashamed, combination of all five) to clothes shopping for several decades, I've recently started to relish the experience. It's crept up on me. A couple of years ago I was, in spirit at least, solidly with the old gents in their anoraks rolling their eyes while their wives tried to make a decision in the fitting room. Now I'm practically Victoria Beckham: I'll have that, that, that and that. And *that's* nice too. And that. Possibly hormone-loss has kicked in early and I'm actually turning into a woman. Possibly it's because too much time in the spendthrift South has finally eroded the residue of a northern puritan upbringing. More likely it's because I'm carrying more money and less fat than I was as a younger man.

But this huge shift also owes a lot to the transformation of both the clothes on offer and the shops they're sold in. Clothes shops used to be overheated, overcrowded and, for anything decent, overpriced. Now, apart from maybe Footlocker, they're none of these things. Also I've noticed that their walls tend to be covered with gigantic black-and-white photographs of gorgeous people about to have sex, or just having had sex, or, in one or two cases, unless my eyes deceive me, actually *having* sex. You never saw that in C&A in 1983. So I find myself shopping more and more frequently: lunchtime pootles down to Canary Wharf, late-night binges in Islington, mincey little detours into Bluewater on the way down to the Kent coast, ooh, all-cotton shirt, £19.99, bargain, etc., etc.

And then there's the clothes. Some time in the nineties, I must have had my eye off the ball, men's clothing got really good. Used to be that I'd have a look around, sigh, and end up in Next. Or Millets. Or Primark. Now, there must be two dozen chains where I'd happily buy half the stock, money and storage space permitting. No wonder the decade-long consumer boom refuses to lie down and die, there's just too much quality stuff around for people to stop spending. Not just clothes, but cars, furniture, holidays; they're all so much classier, cooler, *better* than they were even ten years ago. Critics see such consumption as evidence of a meaningless modern existence. I prefer to see it as part of the eternal human desire to bring beauty and excellence into our lives.

Or at least that's what I told myself when, after a diligent three-hour trawl in York, right at the death I found a delightful grey cashmere jumper for £99 and dammit if I didn't buy the thing. No getting round it, £99 is a lot for a jumper. In the car heading back to my parents' in Hull, a bit guilty on my own account, for sure, but mostly because my dad's reaction was all too imaginable, I came up with this by way of justification. First, I got a cashmere jumper, a present, six months ago. I've worn it every day since and now it's gone square and there's biro on the shoulder, wax on the elbow and holes in the neck. If I buy two a year, realistic at my current rate of usage, that averages out at £4 a week on cashmere jumpers, not so much in the great scheme of things. Second, I barely drink and go almost everywhere by bike. Third, the jumper is useful. Fourth, it contributes to my wellbeing, and thus to that of those around me, immeasurably. Fifth, the goats don't mind. Convincing?

As it was, my dad didn't ask and I certainly didn't tell him. But I have now. I'm expecting the phone to ring any minute.

16 April 2005

Back in my own bed, always a relief. The hotel where we stay in Pembrokeshire is built on a wide ledge of flat(ish) land, four fifths of the way up a cliff. Fifty feet out front is a two-hundred-foot drop to the beach. Fall the first ten feet or so and you might have a chance, maybe grab a gorse, haul yourself back up. Beyond that, the slope goes sheer and you'd be toast, even at high tide. I remember reading in *Golden Gate* by Alistair MacLean that, above two hundred feet, hitting water is like hitting concrete, and in such matters (jumping between cable cars, sabotaging massive German artillery pieces on fictitious Greek islands) I think we can rely on MacLean as an authoritative source.

So there's the cliff to worry about. And then immediately behind our usual room the slope continues up another fifty feet to the road. That makes me anxious, too, especially when it rains, especially because I once more or less memorized a pamphlet about the Lynmouth flood disaster of 1952. No visit to Pembrokeshire is complete without my having a nightmare in which this slope collapses to engulf the hotel in a devastating torrent of mud, water, bracken and moles. (And adders, which I know are roundabout in large number.) The last thing I do each night, no matter how drunk, is rehearse exit strategies: wake Nicola, snatch the children, kick out the window, etc. It pays to be prepared.

The reality is, I'd sleep through it. Once, our burglar alarm at home went off in the middle of the night. Nicola tried repeatedly to rouse me, but I am an exceptionally deep sleeper and after a while she gave up, went downstairs, spoke to the alarm company, gave them the code word, turned the thing off, checked the doors and windows, fed the cat (whose immense bulk, we later worked out, had tripped a sensor), came back upstairs and fell asleep. She told me all about it in the morning. Not my finest hour.

Not, I hope, that I lack courage while awake. Any loud bangs in the park and I'm out there (fairly) quickly to see if anyone needs taking to the Homerton, where the A&E's expertise with gunshot wounds enjoys worldwide renown. One time, I hastened to intervene when Nicola heard a woman outside shouting in an urgent fashion. I got to within ten feet of this woman, then stopped when I saw she was holding a gun and standing over a man with his hands cuffed behind his back.

'Stay back, armed police!' she shouted, so I did: she seemed to have the situation well under control. In Hackney, the subconscious is superfluous: real life provides all the entertainment you need.

Back in Wales, the revived *Doctor Who* added to my troubles. Not the shop dummies shooting people or the big lump of pulsating plastic, I can cope with those, but the line about the

Doctor having been on the *Titanic* in 1912, a throwaway line but sufficient to trigger comatose panic at 5 a.m. Back in 1997, *Titanic* (the film) had a profound and, it has turned out, resonating effect on me. (I had just become a father: exhausted, emotionally vulnerable, etc.) That scene where the mother, all hope abandoned, tucks her children in their bunk as the ship goes stern up . . . my eyes prick just to think of it. My colleague Alan Franks and I have given up trying to persuade others of the merits of *Titanic*, now we just shut the door to our little office and chat quietly about icebergs and 'Nearer My God To Thee' and (we're both especially keen on the marine engineering aspects of the tragedy) transverse bulkheads that should have been built higher. I know I'll pay for it later in the small hours, but I can't help myself.

Ambivalence, I find, characterizes my whole relationship with water. I have the fear (icy depths, jellyfish, crocodiles, piranhas, giant squid, U-boats, gungy plants wrapping themselves around your ankles, the usual stuff), but then I'm a good swimmer, swimming (as with darts, excess body fat is not heavily penalized in the pool) being the only sport at which I excelled as a child. Mr Riley the games teacher would ask me to demonstrate my leg kick to the rest of the class, a kindness not common in his profession and one which I have never forgotten. I even once represented Haltemprice Sports Centre in the fifty metres breaststroke (third in a field of three, saturated three rows of spectators with a cracking bellyflop).

On Saturday, having neglected my goggles since adolescence, and in pursuit of the elusive hobby mentioned last week, I got back in the pool. Did OK, actually. Did twenty-eight lengths of a thirty-three-yard pool, a shade over half a mile if my calculations are correct, which they are. Predictably, I went in the fast lane and, equally predictably, I got overtaken by a couple of teenage girls. Yet it wasn't that I was so slow, just that they were so *quick*, and they could do proper tumble turns as well, which I never properly got the hang of. Neither, I suspect, were they hampered by the worry that somehow, weirdly, a great white shark was about to be let loose in a public baths in Bethnal Green.

14 May 2005

I was going to write about being bitten by a dog on the way to a party in East Sheen on Saturday night. We were just leaving the house after *Doctor Who* when we saw a fire extinguisher lying in the road. My wife said I ought to do something about it. I was carrying the fire extinguisher to the big council bin across the street when my path became blocked by a menacing collie/ Rottweiler/wolf-type creature. It saw the fire extinguisher and growled. Hold on, I thought, this doesn't look good.

The dog growled again. I felt I ought to do something. Failing to appreciate the full implications of meeting a dog with a visceral dislike of fire extinguishers on the unique occasion that I happened to be carrying one, I shook the fire extinguisher in front of me in an attempt to get the animal out of my way. Growling a third time, and circling round behind me, the dog bit me smartly on the calf and ran off. After ten yards or so it stopped, turned, and looked back at me with, I fancied, a triumphant gleam in its barking-mad eye. I told it to f*** right off.

After that, I didn't really know how to proceed, except dump the provocative fire extinguisher in the bin as planned, limp back to our car and tell my wife that, in the thirty seconds since we'd last spoken, I'd been savagely attacked. 'Really?' she said. Yeah, look, I said, rolling up my jeans to reveal two bleeding punctures and a purpling bruise. She asked when I'd last had a tetanus jab. I said I couldn't remember. She said I'd better get one.

After that, we agreed there wasn't a lot else to be said or done, so we made our way south of the river, where we enjoyed a pleasant evening discussing Hull City's recent promotion (any more success, and I might start having to go to watch them play) with some friends. Once or twice, a full ten minutes passed without me thinking about rabies. The dog incident, I decided, fitted nicely, both with this column's title and with its usual themes of idiocy and ill-luck. I also thought it was funny, and we might get to use the immortal phrase Dog Bites Man in the headline. This only occurred to me later, though, once the pain had worn off. (I've never been bitten by a dog before. It hurts.)

My wife, however (along with my mother), has been on at me for ages to do a column about some (rare) success I've enjoyed rather than writing endlessly about my far more frequent failures. Failures, I argue, are funny. Achievements are not.

'But you always make out you're this hopeless loser,' says my wife, 'and you're not.' (There's usually an uncomfortable silence at this point.)

For instance, she goes on, when we kept coming fourth or fifth in the pub quiz, you wrote about it. Twice. When we won, not a mention. That's because I'd look like a conceited berk boasting about trivia I picked up as a kid, I say.

'So,' my wife says, 'regard it as a challenge, and besides, you should always tell the truth.'

Eventually, she wore me down. (Setting 'challenges', banging on about The Truth, getting you to put rogue fire extinguishers in bins, they don't make it easy, women, do they?)

OK, OK, I said, I'll do the damn quiz. But only one paragraph and, I warn you, it won't be funny.

In the new spirit of unfettered arrogance, I won't deny I made a big contribution to our victory. I thought it might be our night when the quizmaster announced the theme of the second round, the Wild West having long been an enthusiasm of mine. Indeed, if I had to list the ten books (not counting the Ladybird *Book of Pirates*) that influenced me most up to (and, in truth, including and beyond) adolescence I'd have to say *The Guns of Navarone, The Day of the Jackal* and *The Godfather*, obviously; and then probably *Animal Farm, Catch-22* and *Slaughterhouse 5*. I think those three novels administered a useful pacifist and satirical corrective to the thirst for violence and moral absolutism engendered by the first three.

But next (this has turned into two paragraphs, another promise casually broken) I'd have to say any atlas, and the *Junior Pears Encyclopedia* and then the *World of Chess* by Anthony Saidy and Norman Lessing. And last but not least would have to be the superb *Pictorial History of the Wild West* by James D. Horan and Paul Sann. Billy the Kid, Jesse James, Butch and Sundance, I know that stuff back to front. The first question in the Wild West round at the quiz was: at which encounter in Tombstone were Billie Clanton and the McLowery brothers shot to death? Elsewhere in the pub people scratched their heads. Me, I laughed out loud. I've known the answer since I was nine years old.

Want to hear any more? Number of shots fired at the OK Corral? Date? Weapons used? Precise weather conditions prevailing in south-eastern Arizona on 26 October 1881? I didn't think so. Try as I might, I just can't seem to find a way to make my possession of these facts amusing, entertaining or even mildly interesting, though I suppose it is revealing. I should have stuck with the dog.

25 June 2005

If you had to choose between being able to turn invisible, and being able to fly, which would you go for? It's not always work, sport and bad jokes; sometimes, when we chaps are alone together, we also discuss important issues such as this, the old invisibility vs flying conundrum. My friend David and I debated it recently. It's a tricky one.

Actually, it's not. Skulking around without apparent spatial form may carry attractions in terms of robbing banks, going into women's fitting rooms, tracking down old PE teachers to wreak pitiless and implacable vengeance, that kind of thing. But when you talk it through, invisibility also brings with it a lot of potential problems. What about stuff you're carrying? Is that invisible, too? Would the cashiers see the sacks of cash floating out of the safe and off down the street? What if the PE teachers managed to hem you in a corner and had the brains to start jabbing around with a fork? These questions have posed problems for H.G. Wells, David McCallum and Harry Potter. David and I agreed we weren't going to solve them in half an hour in the pub.

And then there's what might be called the Robbie Burns issue. You're going to start hearing what other people *really* think of you – never a good idea. In fact, the more we discussed it, the more we reckoned invisibility was your *novelty* special power, your pogo stick or water pistol, great fun for a morning, soon forgotten for ever. Besides, if you really want to be invisible, there's no magic or mystery to it, you just go along to a media party and make sure you're the least important person in the room. Works for me.

Flying, though, that'd represent a different order of pleasure, wouldn't it? What could compare? X-ray vision? Superhuman strength? Going all bendy? Not even close. Flying's the one. I tell you, this cycling I do, late at night in the park, it's a flying substitute, that's all.

Imagine: 'I'm off out, back for *Newsnight*.'

'Oh, OK. Can you get me some chocolate?'

Righty-ho. Trainers on, goggles, gloves, cloak too, *obviously,* helmet while you're learning, out into the back garden, quick look around, left, right, up, coast clear, away you go. Vertical take-off, gentle ascent to treetop height, stabilize, vroom, give it some welly to five hundred feet, level out, bit of a hover to get yourself organized.

Still with me? City spread out below, tuck your trousers into your socks, head down, arm out and off, a sweeping diving arc, couple of hundred mph, sixty seconds later you're coming in low over the Thames, or the Trent, or the Tyne, or wherever's good for you, skimming the waves, rocketing under the bridges, piling on the power to find some empty sky for twists and somersaults and massive big show-off loop-the-loops, then it's victory rolls up The Mall, waggle those wings and home via the off-licence with a Kit Kat. Pylons? Planes? Tall buildings? You'd soon get the hang of those. Got to watch out for bird strikes, of course.

Getting seen is a bit of an issue, though, isn't it. The MoD would get anxious, and even if you managed to stay off the radar, you couldn't keep it quiet. Man flying around unassisted? Big story that, *enormous* story. You'd have the *News of the World* all over your doorstep within a week. David and I chewed this over. I said (these debates usually end like this) that I might have to claim special dispensation to be able to fly *and* be invisible at the same time. He said OK, fair point. Then we had another drink and talked about time-travelling. Two hearts, nine hundred years old, distant galaxies, long-gone centuries, cooped up with crumpet assistant in a police box. What a life.

I hate to generalize, but experience tells me most women feel a certain impatience with these sorts of conversations. They mark, I find, a dividing line between the genders, like cricket, heavy metal and continuing to believe bodily functions are amusing beyond the age of six. See that river, I'll often say to my wife, I'd jump into it for £200, what about you? No? £300, then?

£500? What? You'd want *more* than £500? Come on, I say, brief-case full of money, £1,000? £5,000? £10,000? OK, you'd do it for ten grand. What about £9,000 then? Why ten and not nine? River's not deep, you get wet, you swim to the bank, maybe get your stomach pumped, no big deal, it's a lot of money, £9,000 . . . and so on. However hard I nag, she won't really engage, not *really*.

My son, though, he's showing promise. Hey Sam, I said the other day, Jimmy Bond or Indiana Jones, who would you rather be?

'Difficult one, Daddy,' he replied.

So we discussed it, me leading him gently away from questions of comparative arsenals and gadgets and towards questions of character, and thus to the correct conclusion (namely that 007 is far too fond of himself, and a shocking snob to boot). Yet the real breakthrough was that Sam had taken me seriously in the first place. He's only eight, and already a whole world of vital male drivel is opening up for the two of us, father and son together.

2 July 2005

Shortly after I got together with my wife, we went on holiday to Turkey.

'Why are you packing that great big jumper?' she asked me the night before we flew.

To wear in the evenings when I'm shivering, I said.

'But it's July in the Mediterranean,' she said. 'You won't be cold.'

Oh no, I will, I replied, I'm always frozen after a day in the sun. Aren't you?

'No,' she said, 'I'm not actually. If anything I'm the opposite. I think that's true of most people.'

Turned out I'd been overdoing it, turned out I'd been suffering from sunstroke every summer for years without realizing it.

I've always loved sunbathing. It's practically a hobby. When I say 'a day in the sun', I mean it literally, as in lying in a boiling slather for six or seven hours, longer if practical. As a single man, you get into these habits, don't you? Don't know any better until a woman tells you different. I used to buy my trousers from Burton's, nice grey slacks, double pleat at the top, thin plastic belt thrown in, nothing wrong with that, but she wasn't having it. Put a stop to the tinned ravioli every night as well. I held the line at loose tea for a year or so, then that went too, we've been on bags for years now, I'm not even sure where the teapot is any more. I still resent that a bit, come to think of it. And the ravioli.

But you know, the years pass, you reassert your independence, by degrees. I'm older now, and busier, but still I get out there in the glare whenever I can. The week before last, for instance, I had the morning off, it was midsummer's day, it was hot, Nicola was at work, the children were at school, no way was I going to pass that up. Midday found me star-shaped on a rank old futon in the garden, soaking up some rays, half an ear open for the sound of an unscheduled key in the front door. It's not that Nicola disapproves of sunbathing, just that she's an everything-in-moderation type of person, and I'm more of a few things taken to an extreme. (Or so I tell myself, makes me feel all edgy and exciting.) I lay there heating up nicely, occasionally hoisting my special direction-finding, shadow-throwing broom for re-angling purposes.

Now I know that (one, two, who knows, three?) readers are thinking, hold on, he's done sunbathing before. Indeed I have, column 95 it was, according to the agreeable trawl I've just made through my cuttings book, but two years on, at column 196, I think I can be forgiven a modicum of repetition, of subject matter if not sentences. Besides, there's a twist: this wasn't any old, pants-scrunched-up-like-a-nappy sunbathing, it was full-on red-monkey-bum *naked* sunbathing. (I say bum, I actually prefer the more graphic *butt*, my children having adopted the Americanism from Cartoon Network and won me round.) Does life hold any greater pleasures than naked sunbathing? A few, perhaps, not many.

One of my earliest memories is from the late sixties, I must have been four or five, and we were in . . . Weymouth, I think it was, or it might have been Lyme Regis. A woman came up and gave my mother an earful for letting me run around naked on the beach. The sheer stupidity of the old trout's attitude always stuck in my mind. We've come a long way as a country since then, not far enough though, or else I'd have brazened it out in plain view, instead of wedging myself in the one blind corner, the corner where the man in the office above would have to be using a periscope, on a stepladder, on tiptoe, to see me. Frankly I don't think he's that interested in my bottom. Or butt, even. Yet still one must be careful not to offend.

We've been in this house ten years, and it's taken me that long to go even this far, wriggling free of my shorts in close to total seclusion. The fear of exposure is strong, but in my case the thirst for an even tan is stronger. I did two hours, a mere introduction by my former standards, turning conscientiously, cursing the strapping on my broken toe (full explanation next week), which meant, despite all this expended sweat, I would fall short of the desired perfection, rolling over, grimacing at the alabaster shank on view, remembering my youth. The summer of 1990, England in the semi-final, my naked-sunbathing, freezing-evening, tinned-ravioli heyday, the only time since childhood I got close to my dream. I'd just come to London, I had my first proper job. The bedsit I was renting had but one thing to recommend it, a roof terrace overlooked only by the birds.

You could stretch out in the light and watch the TV in the shade. Highlights, build-up, two live games, though the second one got a little chilly, analysis. Happy, lazy days. I lost my job (it was naked sunbathing versus naked ambition, tan versus career, I chose tan) but it didn't seem to matter too much at twenty-five. The story of the fifteen years since has, in many ways, been about getting into a position where I could occasionally combine both choices. Which I have now managed. Twice indeed. That's not bad going. Another couple of years, I'll see if I can make it three.

16 July 2005

You will of course recall my slipping on an icy wall as a teenager and falling into the jagged remnants of four pints of milk? Yes? Well, the reason for taking such a foolhardy risk with half a gallon of milk was that from the age of fourteen to eighteen I worked for the local milkman. Three hours on a Saturday for £1.50 plus a litre of limeade, a generous rate for the late seventies (although the amount never rose, I noticed, despite the ruinous inflation of that period). Often, I did Sundays, too, and then there was the Herculean effort in the run-up to Christmas. Double orders, Christmas. Cream, juice, suburban matrons treating the family to gold top, extra steri for the pensioners, all sorts. A few people were even starting to ask for semi-skimmed. We thought they were weird.

I had some of the best times of my life delivering milk. Summer morning, 7.30, the streets still, the sky cool and clear, Lennie the milkman at the wheel, me on the running board, the two of us giggling away at some daft joke, whaling that float along at, oh, 17, maybe 18 mph . . . it felt good to be alive. You think I'm joking? You're fourteen, fifteen years old, energy to burn, you leap off the float full tilt and hit the pavement just right, little chicane through a half-open gate, jog up a drive, couple of pints there, dodge through a hedge to the next door, two more, sprint back; it's a blast. You've got no responsibilities, you're not trying to make a decent wage, you don't have to do it every day, where's the problem? I don't think kids these days do casual jobs in the way we did twenty-five years ago. That's a shame. In the winter, perversely, it was even better. Character-building.

I learnt a lot from Lennie. About milk, obviously, but also maths, and memory, and man-management, and the worth of a big smile in almost any situation. Yet the real lessons came informally. Nine-ish, we'd stop at Willerby Square for a rest, a ham sandwich from Skeltons, and the chance to catch up on each other's news. My weekly grapples with photosynthesis, quadratic equations and the Tudors and Stuarts being of limited interest to both of us, the conversational burden naturally fell on my boss. He was great, Lennie. Married, early thirties, live-for-today, extrovert, spectacularly forthcoming about his sex life. He'd bang (so to speak) on and on, me nodding away like a right old man of the world, scarcely understanding a word he was saying, nonetheless loving the breather, the ham sandwich and the illusion of manhood come thrillingly early. And the ubiquitous pint of milk.

The funny thing was, Lennie operated on the assumption that my sex life (non-existent) was not only up and running but was also every bit as colourful and varied as his own. 'You know how you get a porn film off the butcher and invite your neigh-bours over to watch it, Bob?' he'd say, and I'd go, Oh yeah, Lennie, as if that was something I did all the time, after finish-ing my homework and before *Grange Hill*, maybe. And what of the real-life sexual opportunism associated with milkmen?

Housewives in negligees leaning suggestively against door frames? My husband's playing golf all day and I'm *soooo* bored? Nothing doing. Not even when I wore my Kool Kats Drink Milk bush hat *and* my filthy white dairy coat with Whole Lotta Bottle on the chest.

Still, my education continued in other ways. Christmas Eve, we'd trade the ham sandwich for The Wheatsheaf and sit downing Bell's in the bar for an hour. After that, our customers, the decent ones in the smaller houses, would ply us with whisky, too. By the time we'd dropped the last turkey at 2 p.m., I could barely stand, awash with laughter and booze. When William Hague said he drank fourteen pints of beer a day during his holiday job, many commentators jeered in disbelief. I knew Hague was telling the truth, knew his job had been an important, instructive time for him. For me (please excuse the trumpet-blowing), my exposure to male working-class culture taught me never to sneer at people with less money or different taste, an unpleasantness which many columnists seem to regard almost as a professional requirement.

And I learnt an even more vital lesson. I remember one man, a customer, big house, *massive* house. I'd dropped off his usual order and was halfway back up the drive when he whistled at me, whistled as in peremptory, not whistled as in happy tune. He wanted something else. Not knowing any better, I half turned to go back, and then I heard Lennie on the float at the end of the drive.

'Keep walking,' he hissed, 'ignore him.'

So I did. The man whistled again, shriller and louder. And I kept going, and hopped up behind Lennie, and it felt like freedom.

'Always remember,' said Lennie as we gathered speed, 'whatever you end up doing, you're a man, not a dog. Don't let anybody forget it.'

5 November 2005

This half-term just gone, at huge risk to any man-of-the-people credentials I might have accrued, I took the family to New York. An improbably glamorous destination, surely, for someone who habitually patrols only the quadrilateral extending from Hackney over to Pembrokeshire, up and across to Hull, down to Deal and back to London? Indeed, but the children have been clamouring to see their godfather in America, the opportunity arose and, you know, sometimes you gotta roll the dice. Besides, the trip was for the *Magazine*'s January travel issue, so it sort of counts as work.

All right, so it doesn't count as work, except, perhaps, for one element: getting there and back. Ever since I became a father, I've hated flying. Everything about it (bar the food, I like the food): the queues, the claustrophobia, the loss of control, the being told what to do by people in uniform, the fatigue, the knowing your life could end in a blazing fireball at any instant, that kind of thing. Actually, that bit about since becoming a father is a lie. I've hated flying since they stopped letting you smoke. When you could sit there fagging it up, drinking back-to-back Bloody Marys for seven hours, I never had a problem. But having children made it worse. September 11 didn't help much, either.

I spent the week before departure in the usual numb panic. And the Friday night beforehand I barely slept, mostly out of fear, obviously, but also because I realized I had head lice. We had to be up at half six. I woke at 2.10, 3.25 and 5.15, clock racing, scalp crawling. I dozed and dwelt on the fanaticism of strangers and debris on the runway and sparks in the fuel tank and what less than eleven pounds of plastic explosive in its forward cargo hold can do to a 747 at thirty-thousand-plus feet. At some stage, too, I had a dream of exquisite clarity that Commissioner Sir Ian Blair was on the radio solemnly forbidding all travel out of Heathrow. At 6.15, my son came in and said a hamster had run over his foot.

'Mummy,' he announced, constructing a sentence I'm confident has not previously seen the light of day, 'Tincey, Wincey and Sooty have escaped, and we're going to America!'

My wife hurried to the search. I hung back, scratching, sensing the glimpse of a reprieve. A self-sacrifice along the lines of, 'You go, I'll stay and look for the hamsters' was forming in my mind. But Nicola quickly rounded up two of them and, while the whereabouts of the third (it's Wincey, not the biter, sadly) remains a mystery, I couldn't whip up anything like enough concern over her fate to suggest a postponement. Fickle creatures, children.

Moving smoothly on to plan B, I told Nicola I was lifting with nits, and 'I can't see Homeland Security being very happy about it, they're real sticklers, you know.' She found me a comb and told me not to be silly. Three hours later, I was slouching into Terminal 3, final cigarette extinguished, handing over life, liberty and, these days, lighter to people of whom I know nothing and with whom I share no bond whatsoever. Hateful. Absolutely hateful.

But, you know, this sounds corny but it's true, the children, who'd never flown long distance before, their innocence, and the requirement upon me to preserve it, somehow turned the next 3,445 miles into something perilously close to fun.

'This is just ... *luxury*, isn't it, Daddy?' sighed my son, settling into steerage and opening a steady barrage of questions which he kept up for the next seven and a half hours (and indeed, the next seven and a half days).

'What's a life vest?' 'How cold is minus 57 degrees Celsius?' 'Would we be alive at that cold?' 'What speed are we going?' 'How does the plane fly?'

Well, since you ask, four Pratt and Whitney turbofans give it thrust that counteracts the drag and causes air to flow over the wings, which generates the lift needed to counteract the weight. (That took him by surprise. Man across the aisle gave me a funny look, too.)

'How do *you* know that, Daddy?'

I've made a study of it.

And later, 2,500 miles to the good, standing by the rear loo, looking down at Newfoundland, starting to relax, 'Are there parachutes? There should be parachutes, shouldn't there, Daddy? Why aren't there parachutes?'

I don't know, Sam, parachutes would be a good idea in my opinion.

'This big handle, what does "rotate to full open position" mean?'

Probably best not to touch that, Sam.

'What would happen if the wing fell off?'

The plane would crash.

'What?' said my daughter, who had joined us without me noticing. 'The plane would go splash in the sea?'

Something like that, yes.

'And we'd have to get our life vests on? And use the seat cushions as a floatating advice, like in the film?'

Absolutely, sweetheart, I said. We'd land in the sea, put our life jackets on and take our shoes off, slide down the big chute like at Hull Fair, and tread water for a while using our seat cushions as a floatating advice before a big ship arrived to take us the rest of the way to America.

11 February 2006

While the cat's away skiing, the mice will play . . . ping-pong. Yeah, wife on the slopes, had the boys round Friday night. Beer,

Scotch eggs, Pogues on the stereo, table tennis till two in the morning; it's the simple things in life, isn't it? The guest list was seven (plus me), but Mark wasn't well, cousin George got tied up, not literally, at a Chinese restaurant up west, and the two young Turks, Harry and Ben, had other plans, funnily enough. They'll learn. And here's one lesson *I* learnt from them: if you're forty-one and you ask two guys in their mid-twenties round to play ping-pong on a Friday night, when they say 'I'm waiting on some texts' or 'I'll pop round later' or 'I'll see if I can make it,' what they *really* mean is, 'Listen, you sad old fool, we've got better things to do, OK?'

Never mind, their loss. So it was me, Tim (42), Chris (40) and Nigel (38), all of us of an age to appreciate the aesthetics, the balletics, the aerodynamics, the sheer truth, grace and beauty of the sublime ping and the superlative pong. But first we had to get the darts out of the way. Actually, no, first we had to get the children to bed. Not easy, when they see Daddy and his pals swilling Kronenbourg, scoffing cheesy twists and watching in slack-jawed appreciation as Traci Bingham, three-quarters undressed, is evicted from the Big Brother house.

'That lady's got massive boobies, hasn't she?' said Sam, the echoing grunts of assent showing how precisely the eight-year-old had caught the mood of the living room.

Rachel, six, was more interested in the chart I had drawn up to record the forthcoming hostilities.

'Fast Bobby versus The Grinder?' she read out. 'Tornado versus Sicko? Why have you all got silly names?'

Because, I explained, when we have these competitions we like to give each other nicknames and use them all night.

'And is that funny?' she asked.

Well, *we* think it is, I said.

'Why?'

Er, um, I don't know, sweetheart, it just *is*, OK? And by the way, it's Psycho not Sicko.

At that point Sam tore himself away from the telly and sank a left hook into The Grinder's groin, just because he could.

'Your kids are really nice and polite when they come into the office,' gasped The Grinder, his head between his knees. 'Different story at home, isn't it?'

Welcome to the world of the parent, I replied.

Rachel then hit Psycho with a cucumber she had turned into a lightsaber.

After I'd bribed and wrestled the little blighters into their bedrooms, it was down to business. Chris, sorry, Psycho, unveiled his buffet (he'd very kindly assumed responsibility for the catering). This mainly involved ripping open packets of cocktail sausages. I said I'd have got him a nice hostess trolley if I'd had more warning. Very genially, he told me to piss off. Then it was darts in my office. We had the board wedged on a tower of boxes in front of my Kings and Queens of England poster, and an Anglepoise lamp balanced on a stepladder to give proceedings that glamorous televisual glow. Two played while the non-combatants took turns to score in bad Geordie accents with guttural sound effects.

'Grindaaaah you requirahhh . . . urghhh . . . doooble wooon!' and so forth.

Most of the games went to a double-one finish (for the reader unfamiliar with the ways of the arrow, that means we weren't any good). Richard II took a bad hit in the eye. Should have been Harold, but there you go.

'She's a fickle mistress, your dartboard,' said Tornado, after registering a big fat zero on one visit to the oche.

We all nodded our heads sagely. One game lasted for the whole of the second side of *Rum, Sodomy and the Lash*. By

11 p.m. Psycho was drunk enough to write Physio instead of his real false name.

'What's Physio?' said Tornado. 'A Hitchcock film about some nutter who kills his victims by rubbing their shoulders *really* hard?'

I went to check on the children and get more beer.

'Any chance of you bringing some more mini-sausages through, Fast Bobby?' asked Psycho.

He won Quote of the Night for that.

Then it was time for the main event, outside on the deck in sub-zero temperatures, outrageous wind-chill, hats, coats and scarves all round, four muffled-up maniacs smacking it around addictively until the small hours. What brilliant fun. Friendly, too. We play football together, the four of us, and barely a week goes by without some ghastly finger-jabbing falling-out. And yet at the table, loved-up on lager and chorizo, it was all great shot, well done, oh hard luck, mate; the sins of the AstroTurf expiated through a paddle and a plastic projectile. But for the mutual onset of hypothermia around 2 a.m., we would have gone on all night.

'We'll have to club together to send Nicola away again,' said Chris.

Absolutely, I said.

This is the third column I've wrung from her absence, and she was only gone three days.

Next week, *inshallah*, it's off to Qatar.

25 February 2006

One Sunday in Spitalfields Market, east London, about two years ago, a tall man of my own age came up to me not far from the delicious and very reasonably priced goulash stall and asked if I was Robert Crampton. This has happened to me five times now, one for each year I've been doing this column, and I have to say it is immensely gratifying. I puffed out my chest and said, well, yes, as it happens, I am that man. He said he was from Hull, too, and we started discussing schools and streets and people we might have in common.

At which point my wife walked up to see what was delaying me.

'Well,' said the tall man, 'I know *her* for a start.'

My eyes immediately narrowed, suspecting he might be an ex-boyfriend I didn't know about . . . but no, it turned out Nicola and this man, Joe he's called, had done Saturday jobs in Habitat in Hull together, twenty-five years ago. We chatted. Joe, and his wife Di, and their three girls, Rose, Amy and Emma, they were delightful. We arranged to meet again properly. Thus was a friendship rekindled.

And thus did we find ourselves enjoying a fine time in Qatar a week ago, Joe having gone there with his family on a three-year contract last autumn. Random business, life, isn't it? We imagine there's some kind of rational progression, but so often, it's just a succession of accidents. If Joe had spent thirty seconds longer parking his car, or whatever, at Spitalfields two years ago, we wouldn't have spent this half-term in the sand, gravel, rubble and heat of the Persian Gulf. But he didn't and we did.

We were due to fly on the Saturday. On the Friday morning, my son Sam bounded in shouting 'We're going to Qatar today! Er, no . . . tomorrow! Er, no . . . Toyota!' A tribute to the power of advertising, for sure, but also, I like to think, to the family business of turning cock-ups into low-ranking jokes.

And it was an appropriate slogan for Sam to choose, as it turned out, the Land Cruiser being the Qataris' favoured mode of transport – no surprise when they can fill them up for a tenner. And when they don't pay any income tax, electricity, gas or water bills. In fact, it's not a bad ticket to draw in life's lottery, being born Qatari. Especially if you're a bloke. More of a mixed blessing for the women: you get to wear diamonds as big as golf balls, but your fashion palette is rather limited. Still, very slimming, black.

Speaking of low-ranking jokes, when I left work that Friday night, my colleague Alan Franks came up with a good one.

'Well, Bobbly,' he said, 'I suppose it's Qatar for now.'

Al, I said, you're the man, I'll see you in ten days, or sooner if things go badly and I turn up in a jumpsuit on the internet.

'I'm sure it won't come to that,' said Alan, and of course he was right. His Highness the Emir Sheikh Hamad bin Khalifa al-Thani runs a tight ship. I've no doubt that his capital, Doha, is a safer place to be than London at the moment.

We gave the children the multicultural pep talk on the plane. Fat lot of good it did.

'Why's she got that over her face?' Sam said loudly within minutes of arriving at the souk. 'How can she see where she's going?'

To be honest, a rational answer eluded me, beyond saying that is the way most Qatari husbands want their wives to dress, and the husbands are the ones in charge. (Sam and Rachel both struggled to grasp this concept.) Western women are supposed to cover their shoulders and legs in public, although I saw one mother picking up from one of the international schools wearing a skimpy vest with 'Jezebel' printed across the chest. I thought: superb effort, there goes a true twenty-first-century revolutionary.

Mind you, I caught a glimpse of the appeal of the pre-feminist society. After one meal out, nicely stoked up on kebabs and lemonade, practically horizontal on our respective sofas, Joe and I treated ourselves to a shisha. A shisha is perhaps better known as a hubbly bubbly, or a hookah, although don't get the wrong idea, it wasn't a prostitute, rather one of those ornate pipes that resemble a shower attachment crossed with a paraffin lamp.

Muslims may not drink, but they smoke for Arabia, and all around men were puffing away like the refineries out in the desert. For an hour, Joe and I sat there beaming indulgently and trying not to cough: sophisticates, men of the world, princes, sultans even. Our kids loved it.

'Blow some smoke at me, Daddy!'

'No, *me*, me, blow it at me!'

'My daddy can blow it out of his nose!'

'Well, *my* daddy is a dragon!'

'Daddy! Daddy! Daddy!' etc., etc.

I turned to my wife, eating her ice cream, half amused, half disapproving. About time, I said, finally I'm getting some credit for something I'm good at.

8 April 2006

Although almost all of your mails in response to my last-but-one column were positive, complimentary even, it's in my nature to dwell on the one that wasn't. 'Robert, read your column for the first time this weekend and think the title a misnomer . . .' (neutral enough start) '. . . perhaps Beta Male could become . . .' (still OK up to now) '. . . Castrati, which would be a better description . . .' (aye up, don't like the sound of this) '. . . of your whining, effeminate drivel . . .' (woah, that's *nasty*) '. . . Your column made me wretch [*sic*] . . .' (shame the spelling goes wrong there, but that can happen to the best of us) '. . . Yours, Jenny'. (*Love* that sign-off: so polite, so homely, so utterly at odds with what has gone before.)

Whining, effeminate drivel. That's quality abuse, is that. And respect to Jenny for using her full name. This kind of thing usually arrives unsigned. In green biro.

I am confused, though. The piece Jenny takes such exception to was about my not wanting to go to a party, then going anyway, enjoying it, getting drunk, meeting a like-minded chap who enjoyed swapping trivia, and, er, at the risk of belittling my own output, that was about it. Drivel it may have been, everyone's entitled to their opinion, but I've scoured the text for whining and effeminacy, and I can't find evidence of either. If anything, it was one of my more *butch* outings, not a hamster or thong in sight. Beer, lewd jokes, male bonding . . . I mean, how macho do you have to be? Some women, eh? There's no pleasing them.

Or maybe there is. Listen to this, Jenny: when I was at school in the seventies, vast comprehensive, not much use academically, but educational in other ways, we had *fights* all the time, proper tear-ups: split lips, black eyes, blood and snot on your shirt, crowd five-deep chanting 'Fight! Fight! Fight!' I won't con you, Jenny, I wasn't good at fighting, but I wasn't bad either; I was mid-table, Charlton Athletic if you will, doing OK with scant resources, steadily improving over the years. Won a few, lost a few, drew a few, ten or twelve bouts in all, not counting altercations on the rugby pitch or unprovoked assaults, the peremptory headbutt, the Doc Marten to the groin, can't legislate for them, can you?

Or how about this? When I have a spare moment, and sometimes when I don't but fancy it anyway, I play Camper Strike on the net: moving targets (not people, don't approve of that), hit the space bar to choose pistol or rifle, left click to fire, get the head and your computer says 'Head shot!' in a corny Texan accent. No false modesty, I've featured several times on the interim top-three listing, that's the best three scores from all over the world in the previous quarter of an hour. Once, I even got to number one. There I was, 'Bobc', next to a little Union flag. Some Finn and a couple of trigger-happy Turks knocked me off in no time, but for a while there, life was pretty sweet.

What else? I cycle around Hackney a lot after dark. And I once went to a lap-dancing club with Andy McNab and a bunch of FBI agents, some of whom were armed. Glocks, I think. Or was it Brownings? Can't remember. Either way, those Feds were packing. And I'm not scared of dogs. In fact, I go out of my way to pat them in the park, unless they're those little yappy ones – gotta watch them. And pornography? Well, I've grown out of it, but I used to have this friend whose collection grew so extensive his wardrobe toppled over under the weight and nearly crushed him to death. How about all that, Jenny? Impressed?

Not yet? Well how about *this*? The other day I was in a book-shop, checking on the sales of various contemporaries, thinking I really must get round to knocking out my own critically acclaimed genre-busting monster worldwide bestselling publishing phenomenon some time soon, when I saw this book with a soldier on the front firing a machine gun. It was Jane's *Guns Recognition Guide* by Ian Hogg and Terry Gander, and as I leafed through it, I saw that it did exactly what it said on the tin: page after page of specs for pistols, rifles, shotguns and machine guns, Smith and Wesson, Samuel Colt, Professor Kalashnikov, the gang was all there. How absolutely thrilling.

Now the thing is, Jen, I wouldn't normally admit this in print in the current climate, but congratulations, you've flushed me out of cover: I have an interest, a minor interest but an interest nonetheless, in guns. Not in all weaponry (don't give a fig for rockets or tanks or swords), but I do enjoy a good gun book. I don't want to *shoot* anybody (well, only a couple of people, no *three* actually, all right, definitely no more than five), I just like having the information, in the same way that some men, and my wife, read *What Car?* for pleasure. So what I did with Jane's *Guns Recognition Guide*, Jenny, and I'm not ashamed to admit this, OK, I am a bit, but you've goaded me into it, is I *bought* it. Whaddya reckon to that, then?

20 May 2006

When we moved into Hackney eleven years ago, where the next-door house had once stood was a bombsite. A literal bombsite, created overnight by the Luftwaffe in 1940. Post-war, a builder had used the land as a yard. But by 1995, the builder's nephew had inherited and – a stroke of luck – wanted to sell. So we bought the plot and slowly, as time and money have allowed, we have created a garden. And although that's 'we' as in 'my wife', with me leaning on a broom going 'eeeh' a lot, it doesn't stop me, on fine May mornings such as these, getting out there and doing a proprietorial circuit of the fiefdom. Takes about twenty seconds. Five to walk around the garden, fifteen to inhale deeply while slapping my chest feeling smug.

I squint into the sun coming up over the railway line, and I congratulate myself that I, we, my wife, have transformed this speck of city sprawl into something alive and green, give or take an electric-blue paddling pool and a fair bit of moulded plastic. And I think how fortunate we are to have the cachet of living in a hip 'n' happening mixed-use brownfield inner-city regeneration action enterprise doo-be-doo while getting to enjoy this oasis too. And then I inhale again and wish with all my heart that the Hong Kong Noodle factory behind our garden would close down. Or at least cancel its especially stinky night shift.

That's the problem with your semi-industrial: the bit after the hyphen makes a noise and smells. I keep meaning to stomp round there and demand that the owners install some sort of filter, but the thing is, I'm too frightened. So I make the best of it. I say to my wife, look, the British economy needs noodles, can't get enough of them, maybe we should regard enduring the ghastly stench of industrial noodle manufacture as a patriotic duty, like people in Cumbria who put up with RAF low-flying exercises. She isn't impressed.

Still, shoving the noodles to one side (I always do, slimy, slippery things, the offal of the carbohydrate world), the garden's looking good. She's gone for a seasidey, marshlandy, beachy, windswepty, stony-ey theme, a homage, if you will, to our native east coast. Random rocks, metal containers, plenty of concrete, a selection of grasses, it's all very Humber estuary. No howling wind, shredded polythene or dead fish, but you can take the search for authenticity too far, don't you think? I don't think eucalyptus and bamboo are indigenous to East Yorkshire, either, but they grow like the clappers and we needed foliage in a hurry. Avidly, I monitor their progress, willing them on to greater height, width, bulk, leafiness.

My special area of responsibility, however, in time-honoured fashion, is the lawn. It's an extremely small lawn. Circular. Eight feet in diameter, so that'd be πr^2 (quality dredge, Bob), 3.14x4x4, barely 50 square feet of turf. Is that right? If you have access to the very thrilling Google Earth, kestrel-keen eyesight and, of course, the slightest interest, you can see for yourself by typing in London Fields, Hackney, and looking in the south-east corner of the park . . . See the big digger? (Flats being built when the satellite went over, lawn lost some light but preferable to having that site squatted every summer, although having said that the Italian squatters were charming young people. Good-looking too, but that's Italians for you, even the squatters look like film stars.) Just above and to the right of the digger is a green pinprick . . . got it? That's my lawn, that is. My pride and joy. Looks good, doesn't it, from a hundred thousand feet? It's even better from ten.

And to think I didn't want it at first. Lawns, I explained to my wife, are bourgeois. But she stood her ground. No, Robert, she said, actually lawns are not political in any way, and the children will like it as they get older. I said, well you can look after it then, and at first, she did, but little by little, willingly, I've taken over. Each year, I invest a bit more of myself in the lawn: physically, in time spent mowing and snipping and watering; emotionally, in worrying about its success or failure. Given the combined effect of Sam, Rachel, their friends and the poor drainage properties of London clay, failures outscore successes. So far, this hasn't bothered me. But the way it looks right now, all vibrant, vivid, emerald almost, then if we're relaying again next April, I'll feel pretty ripped up myself. In terms of lawn commitment, I've taken the plunge.

Didn't Michael Heseltine once say he'd prefer to be remembered for his arboretum rather than for anything he'd achieved in publishing or politics? I think he did. He did now anyway. I'm starting to feel the same way about my lawn. Oh yes, long after the lukewarm accolades for the tolerably entertaining column have yellowed and withered, that tiny shining disc of green will, I profoundly hope, endure. I shall shuffle off to Kent, or possibly Greece (superb weather, low population density, excellent starters), and thence to the great cuttings book in the sky, and those fifty square feet of grass shall be my legacy.

12 August 2006

When I was eighteen, in the summer of 1982, 'Come On Eileen' at number one, my then girlfriend and I went to see an old VW Beetle advertised in the *Hull Daily Mail*. I'd just passed my driving test at the fourth attempt. We had a long look at this car, built before I was born, a million miles on the clock, got in, got out, walked round it a couple of times, got in again, made small talk with the owner. Naturally I failed to realize that the engine was in the boot and vice versa, but we all smiled about that and moved on.

The conversation started to dry up. I sensed that both my girlfriend and the vendor were waiting for me, as the male half of the potential buying team, to ask a few pertinent questions. So I nudged the front wheel with my toe and, making what I hoped would be a grimace conveying both extreme manliness and sophisticated scepticism concerning the second-hand car market, I thickened my Hull accent and said, 'So, I suppose these are still the original tyres, then, right?' There was a dumbstruck pause and then my girlfriend and the man selling the VW both laughed their heads off.

Walking home, my girlfriend, who had just discovered that knowing next to nothing about cars meant she still knew more than her boyfriend, explained that vehicles of all descriptions require new tyres more often than every twenty years. Usually quite a lot more often. Our relationship never recovered. Shortly afterwards, she went to her brother's wedding in Plymouth and got off with a corporal in the Royal Marines. It was just a couple of months since the Falklands, the smoke had barely cleared over Stanley, obviously I was dead meat. Yes, even with my Kajagoogoo haircut and B in General Studies.

Anyway, you'll understand when I say that the British International Motor Show is not somewhere I ever expected to find myself. My wife, however, who reads *What Car?* the way other women read *Cosmo* or *Elle* and knows only slightly less than everything about cars, had other ideas. On and on and on she went, hinting, cajoling, badgering, until eventually I did the (marginally corrupt) string-pulling necessary to secure us both passes to the press day.

Here I am, I said to her as we parked up at the venue, not smoking, not moaning and about to spend several hours looking at and talking about cars. I feel like the *Wehrmacht* generals surrendering to Monty on Lüneburg Heath. I feel like the war is over, I'm beaten, your victory is complete. She made no comment. You realize this isn't normal, I went on. In films women always want a handbag or a weekend in Paris, not a sneak preview of the all-new Dodge Nitro. If we hurry, she said, consulting her programme, we can make the launch of the Ford S-Max.

We do need, as it happens, to buy a new car: current one too small, warranty about to expire. So Nicola was able to sell the show as a chance to see all the possible replacements in one go, no need to yawn my way through a succession of showrooms. Which is why I agreed to trail round, getting in and out of perhaps thirty cars, not one of which had a semi-naked young woman draped across the bonnet, the motor trade having dispensed with gratuitous sexual fantasy as a retail tool at the very moment I decided to take an interest. (Instead, men in suits make earnest speeches about carbon neutrality.)

We soon established a routine. Nicola would climb into the driver's side and engage some young gun with hair out of McFly in suspiciously flirtatious torque talk. They'd banter on about mpg, SUVs, LPG and MPVs, build up to some serious petrol-head bhp and 0–60 exchanges, wind down with the light relief of seat configurations, in-car entertainment and aircon-as-standard. I'd sit there in the passenger seat, opening and closing the glovebox and fiddling with the drinks holders, feeling like the proverbial spare p . . . part at a wedding, thinking, if he says split tailgate one more time, I'll 'ave him.

After a while Nicola would turn to me and ask what I thought. And that was my cue to say either 'I like the armrest' if I did, or 'I don't like the armrest' if I didn't. At which Nicola and her new buddy would have a little giggle. And I'd think, yeah, you can laugh, son, but once you get to my age you appreciate a nice armrest on a long haul. Occasionally, I'd essay a remark about the bodywork. 'I like this red colour' – something penetrating like that. And once or twice I strayed into sunroofs, but mostly

I just sat there, dutifully silent, feeling pride in my wife's prodigious knowledge, plus envy, plus boredom. As the day wore on, the boredom edged out the pride and the envy.

As we left, her at the wheel as ever, me collapsed gratefully to her left, she said she'd decided new cars are a mug's game and we'll save ourselves a packet buying our friends Karen and Peter's Volvo if it's still on offer. I said that's fine by me.

16 September 2006

I went out for dinner last night and guess who was two tables away, discreetly half-hidden by a pillar? Only Chantelle and Preston from *Celebrity Big Brother*, that's who! It was definitely them, my wife made an entirely spurious visit to the lavatory to get a better angle to check. I thought about ringing my colleagues on the *News of the World* but decided to save the scoop for my own loyal readers, to whom I can now reveal that, while Preston had the apple crumble for pudding, Chantelle didn't have anything. And, they held hands a lot. And, my wife didn't like Preston's jumper. And, er, that was it. Still, what excitement! It's the kind of thing that makes living in London worthwhile.

After that little detour, and following on from forays to Pembrokeshire, Cardiff and Marlow in recent weeks, the action stays in the west, yet sweeps dramatically northwards, to Cheshire and the Shropshire Union Canal. Here, you find me, the family and our hosts Karen, Peter and daughter Loulou barging it up at three and a half knots on the *Just Today* out of Nantwich. I'm on the roof, leafing through the latest issue of *Towpath Talk*, thinking how I absolutely love wearing shorts. As with underwear in medieval winters, stitch me into my shorts in April, I say, and don't dare cut me free till October comes around.

Not everyone is as pro-shorts as I am. It is many years since

Don Estelle graced our TV screens, even so I get *Hello Lofty lovely boy* in a bad Welsh accent once a week or more, plus a fair few dib dib dibs. And the night before the canal trip my shorts had been refused entry to a bar.

'Sorry, fella,' said the doorman at Ninotchka, 'no trainers on a Saturday. Or,' he added with a sneer, 'shorts.'

So we went next door to Curshaws, lady bouncer, spiky hair, Crombie, lovely smile, in you go, no bother. Fellow short-trouser enthusiasts might like to bear this in mind when next they're out on the beer in Nantwich.

Just Today chugged on, my wife at the helm, waxing nostalgic for her coxing days at university. I'd had a brief stab at being Captain Bob, but that steer-one-way-to-go-the-other routine was never going to work out for a man with my limitations. One brutally abrupt zigzag too many and the mutiny was swift and ruthless.

'Come on, Captain Bob,' said Nicola, grabbing the tiller with one hand and shoving me towards the galley with the other, 'time for you to make everyone a cup of tea.'

Now, I yield to no man in my passion for an inland waterway, but I must confess after an hour or two on the Shropshire Union when Rachel, my daughter, wailed, 'I thought it would be funner than this!' I felt a degree of sympathy. So I amused myself and the children by holding the safety rail, leaning backwards over the water and shouting, 'Look! I'm Ellen MacArthur Bob!' And then I did Figurehead Bob and then I clambered around the very edge of the boat (in forty-two seconds, if anyone wants to take it on as a challenge, be sure to avoid getting chopped to pieces by the propeller) and announced that was called Double Oh Bob. Or Bond Bob, if you prefer.

Sadly I couldn't do Pope Bob, my favourite, because you need a big Jiffy bag to jam on your head for Pope Bob. Same goes for Bank Robber Bob, except you have to cut a couple of eyeholes out for that, as you do for Ned Kelly Bob too, whereas for Crusader Bob you join the eyeholes up to make one long historically accurate slit.

'Why do you have to do these things?' asked Nicola. 'You could have fallen in.'

What, and been eaten by giant voles? I said, and then we had our familiar set-to where I say she's too risk-averse and she says I'm an idiot.

But I'm not ready to put away childish, or indeed shortsish, things just yet. Someone at work, it was Rebecca, asked me recently whether it was wise to wear shorts to the office all the time. Listen, I said, all fifteen and fervent, dress codes are an assault on personal liberty! It's our duty to smash them wherever we can!

'No,' she said, 'I was thinking about that blobby thing on your knee, why draw attention to it?'

Oh that, I said, deflated, it's only a wart, you make too much fuss about these things, you were the same that time I had head lice.

'Well, I don't like nits and I don't like warts,' said Rebecca, adding defiantly, 'and I don't like it when you eat tins of mackerel, either.'

Leaving Rebecca's fastidiousness to one side, and ever since another colleague, Lucia van der Post, wrote that a man coming to work in shorts could forget about promotion, I've worn mine more assiduously than ever, warts and all, the (frankly unlikely) prospect of preferment worrying me almost as much as the old heave-ho. Not that it will matter soon. I reckon shorts are now where open-necked shirts were about five years ago, another few years and short will be the new long, and it'll be knees out every summer in the Shadow Cabinet, mark my words.

20 January 2007

When I was in the fine city of Birmingham before Christmas, I met a friend, Susie, for a drink. We discussed the future of secondary education for a while and then we got on to the good stuff. She knew, Susie said, that Nicola does pretty much everything relating to the car, the house, the children, finance, DIY, holidays, interaction with friends, extended family, teachers, bureaucrats and tradesmen. What, therefore, Susie wanted to know, did I do? Very good question.

Susie, I said, gathering my thoughts, I believe you could break down my domestic responsibilities into three areas. The first of which is, as I think is well known, unskilled labour. First and foremost this means anything to do with sanitation, namely: bin-bag management; cat litter; bog-roll resupply; wiping surfaces with kitchen roll. If a sink needs unblocking I have a go at it before we call the plumber. I also do drains. And gutters. My gutters are exemplary. You could eat your dinner off them.

I also make the children's breakfasts, including administering the requisite three teaspoons of Omega 3 fish oil each day so they grow up to be properly middle class. Moreover, I provide a fully comprehensive shop-to-box packed-lunch service, and (my wife would dispute this but I know I'm right) I assume the lion's share of dishwasher responsibility too, including filling the salt tray and the rinse aid and detergent slots. I realize the march of the three-in-one tablet is now sadly unstoppable, but as long as there is breath in my body I shall continue to perform each function individually because I really enjoy it.

Staying with drudgery, I said, I handle tea, coffee, a range of other hot and cold beverages, alcoholic drinks, snacks and light refreshments. My son has now started drinking tea, so this duty has become 50 per cent more onerous. Still, it's rewarding. If I get the milk/tea/sugar dosage right, he has a sip, smacks his lips and goes 'Aaaah!' in a satisfied fashion.

'That's the tea noise, isn't it, Daddy?' he says.

When I'm not tutoring my eldest child to make the tea noise correctly, I also preside over indoor plants. And the bottle bank. Once in a while, I might oil a lock or hinge.

Outside, I tend to the front yard and the back garden, stopping short of any action requiring an aesthetic decision. I sweep, I weed, I strive officiously to keep the lawn alive. I also undertake late-night mercy missions to Mustafa's for milk, Diet Coke and Turkish delight, and occasionally, if supplies are very low, I brave the beggars, muggers, crazies and joyriders and risk a trip to the twenty-four-hour Tesco in central Hackney.

Susie was gripped by a near-uncontrollable yawning fit at this point, but even so, she was, I think, quietly impressed. (I happen to know she has issues with her own husband's bin-bag commitment.) Coming to the second category, I said, this is essentially a portmanteau of things I know a little bit about, and therefore take the lead role on within the family. These include front crawl, butterfly, football, North American Indians, the novels of Alistair MacLean, light bicycle maintenance, geography, war, situation comedy of the seventies and popular music 1977–84. Surprising how often these subjects crop up. I used to do sharks and crocodiles as well but Sam has now usurped me on both creatures.

And finally, I said, there's one other thing I do that bears no relation to what has gone before. What's that? asked Susie, jolting herself awake. Making difficult phone calls, I said. Really? she said, I would assume Nicola would have done those. Precisely, I said, so would most people. I admit it's a strange role for me to have, doesn't fit with the rest of the Bob portfolio at all. It's like when you find out that Rowan Atkinson has an HGV licence.

And yet, if a dinner party needs wriggling out of, or an absentee builder given a boot up the backside, or a neighbourhood turf war starts to spiral out of control, it's me who makes the call. Basically (not sure what this says about my character but there you go) if anything requires either the telling of lies or the implied threat of violence, I swing into action.

But only over the phone. With face-to-face confrontation I have, like many men, just the two modes: appeasement or nuclear, doormat or all-out escalation. Neither is much good for solving a problem. Say I've got a relationship, professional or social, that isn't working properly. I won't think constructively about how to mend it. What I'll do is moan and whine and whinge for months, years possibly, decades in one or two cases, and then eventually I'll lose patience and take the relationship and break it irretrievably into pieces.

Rather like the American military, I find it easier to either Go Big or Go Home, but to Go Long and sort the thing out, like the British Army did in Northern Ireland, is beyond me. Finding a middle way to resolve disputes, potential or actual, is something I really want to work on this year. Susie thanked me for the information and we went our separate ways.

24 February 2007

'Just for once,' my wife says, 'maybe we could go out without you moaning about it. Maybe, even, *you* could arrange something, you know, *book* somewhere, organize a *babysitter*, get *dressed up*, make a bit of an *effort, surprise* me.'

OK, I say, I'll do all that, but you've got to reciprocate, you've got to insist we're going to such-and-such one Saturday, and then about six o'clock, say it was all a joke and you've ordered up a takeaway and a DVD and I can lie on the sofa in my tracksuit scratching my armpits all night.

I'm still chuckling away at my own dry northern wit as we arrive at a club later that evening. I say club, it's more of a hall. A dance hall, even, because dancing is what everyone has come to do. We're at Rarely Groove, which started life as a one-off benefit for the tsunami victims and has since become a bi-monthly bash and the hottest ticket in Hackney. Provided you were born before the Beatles split up, that is. And preferably before they were famous.

The premise of Rarely Groove is brilliantly simple: a disco for grown-ups. No kids, no food, no frills, and most importantly, no irony. So no Abba or Wham! or Bee Gees, plenty of funk and soul: James Brown, Rose Royce, Marvin Gaye, proper dance music put out by black people basically.

Now I'll never amount to anything on the floor, dancing being all hips, me being all shoulders, chest and head. Obviously, up to a point, alcohol helps, but even after five pints fourteen stone is a lot of booty to shift around in even a moderately rhythmic fashion. Shunned by our respective wives, I spend most of the evening dancing with my friend Gary.

Gary is the same height and build as I am. We also share an identical level of balletic grace, i.e., none whatsoever. I should imagine that Gary and I, shoulders rolling away threateningly, look a lot like a couple of prop forwards in need, as it were, of a hooker, who I have to say would have completed a rather tasty front row. An appropriate image as it happens, since for a good hour we right the wrongs of English rugby, shouting stuff about second-phase ball and territorial kicking alternately into each other's ears.

Around us, the floor shakes to the combined weight of a hundred or more Hackney mums and dads letting their hair down. Up and down, back and forth, I try to stick all the while to the golden rules of white male heterosexual dancing as set out by Will Smith in *Hitch*: minimal foot-to-foot shuffle; no fancy moves; no finger-clicking and, most definitely, no lip-biting. It's dad-disco stripped to the essentials, and it gets me by without too much sniggering. Then Steve, quite the mover in his own idiosyncratic way, stamps on my big toe and I have to have a breather.

'Ingrowing toenail,' I explain.

Steve apologizes and tells me how a Chinese masseuse had sorted out his troublesome neck.

Sitting one track out, taking in the scene, I see Gary gamely plodding on alone, a tighthead isolated in a ruck, and Steve, elbows flying, and Phil, moving freely again after his heart op. Filtered through a gauze of Guinness, I feel a warm wave of goodwill wash out towards these men. I can date the start of our friendships precisely: this time of year, a decade ago, a world away.

Our wives had all forced us to go to the same as-it-turned-out absurdly right-on antenatal class, and as you can imagine, eight weeks of sitting on a bucket pretending to be in labour lashed us pretty tightly together (although Gary, to his immense credit, refused point blank to go again after week three). And then our babies were all born within a fortnight of each other that spring, and the next ones two years later, and the women have kept the men more or less in touch with each other ever since, each meeting a bit greyer and more ragged around the edges than the last. That's me, Gary, Phil and Steve, not them, Nicola, Fiona, Hilary and Leone, perish the thought.

And now we find ourselves in the lavatories of this old hall in Hackney, along with a changing cast of other half-familiar dads, meeting up for a secret smoke. Only normal fags, of course, having reached the age where mere tobacco can call down considerable uxorial grief all by itself. Out in the hall, they're still dancing and talking, schools, holidays and houses, and, mostly, the children, always the children.

And back in the bogs Steve says there should be a revolution, and Gary and I say what are you talking about, and Phil smiles in a scholarly way and says, well, Hackney does have a fine radical tradition, and Steve says take over the City, the banks, something big has to change, and Gary and I say, yeah but, c'mon, nothing big *does* have to change, does it? Something *small* perhaps, pave over the lawn, get a new stepladder, something *medium* maybe, do out the loft, carve out that extra bedroom, but nothing big, not really, because isn't life pretty good as it is?

14 April 2007

So, interiors. It's a big ask, but on the bright side, at least it's not fashion. I may have run out of things to say about clothes, but as regards chairs, tables, *finials*, the swag-Roman-Venetian conundrum, beta male has opinions to spare. I suppose if I were an alpha type, I'd either leave it all to her while I got on with clawing my way to a better parking space at the office (or indeed, *any* parking space), or else I'd be able to impose my own taste. But I haven't sufficient testosterone to pursue either option.

Instead, what I've done over the years is fight a protracted rearguard action, rather like the *Wehrmacht* as the Red Army rolled them back across the steppe in the years after Stalingrad. Very like that, actually. I imagine if my wife sat down with Marshal Stalin to discuss the status of individual liberty vis-à-vis the need for order, authority and control, a consensus would soon emerge.

Room by room, inch by inch, bitter hand-to-hand combat has seen me withdraw from the bedroom, the bathroom, the living room, finally the kitchen. As I have relinquished this territory, cushions have proliferated. Patterns, too. Weird, to my mind wholly superfluous, covers have appeared on the sofa. Dried flowers have been placed on shelves. (The wife–Stalin parallel diverges at this point, I admit. I don't think Joe was big on floral arrangements.) Worst of all, I am no longer allowed to store the spare cat litter out in the open for ease of access.

Elsewhere, such toilet accessories as I possess (razor, shaving foam, toenail clippers, large bottle of surgical spirit for all your perfumery needs) have been consigned to high-shelf oblivion where they cannot offend any of my wife's friends or female relations who might stray in. Similarly, recent mopping-up operations in the fiercely contested kitchen pocket have led to much indispensable stuff being tucked and tidied away. Absolute staples of my regime (bran sticks, prunes, cod liver oil) have all been swept from sight.

I am now holed up in my shed/office next to the garage, like a loony survivalist waiting for the Feds in his cabin in Montana. There's been talk about converting my sanctuary into an extra family space. Once I heard the phrase 'garden room' employed, I went into shameless Churchillian. I shall not flag or fail, I shall go on to the end, I shall fight in the hallway, I shall fight in the bog next to my shed/office, I shall fight with growing confidence and growing strength in the air above my shed/office, I shall defend my shed/office, whatever the cost may be, I shall fight on the, er, beaches, I shall never surrender, etc., etc. She beat a tactical retreat.

I look around at the bare MDF, the album covers Blu-tacked to the wall, the posters, the maps, the pictures of Oliver Cromwell, William Sherman, Mikhail Tal, Primo Levi, Stuart Pearce and Viv Richards, the shelves of *Viz* and *Prospect*, the dartboard, the trunkload of old diaries and notebooks, the bicycle gear, the rubbishy CD player, the boxing gloves, and I sigh and think: if only the rest of the house could look like this, a cross between a gym, Bomber Command and the clerical section of an ailing factory. But I know it won't happen now.

Sometimes I think I should move in here full time. All I'd need would be a barricade, a stove, a camp bed, a bucket, a fridge for my chicken, maybe a dishwasher for company, a massive one such as I used to load at the Willerby Manor hotel for peanuts in 1980; any crockery coming out still cruddy got shoved into a skipful of rotting food out the back. And if not a dishwasher, then some other piece of kit, maybe a version of that magnificent steam engine at the Science Museum, Burnley Ironworks Company 1903, or the Toyoda loom they've got there, too. Never mind simulators and touch screens, give me lumps of metal. Those twin fifteen-inch naval guns outside the Imperial War Museum? Awe-inspiring, they are.

And then I look out into the garden, where over the winter I have prepared what really will be my last line of defence. That lawn she likes? I've dug the bugger up. She wants it returfed, I want to put some rhubarb in. Stand-off. Meanwhile, there's a covered deck bit: I've colonized that, got my punchbag hung up on a chain, a selection of weights, a mat for sit-ups, a rugby ball. Too bad there's still a pink chair out there, in among all the Lonsdale. I tried to get rid of it, but she spotted me; says it's Lloyd Loom, one of those brands women go crazy about.

I've also faithfully stuck up those freebie movie posters *The Times* gave away, *Rocky, Platoon* and *Gladiator* at least. I say look, What We Do in Life Echoes in Eternity, aren't they the best eight words ever strung together? She says she wants them down anyway, Russell Crowe in a skirt and all. Another stand-off. But spring is here now, the fighting season is upon us. She will strike again sooner rather than later. I shall have to be on my guard.

12 May 2007

Another country, another camper van, another crash. There was a debacle last year, when, slowly, carefully, precisely, I reversed a cumbersome German *schlafenwagen* into a Sardinian tree. 'Look out for that tree!' said Nicola. 'What tree?' Crunch. Five hundred euros down the pan.

Twelve months on, pretty much the same thing has happened. I'm in a motel car park in Monterey, California, trying to squeeze our hired VW through a narrow gap, again under guidance from my wife. I'm doing fine, back and forth, left hand down, all that business, when my attention is diverted by the most astonishing tree, emerald green, laden with spiky red flowers.

'Look at that,' I say, 'that's just beautiful, isn't it?'

'There's a low wall on my side,' replies Nicola, 'and you're about to hit it.'

'Why is it,' I say, picking up a theme already well explored on this and other holidays, 'that whenever I go a bit lyrical, you start criticizing my dri—'

Bang. The impact was just where the slidy door meets the rear panel, instantly doubling the repair cost: 952 bucks, not to mention 34 cents. Bad hit that, even with the dollar as cheap as it is. Rather undermined my case, too, in the ongoing big picture versus little details debate.

Low-speed, medium-sized vehicle manoeuvring is starting to look like a weakness. Certainly, my shortcomings keep adding tiresomely to the expense of going on holiday. Nicola says I don't make sufficient, or indeed *any*, use of the wing mirrors. And it's true, I do regard these fixtures as deeply superfluous, hanging about making your car wider while not working their passage in any way. They have long been, as it were, a blind spot.

Still, it could have been worse. (A fortnight among Californians can turn even a middle-aged Protestant from the North of England into an optimist, at least for a while.) In the mountains, one old-timer warned me if a bear smells so much as a packet of toffees in your glovebox, he'll take off your car door, or your arm, or your child, or all three, without breaking stride. Got to watch out for the cougars and coyotes, too. And the heavily armed psychopaths. In that context, one bump in 1,500 hard-driven miles up and down the Pacific Coast Highway isn't so bad.

Among the most enjoyable of those miles were the handful spent in Beverly Hills, where I vetoed the rest of the family and bought a map to the stars' homes. Even my eight-year-old daughter, who has a sneaking interest in celebrity, knew this was a desperately unsophisticated option.

'Look,' I said, 'we're on a glorified suburban housing estate here, it's Kirkella [affluent Hull suburb where I grew up] with palm trees, there's really not a lot else to do.'

My friend (and the children's godfather) Michael was with us. He navigated, I drove, the rest of the van sat in sullen protest.

'Up Sunset, second right, first left for Lieutenant Columbo,' Michael would announce, 'after that I can do you Kirk Douglas, swing by the Fonz and then head up to Bel-Air for Barry Manilow, Britt Ekland and Red Buttons.'

Sounds good to me, I'd say, and sing a snatch of 'Can't Smile Without You'.

'Who's the Fonz?' asked the children.

'A hugely significant cultural figure,' I replied.

'What did he do?'

'Well,' I began, 'he was on the TV when me and Mummy and Mikey were young and, er, he could get stuck vending machines to work by kicking them in a certain way and, er, when he'd done that, he would lean back, put both thumbs up and go "Heyyyy!"'

In the rear-view mirror, the children's faces registered part confusion, part boredom, part pity. Mostly pity.

I've got to say. Columbo's place was a let-down, surprisingly pokey given the enduring popularity of the dishevelled tousle-haired one-eyed raincoat-sporting henpecked early-seventies maverick police detective.

'Oi! Columbo!' I shouted, something snapping inside me. 'Your house is *rubbish*!'

'Yeah,' yelled Michael, leaning across me out of the window, 'it's crap!'

Poor form, I know, but the conformist nature of American society (rugged individualism, my arse) can sometimes give rise to unstoppable infantile urges. At least the children enjoyed hearing their godfather say crap, bless 'em.

After Columbo, we got lost trying to find Gene Hackman's spread. Energy leaked out of the enterprise, reviving briefly when I said I'd seen Matt Damon on Rodeo Drive but, hand on heart, it wasn't him. I thought I saw Richard Widmark, too, but it wasn't him either, although it may surprise you to learn that he is still, at the time of writing, alive.

In fact, much as I loved California, I could make a very long list of the famous people I didn't see there. No Clint in Carmel, no Bruce Willis in Malibu, no Pammy in Santa Monica, splashing in the surf in slow motion in a high-cut red swimsuit carrying an improbably shaped flotation device, or otherwise. Not to worry.

27 October 2007

I was out for lunch with a friend recently when we passed a security van collecting cash from a shop.

'I always worry when I see one of those vans,' she said, 'in case there's a robbery and I get hit by a stray bullet.'

That's strange, I said, because when *I* see one of those vans, I always hope there is a robbery so I can intervene, preferably incurring a minor non-life-threatening but picturesque injury (the John Terry/Terry Butcher blood-soaked head bandage would be ideal) and be a hero and win a medal and quite possibly a large cash reward as well.

I wondered if there are women who feel the same as me, or men who feel the same as my friend, or whether we had hit upon a fundamental difference between the sexes. But then I thought of some of my heroines, Ellen MacArthur, Katy Hepburn, Martina Navratilova, Sophie Scholl, Condoleezza Rice, those Saudi women who drove their own cars, Eve Arnold, Natalie Merchant, Curvy Kathy Lloyd . . . they're gonna do something, aren't they, those girls? Except the dead ones.

And Curvy Kathy Lloyd, I suppose, might not be up for it, although she could always whip her top off to distract the robbers, allowing someone else, i.e., me, to disarm them, which would impress Curvy Kathy Lloyd no end, blah blah blah. I've just looked up Curvy Kathy Lloyd on the net. The first site is blocked because it contravenes News International's policy on pornography. The second reveals Curvy Kathy Lloyd is forty next month! Can that be true? The years fly past, they really do.

No doubt if it ever came to it, I'd hit the deck along with everyone else. But still, it's vital to think these scenarios through, hope for the best, prepare for the worst, train hard, fight easy, all that business. Being ready to do the right thing makes it more likely you will should you ever be called upon, and when and if you *are* called upon, that moment will be a defining moment, maybe *the* defining moment, of your life. I climbed a cherry tree last year, had to go five, maybe six feet up, to retrieve the neighbour's kitten. Maximus, he's called, daft cat. My children still talk about it.

We were at the Deep a fortnight ago, the new(ish) aquarium in Hull. Obviously, I checked out all the angles, decided what to do in the event of the glass giving way and a tide of sharks, stingrays and whatnot engulfing my family. Later on we went to Hull

Fair so I could have the best part of a hundred quid vacuumed out of my trousers. On the big wheel with my dad, brother and sister-in-law, with my wife, daughter, another sister-in-law, niece and nephew in the next carriage along, the temperature dropping, the fair spreading out below us, I said: hold on, if the rivets start popping out of this thing right now, what's the plan?

My brother and I agreed we'd have to fling ourselves across to the next car to get the kids, your basic Richard Burton manoeuvre, made trickier by the lack of an ice axe.

'What about me?' said my dad.

You used to go rock climbing, I said, you've done worse than this in a woolly jumper and hobnailed boots, you'll be all right.

'That was fifty-five years ago,' he said.

Cycling to work these perfect autumn mornings, I've taken to stopping off at a bench by the Thames. I make a few notes, I swig some of this foul protein mixture I'm taking to turn me into that massive hairy French guy, Chabal. I watch the commuter catamarans heading along to Docklands, willing someone to fall in (though clear of the propellers) so I can take my chances with the tide, cold, hydrofoils and Weil's disease and save them, just as Matthew Parris once hurled himself off a bridge further upstream to save a drowning dog.

I was down there today and there was a young couple on the next bench, tourists, taking pictures, her sat on the railings so he could get Canary Wharf in the background. I thought: one slight miscalculation, and she's in, and he doesn't seem to care. I'm not proud of this but, you know, I'm a good swimmer, she wouldn't have been in the water longer than a minute. And she looked pretty resilient, she'd have got over the trauma in due course. Everybody wins! And it was high tide too, so I could have dived, not had to do that uncool straddle jump I was taught in my pyjamas at Haltemprice Sports Centre about a hundred and fifty years ago.

Sometimes, when my wife and I discuss moving out of London, I think, yeah, let's do it, I could join the RNLI, or one of those rural fire brigades run by volunteers, or get a Land Rover with a tow bar, cruise around on winter nights, owls hooting, hauling cars, sheep, cows, hedgehogs, anything really, out of ditches, ice crackling beneath the tyres, breath steaming in the chill, 'Thanks, Bob, you're my absolute hero,' don't mention it, hedgehog, it's no bother, you take care now.

Meanwhile, I watch, I wait and I hold myself in readiness.

3 November 2007

My wife and I are visiting potential secondary schools for our son. I find I have the same reaction to schools as other people do to hospitals, or museums: fear, anxiety, physical and emotional discomfort evidenced by sweating and giddiness, plus a helping of both extreme fatigue and extreme hunger.

On a recent tour, I slipped out of a classroom to get a few moments to myself in the corridor, leant against a project on, what else, global warming stuck on the wall, and thought, hmnn, while I'm here, I'll restore my spirits with a bit of Ugly Breakfast. I had a stash of the notorious yoghurt, prune, berry and seed-based gunk slopping around in a Tupperware box in my rucksack. Portable Ugly, the children call it.

I didn't have a spoon so, resourceful as ever, I detached a lens from my sunglasses and, peeling off the lid, glancing this way and that, started shovelling down the gloop. And it was in this furtive attitude that, seconds later, my wife tracked me down. As wives do. 'It's like having to bring a baby with me,' she sighed.

Indeed so. Many men, of course, fail to mature properly, but usually the failure to progress dates from about eighteen years of age, fourteen in distressing cases, not, I think, twelve months. I was, for example, researching fear of fireworks (which I have) on the internet, and all the advice related to babies. Or pets. The assumption seems to be that by the age of forty-three a person ought to have learnt to deal with loud bangs.

But I haven't. Which is why, along with the let's-burn-some-Catholics politics and carbonized jacket potatoes, I don't much like Bonfire Night. Neither does my son. Neither do the cats. So out of the six of us in what the children call the nuclear bomb family, that's four of us voting no.

I shall get my head down early with my black woolly hat jammed over my ears, the hat people say makes me look like a burglar, although I don't suppose real burglars actually wear black woolly hats, any more than they wear masks, stripey jumpers or carry bags with 'swag' written on the side and candelabra poking out of the top.

Strange what you pass down the generations. Walking my son to school, if a car horn goes, or a motorbike rips by, it's hard to say who flinches most, the forty-three- or the ten-year-old. I try to play down my own reaction for his sake. Inside, I want to clutch Sammy for comfort, my own as much as his.

Car horns are a real menace. I can't believe the anger, fear and irritation they cause is outweighed by any good they do. I'd get rid of them. Same with fireworks. In our neigbourhood, leading up to 5 November, it's like the Somme. Yeah, sixty thousand people were slaughtered in one morning last week. And that mud gets all over your carpets.

A night inside this Monday will mean missing out on my current punishing exercise routine in the garden. Dull business, exercise, except last week I was doing press-ups and the cord from my tracksuit was hanging down. Tiger the cat came skidding out of the darkness to attack the cord at the precise moment I lowered myself to the ground, squashing him.

'Look, Rachel,' shouted Sam, 'he's trying to sex the cat!'

Rachel was inside making her brother some ear muffs out of

paper and cotton wool in advance of the fireworks. Isn't that the sweetest thing you ever heard?

When I was living on Daws Hill peace camp in High Wycombe in the winter of 1983, we used to go into the woods around the American base and throw firecrackers over the wire. Well, I say 'we', the truth is I would crouch up against the bole of a tree, eyes tight shut, fingers jammed in my ears, while braver boys chucked the ordnance.

The idea was to try to get the sentry to draw his gun. I have a feeling he did once, although I also have a feeling I might have made that up. The fact/fiction distinction has a tendency to blur with the years.

Good word, 'bole', all reassuring and cosy. Some people feel complete by the sea, some in the hills; me, I like woods, full of those lovely boles. Again, noise is a factor. We're supposed to find the sound of lapping waves soothing, or mystical, or romantic, I find it aggravating. Same with wind up a mountain. Meteorological wind, I mean, not flatulence, that can be both helpful and amusing when climbing a hill.

I like being a few feet back into a wood on a slope on a still day, invisible behind the bole of a tree, looking out over open countryside through a screen of foliage, watching and waiting. I like to think that buried deep in my ancestry are outlaws, archers, hunters, ambushers. But not, I hope, peeping Toms.

I've inherited their patience, and by the spring, if I haven't got too bored, I shall have their physique too, but I'm not sure either fully compensates for having the courage of a kitten.

24 November 2007

There's this new coffee bar at work by the lifts as you come in. The Thunderer, they've called it, a reference presumably to the deafening laxative effect of several hundred people drinking a lot more coffee than they were drinking a week ago.

Next to the cappuccino machine they've put in this sort of elliptical shelf at elbow height. No chairs! Rather, the idea seems to be that you hold impromptu brainstorming sessions while leaning casually on the shelf, nursing your tall no-whip skinny decaf latte and thinking networky internety onliney out-of-the-boxy blue-sky-y let's drill down into the numbersy are we all on the same pagey type thoughts.

The day the Thunderer opened for business, always keen to keep up with the latest innovations, my colleague Alan Franks and I went to the shelf.

'This is tremendously exciting, isn't it, Bobbly?' said Alan.

'Franksie,' I replied, 'as ever you speak for both of us.'

After that, we had a slice of fruit cake and, not for the first time, discussed how an uncanny number of the messengers on *The Times* resemble famous sportsmen.

There used to be Alan Shearer and Phil Neville, but they seem to have been given a transfer, which leaves Shane Warne, Steven Gerrard and a tall bloke who Alan thinks looks like Stan Collymore, but I don't. After kicking that debate around the block for a while, we lost interest and pretended to be Japanese soldiers, which always ends with one or other of us miming melodramatic self-disembowelment. If self-disembowelment wasn't a real word before, it is now.

Oh yes, the white-hot heat of technology is burning brightly in my life at the moment. As the nights get ever colder, I go to bed ever earlier, burrowing down deep under the duvet with the cats, my laptop and a DVD. Feels pretty cutting edge, I can tell you. So far, I've rewatched *Das Boot*, *The Guns of Navarone* and a lot of old David Attenborough documentaries, plus all the special features explaining how they were made, because that's the kind of postmodern twenty-first-century guy I'm becoming.

Meanwhile, my wife is downstairs, drawing up spreadsheets and zipping through *Ugly Betty* episodes, having rapidly mastered series link on the new Sky box. Traditionally, men are supposed to hog the remote control; in our house, I can't get near it. Even when she goes out, and I settle down to take in some urban underbelly movie carnage, the telly tells me I can't because she's already recording *Heroes* and *America's Next Top Model* and that's your lot, Bob. I have to trudge back upstairs to *Das Boot* instead.

I think a technological tipping point has been reached in my family. We've had the requisite kit for a while, now we've started using it. Three years ago, my wife bought me an iPod. Two years ago, she read the instruction manual. One year ago, she loaded some music on to it. A month ago, I tentatively fired it up. Good, aren't they? A long lead time, but I got there in the end.

Meanwhile, my nephew is in America on a gap year. He calls his mum and dad every week on Skype, which as you all know features a little camera on top of your computer so you can see each other. Up in Hull recently, I spent half an hour at my brother's looking at a grainy image of my nephew in Connecticut trying to get the thing to work.

'This is f****** pointless,' he emailed in the end, but still, good effort.

My parents have had a mobile for several years, but they had never been known to switch it on, regarding it with as much enthusiasm as you would, say, an irradiated dog turd, were you required to carry such a thing around with you. And then recently I was amazed to discover that not only has the mobile been activated, but my dad and his pal Ted, his best man from 1955, have taken to texting each other a dozen times a day, like schoolgirls, except their exchanges revolve around each other's ailments rather than who said what to whom in Starbucks.

They're not *that* sophisticated, though.

'Ted tried to do this predictive texting the other day,' my dad told me. 'I got a message that said Gnnnhgh who RaGGer doff cruet huff, CLOD Begin?'

Still, it's a far cry from the days I'd get home to find a long message from my mum on the answerphone, at the end of which you'd hear, 'Oooo he's not there, he must be out, I've said we'll try later.'

I'm in no position to scoff. The funereal pace of my own texting is infamous.

'Hey, Rob, wouldn't it be quicker to write a letter?' various teenagers of my acquaintance ask, watching me stabbing away, tongue stuck out in concentration.

They also make fun of my mobile, Nokia's finest from the stone age of 2003.

'Hey, Rob, do you shovel coal in to charge it up?', etc.

And I got a seven-inch single out the other day and my daughter asked what I was doing with 'that big CD'.

Eeeee, the world's changing fast and that's a fact.

1 December 2007

How much do you tell your children of the not nice, naughty, not to say downright nasty things you got up to when you were young? Very little, is the correct answer. And yet when my son and I are alone together and he eggs me on without the restraining presence of our wife/mother and daughter/sister, I am consistently unable to keep my mouth shut.

He knows about trying to persuade a builder to put up an extension on the local newsagent's. He knows about hurling water balloons into a crowded bus three nights in a row and how on the third night the bus driver begged, 'Oh no, lads, not again.' And he knows how Dave, one of my colleagues in the bike factory, succeeded in stealing an entire bike, piece by piece, including, somehow, the frame, until at the last, Ray the charge-hand caught him leaving with a wheel-shaped bulge under his coat.

And then, the other night, Nicola and Rachel were out, Sammy was doing his maths homework at the kitchen table and I was at the sink scrubbing a particularly encrusted baking tray that wouldn't fit in the dishwasher.

'Why don't you just put it in the bin?' Sam suggested, eager for any distraction from calculating the area of a triangle.

And so I told him about when I used to do precisely that.

I was sixteen and had secured a holiday job in a hotel kitchen in suburban Hull. All went well for a few weeks, then I discovered the regular staff got paid twice as much as I did, £1.20 an hour as opposed to 60p. This (the discrepancy, if not the risible amounts) was perfectly reasonable now that I think about it. They were grown women with families to support, I was about to go into the sixth form. At the time, though, it felt unjust, especially as I worked hard and they mostly stood around chatting and smoking.

Within the space of one shift, I explained to my son, his ruler and pencil discarded, I turned from model employee to industrial saboteur. The next time a filthy serving platter with a trout carcass welded to it came through, I announced I was going out the back for a breath of air. Smuggling the unspeakable object along with me, I dropped it into the big bin reserved for slops. Then I hunted around for a stick and poked and prodded until the thing sank, farting and gurgling, beneath the surface of the goo.

'What happened?' asked Sam.

What happened, I said, is nothing. And so, having got away with it, I kept doing it. Over the next few weeks, it became second nature to me, and never mind the tough stuff, *anything* that required even a minimal effort to clean went into the slops bin. And then, after a month, the pig farmer who bought the slops off the hotel complained.

'I know people think my pigs'll eat anything,' he said, 'but they won't eat plates. Or saucepans.'

I was swiftly informed upon and sacked.

Sam giggled away in gratifying fashion.

That's not all, I told him, all paternal propriety swept aside by the adrenalin rush of a receptive audience. In that intervening month, between first going bad and getting the push, I developed another habit. And this one was truly inexcusable.

'Inexgookable?' queried Sam.

Very bad indeed, I explained. Again, the scuzzy few square yards immediately outside the hotel kitchen formed the scene of the crime.

'What did you do?' he asked.

Well, I told him, one day, on my tea break, having as usual disposed of any even mildly distasteful crockery in the slops bin, I had a sit-down and a cup of tea, and then I decided to hurl the cup at the wall, like a Russian necking a glass of vodka and dashing it into the fireplace.

'What?' said Sam, his eyes lighting up. 'Did the cup smash?'

Forget 'smash', I said, it practically *exploded*.

'How many did you throw?' he asked.

Must have been a couple of dozen over those few weeks, I replied. And again, the first time you do it, your heart is racing, you can't believe that you're going to do it, are doing it, have done it. And then it becomes easier and easier until soon it's a matter of routine: finish tea, smack lips, launch cup against nearest wall, go back to work. So much easier than the bind of taking the empty cup back indoors to be washed up.

And that, Samuel, I said, feebly trying to inject a moral at the death, is how evil takes hold, in a man and in a society. You cross that line, and before long, it's hard to cross back.

'How do you know where the line is?' he asked.

You just *know*, Sam, I said, putting on my special stern father-to-son voice, *everybody* knows. And the correct thing is not to cross the line in the first place, but if you do, you must step back over to the right side straight away, understand?

'I understand,' he said gravely, catching my tone.

But even more important than that, Samuel, I said, is that under no circumstances do you tell your mother about this conversation.

22 December 2007

I suppose if forced to choose I would probably rather go into a bra and knickers shop than a ladies' lavatory, but it would be a close-run thing. In the list of Things You Don't Do As A Man, browsing around women's underwear departments comes very near the top. So when John Lewis invited me over to talk about choosing lingerie for Christmas, I mulled it over for a long while, and then asked if I could bring a friend.

Chris and I met up at the back of the shop off Oxford Street, both of us heavily swaddled against the possibility of being recognized, looking as if we were going to rob the place rather than pick out something pretty. I had invited Chris because last Christmas he bought his then girlfriend some gear he thought looked sexy but turned out to be a marginally feminized version of the thermal underwear cowboys wear to hobble to the khazi in comedy westerns. That was the end of that. Now Chris is six months into a new relationship, with Charlotte, and I didn't want to spurn a chance to help the lad.

The chief lingerie adviser for John Lewis Oxford Street is Maria Walker. By the time we met Maria in her domain on the first floor, I was already in a dry-mouthed sweat, all decision-making capacity gone, my head swept clear by the ocean of cotton, lace, satin, silk and Lycra undulating away to the horizon. Also, I got distracted by a rather fetching dummy. Do you find yourself fancying the mannequins? I asked Chris.

'No,' he replied. 'As it happens, I don't, you pervert.'

Christmas and Valentine's, said Maria, men do come in. The rest of the year, 'They edge up to an outer display then bottle it and head for the lifts.' When men do buy, she said, 'they usually go for black or red, and they're keen on suspenders. They're usually buying for themselves.'

Come again? said Chris.

'I mean, buying what they would like to see rather than what their partner might want,' explained Maria.

We got down to business, and for the next half-hour talked plunge versus balcony, Freya versus Fauve, thong versus brief, back size versus cup size and how the Wonderbras were set slightly apart, as if snubbed by the other bras when they start chatting once everyone's gone home. I took the opportunity to ask Chris a lot of questions about his girlfriend's underwear, while also upgrading my general knocker know-how at the feet of the expert Maria. Very interesting she was, too.

Harley Street, for instance, is around the corner, so she sees a lot of customers whose boobs look like, not to mention sound like, two kettle drums in an empty room. And although Jordan may say she's a 32FF, she's more like a 28K and probably has her bras made specially. By an engineering firm in the West Midlands, I think. Or the Ruhr.

Meanwhile Chris kept moaning about how hard it was to choose a bra simply by seeing it on the hanger, illustrating his point by repeatedly grasping two imaginary grapefruits to his chest and sticking his tongue into his lower lip in an attractive fashion, like Sid James telling Bernard Bresslaw the facts of life. Maria pretended not to notice. We ummed and ahhed for ages, brown or pink, patterned or plain, this or that.

In the end, we both plumped for black and went to the pub.

Talking of Sid James, who should I see later that very evening in the stalls at the Hackney Empire (*Dick Whittington and his Cat*, superb show, Christmas in all its camp cloak-tossing cross-dressing glory, what a wonderful country this is) but the Queen of nudge-nudge herself, Barbara Windsor. Contrary to myth, and contrary also to one of the key Carry On gags, Barbara Windsor, I can report, does not have particularly large breasts. Or maybe the recent Jordan-led inflation has skewed my judgement.

Anyway, over there, I said to my daughter at the interval, pointing discreetly to Babs, is one of the most famous women in the country, a titan of popular culture, a heroine for the ages, an English archetype, a true celebrity, a genuine legend, the Empress of the East End and a national institution to boot: go and get her autograph and I'll give you £5.

'Why can't you?' asked Rachel.

I'm embarrassed, I said.

'So am I,' she said.

I told her I'd make it ten and off she went.

Next morning Chris came up to me at work. 'She loved them!' he said. 'Best lingerie she's ever had.'

Mate, I said, I'm delighted.

'How about you?' he asked.

Well, er, um, she hasn't seen them yet, I said.

'What?' he squeaked, utterly bewildered.

Listen, I said, I had to take Rachel to the pantomime, and when I got back from that I had to give the cat his medicine, and make the packed lunches and stack the dishwasher. And after that we had to choose some new radiator taps and talk about secondary-school entrance. Chris nodded slowly, sympathetically, and I could see him wondering if such a crushing late-night routine lay in his own future, too. Which, of course, it does. Merry Christmas.

2 February 2008

I've just made the annual pilgrimage to my accountant, Brian, up in Hendon. The meeting traditionally starts with my pathetic attempt to take command of proceedings. After about seven seconds of me pulling irrelevant letters from the building society out of my pockets, either Brian, or my wife, or most recently, the two of them in unison, tell me to sit down and shut up while they sort out my tax return.

So I eat biscuits and look at the photos of Brian's kids and half listen to the hardcore CGT, VAT and MIRAS chat – no, MIRAS has been binned, hasn't it, but other acronyms have replaced it – and there's maybe a little light taper-relief talk, and I always know they've nearly finished because they like to relax with a bit of politico-economic back-and-forth over what Gordon may or may not be about to do about this, that or the other. And then I shake Brian's hand and we leave.

The formula never varies, and I like it that way. It's the same at the vet, also called Brian. I take the last appointment of the day so Brian and I can have a proper chat.

'I like your cat basket, Mr Crampton,' says Brian, fruitily.

Thanks, I say.

'Do you use the carrying handles or that rather elegant shoulder strap?'

The handles, I say.

'Why?' he asks, eyes twinkling. 'Is it because using the shoulder strap would look camp?'

Brian, I say, I admit it, you're right, it's because the shoulder strap is completely unacceptable to the forty-three-year-old heterosexual male.

Brian chuckles. 'Would you like a Ferrero Rocher?' he says, that being his treat at the end of a hard day's vetting.

It's a similar story at the dental hygienist. Although she's not called Brian, she is called Sairan, which uses most of the same letters. Sairan is an Iraqi Kurd with soulful eyes. (If Sairan isn't on duty, there's a Baltic blonde in a see-through tunic instead, but I plump for the brown-eyed girl if possible.)

'You smoking?' asks Sairan.

'Hardly at all,' I say guiltily.

'Stop the smoking,' she orders, poking around in my mouth, 'stop also the tea, the coffee, the alcohol, the fizzy drinks, the spice, the chocolate, the sweets . . . And then kill yourself because life is over!'

'Arrrrrh,' I say.

'I make joke,' says Sairan.

It's hard to be sure, upside down with her wearing a mask, but even as she's laughing, her people's pain doesn't seem to leave her eyes.

'Your wisdom teeth are hurting?'

Too right, I say, I think we should get the buggers out.

'No!' Sairan commands. 'Keep them in. When you are older, your face slide, teeth hold it up. Is better.'

Yes, these routines, these rhythms, they're vital, keeping the world ordered and stable, or at least giving the illusion that it is. Which is not to say I can't change my routines as the occasion demands. My children, for instance, go to a swimming club every Friday night. They went up a group before Christmas, therefore their starting time changed, therefore I was thrown into confusion and despondency.

And then I realized the shift freed up a half-hour that wasn't there before. Swiftly, with the sort of flexibility required in today's fast-changing world, I located this lovely little boozer near the baths and right there and then started a brand-new routine.

Or here's another example. My son recently reached the second key stage of childhood development, the one after learning to switch the telly on, namely he can now be trusted to make a cup of tea. That is, trusted as in deal safely with boiling water, and trusted as in get his ratios right. After decades making my own and other people's tea every morning, I am only too happy to hand over the responsibility, I hope, for ever.

The signs are good. 'Can I make you a cup of tea?' possibly the sweetest eight-word sequence in the English language, has become Sam's constant refrain. Not just to his parents, but to anyone who comes into, or near, the house: postmen, milkmen, radiator men, stove men, men who need to borrow £7.50 to get to the Homerton because their wife's in labour and they've left their wallet indoors and I'll pay you back tomorrow, mate, they all get asked the same question.

Most of all, Sam likes making tea for the builders, which is handy when you lose your bike key, thus leaving your faithful friend locked out on a busy street for days, all attempts to free it defeated, your precious routines in ruins. Indeed, if you're thinking of getting a bike, might I recommend the Squire D-lock to keep it safe? Attack it with hammer, hacksaw, chisel or bolt croppers, it'll snigger and ask: is that the best you can do?

No, in my case, because luckily I currently have instant access to a man with a cordless angle grinder, a man what's more who owes my son several dozen cups of tea. Yet even then it took Ted a deafening five minutes to slice that steel, sparks flying all over. Of course your bike may still get nicked: a hundred or more people must have passed us and not one of them took the slightest notice.

26 July 2008

The twin perils of driving and navigation are probably responsible for more husband–wife aggravation than anything else. I suppose money, sex and in-laws can create more serious long-term disputes, but for sheer everyday niggliness, getting in a car together must shade it. From the first time we drove together in 1990 (a hired Passat, Prague, I reversed smartly into the car behind) to last weekend on the A40 when it got a bit unpleasant around Gloucester, hitting the road has posed problems.

Satnav has only added to the tension. Instead of having five competing, often contradictory sources of information to synthesize, we now have six. The satnav just goes into the mix with the road atlas, road signs, prior experience of the journey and any advice offered by third parties (plus, of course, the only thing we actually need, namely my unerring, infallible and otherwise uncannily accurate sense of direction). I think my wife sets too much store by the satnav, she thinks I'm a Luddite. It can get quite nasty.

But not as nasty as it does for some couples. A friend of mine, let's call him Harry, told me how his wife once knocked off a motorcyclist. As it were. She phones Harry in a state, telling him what's happened, and as Harry puts the phone down, he says to his mate standing next to him: 'I hope she gets six months. But only if the prison has a crèche.' (Their son was a baby at the time.) Except Harry hasn't put the phone down properly, his wife hears every word. (The guy on the bike was fine, which is more than can be said for Harry.)

Another story about Harry. When his van gets clamped a few years back, instead of bothering with the usual rigmarole, he simply reaches in the back for his cordless angle grinder, couple of minutes, job done. He doesn't hear anything from the authorities, assumes he's got away with it, mostly because the van is registered in his (by now ex-) wife's name. But then the ex-wife phones Harry up in a fury.

'I've just had the police on,' she says, 'they've put out a f****** warrant for my arrest.'

She's a scary woman, Harry's ex. One time, Harry recalls, she gets in some stand-off with another driver, a young bloke. This kid gets out, walks over to her car, reaches in the window, grabs some clothes off the back seat. 'I've got her knickers!' he shouts, swaggering triumphantly back to his car. At which point Harry's ex jumps out, catches the guy up, flattens him with one punch, retrieves her underwear, drives off.

I wouldn't have minded Harry's ex being there the time we turned into Dawson Street in east London to find a big hairy guy blocking the road with his big hairy motorbike. He was manoeuvring the bike out of its space, taking his time, taking the mickey, frankly. We waited and waited and eventually Nicola bipped the horn, at which point the guy totally flipped and started shouting abuse and lashing out at the Crampton Honda with his boot. I was (sort of) thinking about having it out with him man to man when I saw the words 'London clubhouse' above a Hells Angels logo on the building to my left.

'Er, might be an idea to put your foot down,' I said to Nicola.

There's so much anger around driving, so much pride at stake, so much overinvestment, so many men on a hair trigger every time they fire the ignition. We were in a traffic jam on the Embankment last month, it was Trooping the Colour, everything was graunched up. Heading west, there's a right-hand filter up to Trafalgar Square, but the guy in front wouldn't budge, he just sat there with clear road ahead of him. I think he was anxious about guiding his expensive car through a narrowish gap. Nicola duly bipped him (she makes liberal use of the horn, to be fair, my wife), and instantly he was out of his door, snarling, swearing, beside himself with rage.

I'm not usually one for the laid-back approach, I don't go for that relax, chill out, don't worry, be happy attitude, I think it's a cop-out, but with men and motors, I do catch myself thinking: for God's sake, boys, calm down, someone's going to get hurt. And I count myself lucky that while most of the classic male nonsense (job, status, intelligence, income, physique) plays a big part in my good opinion of myself, driving does not, not a shred. Which is I suppose both cause and effect of choosing to ride a pushbike.

And finally, not sure where this fits in but it's funny, I've got another friend who, like me, prefers life in the left-hand seat. His wife does most of the driving, and when they get to a junction, unlike me (he's a military man, hyper-efficient) he says, 'Clear left,' if she can make the turn. Then one day for some reason he was driving, she was next to him, they got to a junction, she says, 'Clear left,' he pulls out . . . Whack, they're broadsided (fortunately at low speed) by an oncoming car.

'Why did you say, "Clear left"?' he asks.

'Well, you always do,' she replied.

1 November 2008

The children's half-term holidays fail to coincide, my wife takes Rachel up north for a few days, Sam and I are home alone, Saturday to Wednesday. It doesn't take long for things to deteriorate. An hour after they're out the door, we're over the market eating burgers.

'What do you want for tea?' I ask.

'Another burger,' he says.

So we buy some more burgers. And rent four films.

Back home, we discuss going to the lido and decide we can't be bothered. He plays Mario Kart on the Wii, I potter about in the garden. Later, we put some sounds on and string up the punchbag. He does a few rounds, I sit smoking and calling the shots. Then we get the axe out and chop some kindling, get the barbecue organized. Sam asks if, in his mother's absence, he can have a licence to swear. Within reason, I reply. Are you getting the picture?

Tufty John and Corinne call round. I think Corinne's just about forgiven me for a shocking miscalculation soon after she and John started seeing each other. They'd come down to visit us in Kent, and we were in the pool, and I went underwater, and then surfaced and – I don't know what possessed me, it was wrong on so many levels – asked Corinne about the birthmark on her thigh.

'It's a tattoo,' she said.

Anyway, Sam invites them to stay for tea, Corinne's a vegetarian so she goes off to buy mushrooms, tofu and whatnot, comes back and sorts it all out. She runs out of skewers, so I improvise some from wood splinters and feel pretty damn good about that. Corinne and Sam knock up a nice marinade while John and I mince about doing nothing much of anything.

The four of us then decamp to the pub, John and I telling self-serving war stories from jobs we've done together. We come back, fire up the barbie, stuff our faces, watch *Ocean's Eleven*. When the Elliott Gould character says, 'Yeah, and even if you do get outta the casino, you're still in the middle of the f****** desert,' Sam beams in appreciation, and I know that's the one bit of the whole film he'll remember.

Sunday morning, it's the full English at a local café. We're just discussing what to do about tea when Cousin George calls. Lourdes, his wife, she's Spanish, wants to come over to make a paella, they'll bring all the ingredients, is that OK? Duh, hello, like, yeah. Sam and I spend the afternoon pottering, boxing, playing Mario Kart and chopping wood, much the same as the previous day. George and Lourdes arrive. She says she doesn't need any help, indeed prefers to cook by herself. I say, Lourdes, crack on.

George has brought a bottle of Penfolds RWT Shiraz 2000. (He's in the wine trade.) We take it outside and get a fire going in the barbecue bucket. George's offerings are usually wasted on me, but even I can tell this is good stuff, and my idea of good is £5.99 instead of £4.99.

How much would this cost in the shops, George?

'About £50.'

Blimey.

'Can I have some?' asks Sam, methodically feeding wood into the flames, the fire-fever upon him.

George and Lourdes leave and I make a tactical error. Instead of having to wake up at 6.45 to take Sam to school, I hit on the brilliant idea of simply staying awake instead, watching films, drinking whisky and eating cold paella. *True Romance*, *Midnight Run*, emails, texts, iPod, I last until about 4.30 a.m., next thing I know, I'm propped up on three pillows, laptop and cats heavy on my legs, head pounding like a drill, Sam shaking my shoulder, wanting to know what a prostitute is and whether I think astronauts' helmets are bulletproof.

Heroically, I get through the day on two and a quarter hours' sleep, and go to collect Sam from his school bus stop. The sky is threatening, for which eventuality my wife has given me instructions about a waterproof, but I hadn't been listening, and on the walk home the heavens open and we get as wet as if we'd jumped in the canal.

'Can we get a pizza and watch *Ocean's Twelve*?' asks Sam, the rain streaming off the end of his nose.

Not on a school night, I say.

'Please?' he says.

Oh, OK, I say, conscious that I am running out of friends and relatives whose wives or girlfriends I can inveigle round to cook our tea.

Actually, there's Ben and Natalie, I could invite them, but then I remember a few months ago I'd bungled badly when introducing Natalie to another friend. (I've made something of a habit of getting it wrong with friends' girlfriends.) This is Natalie, I'd said, she goes out with Ben.

'And I'm also a person in my own right,' Natalie had added, not unreasonably.

Refreshing to encounter some old-school feminism among all the regressive girlie blather you hear these days, but for current purposes, the incident didn't suggest Natalie would react well to being asked over to rustle up some grub. Domino's it was then. And so on.

Normal family life has long since resumed service.

8 November 2008

My friend Joe came to stay. He's a working-class boy from Bradford, 6 feet 4 inches, fifteen stone, used to box for the police. Heavyweight, naturally. He spent some time as a sergeant in the Parachute Regiment, got some medals, knows all the moves, is still in fantastic shape. Basically, and I'm not making this up – if I were I'd make the claim more believable – I think Joe is the hardest man in Britain.

I don't know if you're familiar with Jack Reacher, hero of Lee Child's series of thrillers? Ex-military policeman, enormous, capable of the most explosively efficient violence, Reacher reckons there are only about ten people in the whole world he has to be worried about. Well, my friend Joe is one of them. And unlike Jack, Joe is not a fictional character.

Whenever Joe stays, I find excuses to go out walking in the park with him late at night in the hope that someone will try to mug us. Get £200 out of the cashpoint and wave it about, go up to local likely lads sitting there on the bench doing that horrible long drooly spit they do and poke them in the chest, that sort of thing. No joy so far.

We went out for dinner: me, Joe, my wife Nicola, our friend Karen. Argentinian place; naturally, we had steak and chips. Unimaginative, you may say, but that's pretty much all they serve, and besides, steak and chips is one of the finest achievements of human culture. When the bill came, Joe and Karen made the obligatory move towards their wallets, but I slapped my plastic down in expansive fashion – no, no, our treat – tapped my PIN in without a second glance. It *was* our treat too: the bill came to £1,598,039. And 18 pence.

Needless to say, my lines of credit are not that long and MasterCard was having none of it, which was lucky because we'd had a good time, but not that good, not one-and-a-half-million-quid good. Let this be a lesson to everyone: even after a bucketful of house red, check what it says on the machine. If it's £1,598,039 and 18 pence, or indeed anything approaching that, don't pay.

Back home, we went straight out into the back garden and got the gloves on. It's a ritual Joe and I have, one my wife is familiar with, but which came as something of a surprise to Karen.

'What are you two doing?' she asked.

'We're just going to have a bit of a fight,' we said.

'A fight?' said Karen.

'Won't take long,' I said.

Karen rolled her eyes. 'I'm eternally glad I'm not a man,' she sighed.

Of course, it's not a proper fight, not with me being me and Joe being the hardest man in Britain. It's more like a film fight when the normal-sized hero, Bond or Indy or whoever, tangles with the monster baddy and gets slapped all over the place for a while before winning with some cute piece of footwork and improvisation. Well, it's like that, only with the slapping around but without the winning-at-the-end bit.

Tell you what – and this is a good link, very smooth, smooth move, Dad, as my son might say – I wish I'd had my gloves on the next day on the towpath. Bit inconvenient, cycling in boxing gloves – they're only good for one thing, really – but I could have done with the protection when a fellow cyclist suffered a total brake failure and ploughed straight into me. It strikes me now that it's possible her brake cable had been tampered with, as used to happen in just about every episode of *Charlie's Angels*.

Farrah Fawcett was fine, whereas my right hand got mashed between my brake lever and her handlebars. I was stationary, having seen her coming, she had slowed to perhaps 8 mph by the time of the impact and yet it still hurt a great deal, fingers bleeding all over, middle knuckle turning purple in the course of the afternoon. Rather me than her, though. The price of being a man, eh? With any luck I'll get a scar.

That same stretch of canal, a few months ago, coming home late, I slow to go under a bridge, and as I approach I see some kid standing there in the shadows, blocking the way; your basic Hungry Troll/Billy Goat Gruff scenario. Aye up, I think, what's his game? If he tries any funny business, one of us is going in the water, and it isn't going to be me.

'You've got to say "please",' he slurs, as I come to a stop.

'No, I don't,' I reply, or words to that effect, edging past with my heart in my mouth.

He mumbles and moves aside.

Foolhardy, really, seeing as I'm in no condition to back it up at the moment. Sheer bulk counts for something, of course, but I'd be better off if I could recapture the (modicum of) fitness of a few years ago. Nomadic tribes – I think this is true – when they strike camp, they carry an ember from the fire with them. I'm not entirely sure how, I think they put it in a piece of old leather, or some such. The same fire thus lasts for years. Decades, even. This winter, I need to nurture my own spark of self-denial; fan that dying glow back into life before it goes out once and for all.

15 November 2008

Screwdrivers, pliers, hammers, socket sets, Rawlplugs, the drill, anything to do with the car, anything to do with electrics, any-thing to do with water, gas, paint, keys, locks . . . Most of the tools in the house are unequivocally the preserve of my wife. She knows where they are, what they're for, what they're not for and how to use them. These tools are like most of the houschold tasks (operating the TV remote, disciplining the children): notionally shared, but we both know who's in charge. It isn't me.

I do have my own, limited, low-skill areas of competence. In terms of kit, these encompass the lawnmower, although I have to ask for help if the setting needs adjusting, and the extendable ladder. And the broom. I also husband the bike pump, the bike oil and certain bike-related spanners, two to be exact, keeping them in my very own drawer. Specific items of stationery are also ring-fenced: my stapler, my highlighter, my special felt-tips for filling in my exercise 'n' alcohol stats in my diary, etc. These come under periodic attack from my daughter, who has inherited my office-equipment fetish. Eternal vigilance is required.

But then there's the axe. The axe for me is what diplomats engaged in treaty negotiations call a red line. It's out of bounds, beyond the pale, not up for discussion. I can surrender any amount of tool-related sovereignty and swallow my pride; my, ahem, chopper, though, is my last ditch, my Alamo, my '¡No pasarán!', my so far and no further. Were I to allow the axe to slip into collective usage, be stored in some unfamiliar nook of the house, be swung without my guidance or say-so, I might as well take the article in question to my own nadgers and have done with it.

That isn't going to happen. No one is going to take away my axe. Chopping wood with an axe is one of life's core pleasures. I say 'pleasure', but I hesitate to use the word; I wouldn't want to trivialize the awesome business of splitting timber, for warmth, for shelter, for peace of mind. It's an urge, an instinct, a need. A physical, emotional and aesthetic need. Brick houses, urbanization, industrialization, central heating, the Clean Air Acts of 1956 and 1968, we gained a lot, yet we lost something, too.

And we're starting to realize it. It's interesting, isn't it, how what used to be thought archaic is coming back into fashion? Once we aren't required to do these things any more, they're all the rage. What were necessities two generations ago are now luxuries. Knitting classes are big at my local fabric shop, for instance. Stitch and Bitch they're called, great name. Knit and Natter was good, but Stitch and Bitch is better. Growing vegetables, making stews, eating offal – what used to be done by the poor is now enjoyed by the rich.

Anyone with spare education, time and money doesn't want to be a playboy or a party girl, they want to be a gardener or cook. Aristocrats reinvent themselves as artisans. New media millionaires cash in and run off to their smallholding. At my less exalted level of leisure, skill and ambition, the same simple-life, off-the-grid impulse translates into spending twenty minutes a day engaged in the brute reduction of logs with a metal wedge. In another life, I'd have fancied being a lumberjack. Or an illegal logger.

It's a bit late for that now. By way of a surrogate, I kneel out the back, remembering you're supposed to let the weight and momentum of the axe do the work without really understanding what that means, and halve a log, and halve those halves, and, if I'm doing kindling, halve those halves, trying to stay calm, drifting off into a splinter-flying frenzy, hauling myself back under control, clean white wood multiplying in the basket by my side.

I scoop up the product of all this halving and transfer it from the basket to the big wood box, back and forth, thwocking the axe into the chopping block before I move away, not for safety so much as the sound makes me happy, makes me feel I might resemble Charles Bronson in *The Magnificent Seven*, or Henry Fonda sticking the flick knife into the table in *12 Angry Men*.

I'd rather not be putting the wood in a box. I'd rather it was on display. If I were ever to produce an installation, which I may well do, my installation would be a wall of chopped wood, stacked floor to ceiling, twelve feet high by twenty feet wide, with my axe whacked in about halfway up, the star of the show.

Knives are the villains of the piece right now, but axes, they've had a lousy press for decades. You never hear chilling tales of *sane* axemen on lonely hillsides, do you? Perhaps I should write one, try to reclaim the axe for civilized society. Meanwhile, jobs are axed, hundreds given the chop by corporate hatchet men. Pedants have an axe to grind. Bigots too. Stroppy women of a certain age are old battleaxes. It's a poor way to repay this fine catalyst of human evolution.

31 January 2009

Two days after the inauguration, redeployed to Washington, I walked up Pennsylvania Avenue pretending to be Barack Obama. I tried striding down the middle of the street holding Michelle's hand like he did, but Michelle wasn't available and a traffic cop blew his whistle at me. They don't hold with jaywalking in the US, especially when you're waving to an imaginary crowd.

It was freezing cold, minus six or thereabouts. I had my woolly gloves on but somehow they just didn't cut the same dash as the sexy, semi-fetishistic tight black leather pair Obama wore. Besides, gloves make my hands all hot and sweaty, and you have to take them off to write anything down or roll cigarettes, two of my major activities.

It's about a mile and a quarter from the White House to the steps of the Capitol where the president is sworn in. I walked it quickly and was a bit puffed by the end. That's another difference between the new leader of the free world and me. Although he's said to enjoy the odd crafty fag, he doesn't enjoy fifteen of them a day, and he's as fit as a fiddle, as opposed to two, quite possibly three, stone overweight.

I sat down on a bench to get my breath back and to try to think of any area of life in which I could claim to be superior to this man. I sat there a long time.

Obama looks good in a suit and I don't. He looks good in an overcoat and I don't. He looks good in swimming trunks and I don't. And he's got those supercool Ray-Bans and I've got some silver and black plastic things that cost seven quid at Decathlon. He's taller than me, and there's less grey at his temples, despite his being three years older. And he's got a deep, impressive, commander-in-chief-type voice. My voice goes squeaky under pressure. And while his accent is rich and rolling and mellifluous, mine is a generic northern monotone.

I tried to get up the steps to the Capitol to stand where Obama stood when he took the oath. But of course it was still railed off and the police wouldn't let me through. So I went back to my bench.

I suppose, between us, we have written two bestselling books.

The problem is, he wrote both of them. Although I did once sign a deal to write a book, in 1999, and although it is, incredibly, still advertised as being available on Amazon (for £7.54) under its working title of *Whatever Happened To . . .*, the snag is I got bored and never actually finished writing it.* So despite my making my living as a writer, and his making his living as Most Powerful Man on the Planet with writing as a mere sideline, he outscores me heavily here as elsewhere.

Obama's logistical backup is impressive. He's got hundreds of bodyguards, thousands of staff and close on three million uniforms at his command, if you include reservists. Plus he's got the limo, the chopper and the plane. And a charming country residence in the woods of Maryland. I've got a bicycle, a Honda CR-V my wife won't let me drive and a small share in an editorial assistant whom I'm frightened to ask to do any photocopying. And a chalet in Kent that looks like a large piece of Toblerone.

Before I started up Pennsylvania Avenue, I'd been shopping. Of course there were T-shirts and mugs and stickers, but there were also Obama dolls, Obama board games, Obama bottles of hot Obama sauce. As for Bob memorabilia? Not a trace. Not so much as a fridge magnet.

He's very up with technology, too, Obama. Won't let that BlackBerry out of his hand, does all that Twitter and MSN and Facebook and whatnot. Me, I've got a steam-powered Nokia and I use the internet to do quizzes and play games. I don't think he's sitting there in the Oval Office trying to remember the capital of Honduras and playing stick cricket, is he?

You can tell he's a good dad, too. Those girls, Malia and Sasha, they're clearly delightful, well behaved, well turned out. My kids are delightful too, but that's thanks to their mother not me. I do OK, but can be a bad influence. I saw a mug in a shop

* This selection of columns is not, however, to be sniffed at.

the other day. It said 'More F****** Tea Vicar' in big red and green and blue letters on the side. I knew it was wildly irresponsible, but I bought it all the same. I think Obama would have resisted the urge.

Still on the bench, shivering now, the wind snapping at the Stars and Stripes flying over the Hill, I dredged up two crumbs of comfort. One, judging by his performance at the various inauguration balls, Obama is a rather dorky dancer. My moves, if I say so myself, get funkier all the time. And in terms of oratory, he fluffed his oath and in any case, am I alone in thinking his rhetoric a trifle overrated? Mine, meanwhile (thanks to the ongoing public-speaking tour, of which more, much more, in the coming weeks), is coming on nicely. All, perhaps, is not yet entirely lost.

7 March 2009

So, we're in the desert, down near the Saudi border, and Bob of Arabia is wearing the *keffiyeh* (the chequered scarf popularized in the seventies by Yasser Arafat, surely the most overrated politician of the late twentieth century) that comes out once a year. Bob's pal Joe, expatriate here in Qatar, is at the wheel of his 4x4. In another car a hundred yards back, Mrs Joe drives while Mrs Bob finds herself in highly unusual occupancy of the passenger seat.

We've come down from Doha, the capital, past a million refineries, stopped where the road stops, let the requisite air out of the tyres, and now we're bombing along the floor of a hard-baked wadi between two banks of dunes a hundred feet high. I'm pretending I'm in the Long Range Desert Group behind Rommel's lines in 1942. In another twenty minutes we'll be at the coast, where we're going to camp for the night.

The windows are right down and the stereo is right up, 'Fat

Bottomed Girls' if I remember rightly. In the back, Joe's daughter Rose and my son Sam are singing along. We're having a right old Queen-fest, Queen-fest as in the band, not Queen-fest as in Joe and me pouting and saying, 'Oooo, I love your curtains.' All is well. Or *oil* is *well*, if you will. Hah hah and once more hah.

And then, bang, the car starts wobbling and making a funny noise, audible even above Freddie Mercury's histrionics.

'I think we've got a puncture,' says Joe.

'I think so too,' says Bob of Arabia.

We trundle to a halt. Di and Nicola pull up alongside. Joe and I scratch our heads and inspect the shredded rubber and start hunting around for the spare. I sigh. I've changed five, maybe six tyres in my life and not once has the process been straightforward.

Joe is as impractical as I am. As previously mentioned, Nicola and Joe met when they both had Saturday jobs in Habitat in Hull in the early eighties. The staff were required to assemble some of the furniture, and the chairs and tables that Joe put together were so rickety that, if Nicola couldn't fix them, they'd smuggle them into the Returns pile and hope no one found out.

So neither Joe nor I are looking forward to this business, eighty degrees, wives and children looking on waiting for a giggle. And then, on the horizon, shimmering in the heat, growing ever larger, we spot a figure approaching, like Omar Sharif in *Lawrence of Arabia*, except on some vehicle rather than a camel. Or was it a horse?

The figure comes nearer, resolves itself into two figures, two young men in fact, Nepalese as it turns out, two-up on the same quad bike, the latter-day ship of the desert. They have a shovel, they have a wheel brace, they have a flat stone to rest the jack on so it doesn't sink into the sand. They indicate they want to fix the tyre. Joe looks at me and shrugs.

'Lads,' he says, 'crack on.'

Fifteen minutes later, we're back on our way, 'Crazy Little Thing Called Love'. Fifteen minutes after that we've taken a wrong turn, easily done, round and round in circles, lie down to die, picked clean by vultures, never find the body, etc., etc. We're on a beach, inching through perilously soft, deep sand, Di and Nicola following. To our left, the Persian Gulf. To our right, a small encampment.

Tourism is in its infancy in Qatar: where in twenty years a hotel may rise ten storeys high, now stands a modest circle of tents you can hire for some R&R. And watching us from deck-chairs in front of those tents, a group of young men. Perfect teeth, brutal buzz cuts, massive biceps, aviator shades. Unmistakably American. Unmistakably American servicemen, in fact.

We exchange waves. A minute later, checking the mirror, we see our wives' car stopped, engine screaming, sand spraying, opposite the young men. Joe turns the wheel to head back. But now our car doesn't move. More power. Nothing doing. I get out and squint down the beach. The young men have moved as one to our wives' car and already liberated it from the sand drift.

'Joe,' I say, 'we've got about a minute before they get here.'

Grabbing a child's multicoloured plastic spade from the boot, I scoop and scoop and scoop and Joe revs and revs and revs and we get absolutely nowhere.

I peep over the bonnet and see the platoon jogging towards us in perfect formation and know all pride is lost. And then they're upon us, the boss man instructing Joe about the correct way to drive his car, the others ushering me aside so they can push.

'Leave it to us sir, turn that way sir, no sir, the other way sir, that's no problem sir, you have a nice day sir.'

My mobile rings. Sandy, pink, sweaty, fat, absurd scarf swathed around my head, Freddie Mercury wailing 'I Want To Break Free', I answer it.

'We were thinking,' says my wife, 'that we'd leave you two here and take them with us. What do you reckon?'

23 May 2009

A family of blackbirds has set up a training zone over our garage roof. Bad idea! The cats, agile, ruthless, cold-eyed killers in the absolute prime of life, lie in wait. It's carnage. They're slaughtering fledglings at a rate of two a day. Feathers, gore, baby-bird body parts strewn all over. Messy business.

I'll tell you what chills my blood though, and that's the way the cats don't even look particularly pleased with themselves. Dogs, when they've done something enjoyable, they can't hide their emotions, can they? Cats? They're just, 'Yeah? Gotta problem? I'm a cat, it's what I do.'

They've been more adventurous lately, Tiger and Lucky. Well, not so much Tiger, he still prefers to hang around the house on the off chance of food. Tiger's distinguishing feature is still his extreme stripyness. When his nadgers had to come off, and Brian the vet shaved a patch of fur to do the op, Tiger's skin, his actual skin, was as stripy as his coat. Who knew?

Lucky, she's a girl, she's the explorer, always in scrapes. I find, contrary to popular belief, women are less conservative than men, keener to see the world, less bothered with the comforts of hearth and home. Our cats are no exception.

I did the lawn last Sunday, first mow of the year, came within six inches of giving Lucky's tail a brutal crop along with the grass. Bad moment. Wouldn't have wanted to explain that one to my daughter. Or my wife. My son, he'd have seen the funny side.

I almost took her tail off a couple of times in the winter too, chopping wood. Different seasons, similar hazard. I suppose having your tail mown off is marginally preferable to having it lopped off with an axe.

We keep them both in at night though. I'm not entirely sure why. There is a reason but I can't remember. So the routine is, no food through the evening, that way at bedtime they come trotting in when you call. Never fails.

Except when it does. Tiger, he's never far away, here I am, pad pad pad, any scoff on the go? Lucky, though, she's over next-door's garden, or the one beyond, it can take an age, standing out the back making miaow noises, shouting 'Lucky! Lucky!' feeling like a dork.

Twice recently Lucky hasn't come at all. I go gruff and say forget it, she's a cat, she'll be fine. My wife says imagine if she weren't fine, Rachel (my daughter is Lucky's biggest fan) would never forgive us. This then allows me to do what I want to do anyway, which is locate the cat, but in the acceptable guise of put-upon paterfamilias rather than namby-pamby fussmonger. Cupboards are opened, curtains prodded, beds quartered.

Once when she didn't return we found Lucky shut in a wardrobe. The other time though, by 1 a.m. we had established she was definitely not in the house, so where could she be? Rachel woke up, adding an extra edge of hysteria to the proceedings.

Come on, Tige, I say, where's your pal? Skippy the Bush Kangaroo? Clarence the cross-eyed lion in *Daktari*? Lassie? Tiger doesn't do what they did. No eye-rolling or ear-curling or whisker-twitching or tail-wagging to indicate Lucky is stuck in the abandoned silver mine with the water level rising but we can take the old logging trail through the woods, it's a short cut. Rather, with attention elsewhere, he focuses on stealing Lucky's share of the food.

My wife, in the manner of Velma in *Scooby-Doo*, says, 'Quiet, everybody!'

We all shut up and listen hard and sure enough, a faint mewing drifts in on the night air.

'It's coming from the noodle factory!' wails Rachel. 'She must be stuck on the roof!'

Indeed she is. Shine the torch, get that proverbial glitter in return. Spooky, the way their eyes shine like that. And yet useful. She's jumped across the gap between our neighbour's end wall and the Hong Kong Noodle factory, purveyors of fine noodlized products to the trade. A seven-foot gap over a thirty-foot drop, good effort, but now she doesn't fancy the return leg.

I turf my son out of bed, open his bedroom window, climb on to our roof, then on to next-door's (luckily we're on good terms), creep along to the stranded cat, call for a stepladder. Lucky, pacing back and forth, nervous as the kitten she recently was, doesn't go for that, doesn't like the spaces between the steps.

So I ask for something flat and solid to lay across the ladder. My wife supplies a large print of some flowers, Ikea's finest. Using that, I improvise a rather ingenious sliding bridge, and slowly, under close instruction from my daughter at the bed-room window, coax the cat on to the painting, pull it across the void. Job done.

Grumbling all the while, harrumphing and galumphing, and of course secretly loving it, I get to bed about 2 a.m. It's the sort of situation dads were invented for.

5 September 2009

I'm hoping, even with September under way, that I can wring one more column out of the holiday in Pembrokeshire. Here goes.

For many years now, my wife has wanted to have a surfing lesson during our annual stay in west Wales. One morning this trip, she made good on the threat, taking our daughter along too. My son and I hired a sea kayak instead, knowing, if we went surfing, we'd be treated as light comic relief. Our differing experiences perfectly illustrated one of the major fault lines in my family.

For starters, Sam and I talked at some length about our impending expedition. We'd take the craft miles up the shore, explore caves and inlets inaccessible by land, see seals and dolphins, return with a few lessons in kayak handling for the Inuit.

Our only concern was whether a four-hour rental would give us enough time to cover the huge extent of coastline we planned to survey. It was possible we might need all day.

Nicola and Rachel said nothing about their forthcoming surfing lesson.

The surfing and kayaking were in opposite directions from the hotel. Obviously, there was no question of my having use of the car, so Sam and I were planning to walk until our pals Jeff and Jane kindly offered us a lift. After some sweets, the customary wrestle with the wetsuit and a lot of help from Jeff, we succeeded in lugging the kayak down to the water and out through the surf.

'Which way shall we go?' I asked Sam. 'North to those caves, or south to those caves?'

'Which is nearer?' he asked.

'Those ones.'

'Let's go there, then.'

We paddled for three or four minutes.

'This is tiring,' said Sam.

'Yeah, I know,' I said. 'Let's have a breather.'

We both lay back, panting, thirty yards or so offshore.

'What would you do if a great white shark popped up over there?'

'Tell it to bog off,' I said, yelling, 'Oi! Shark! Bog off!' to make him laugh, which he dutifully did.

'What would you really do?'

'Hit it with a paddle.'

'On the nose? Their noses are the most sensitive area.'

'Fair play, on the nose it is.'

Three seconds of silence.

'What's the most dangerous animal in the sea?'

'This sea? Jellyfish probably.'

'What would you do if a jellyfish appeared?'

'Ignore it. If you're in a boat, a jellyfish is just a floating plastic bag with gunk attached.'

'What about a barracuda?'

'You don't get barracudas in the Irish Sea.'

'You don't get great whites, but you answered that one.'

And so on, facts, fantasy, fatuity in equal measure. We got another fifty yards towards our intended destination, but it hadn't got appreciably nearer, and we were running against the wind and the tide.

'Let's go and have a rest on the beach,' I said.

The run-in to the beach was, of course, a great deal more exciting than battling grimly through the open swell. Having cruised in once and caught a decent wave, we wanted to do it again. Soon, we had abandoned the all-day-up-the-coast plan in favour of the half-an-hour-mucking-about plan.

So, like Rachel and Nicola six or seven miles away, we ended up surfing too, only this was sitting down in a big unwieldy multicoloured plastic shower tray surfing, with paddles and life jackets. And shouting out silly words that actual surfers may or may not use.

'Woh, dude! Serious tube!'

'Yo, er, radical wipeout!'

'Yes, er, extreme barrel!'

'Let's boost some major air,' etc.

We kept up this gibberish for quite a while, amusing ourselves greatly. By the time we drifted back out into the bay the rule was I had to call him Rip Curl and he had to call me Pipe Line. Also, I'd taught him the theme music to *Hawaii Five-0* and explained the innovative use of a wobbly camera in the opening credits.

We spent another twenty minutes discussing how we were definitely going to buy a kayak once we were back in London. A two-man kayak, light enough to fill full of food and yet still carry down to Regent's Canal and lift around all the locks.

Our kayak is going to be painted black, we decided, and we'd take it on night-time missions up the River Lea, developing huge shoulder muscles while gliding soundlessly in among the enemy fleet, attaching limpet mines, sending thousands of tonnes of Nazi shipping to the bottom, and so on and so forth.

Then the sun went in and Sam started to get cold.

'Better carve this plank inside, Pipe Line,' he said.

We surfed in a final time, Jeff helped us get the thing back to the rental place, Sam had some more sweets from Londis, we sat with Jeff and Jane on the front and steadily began mythologizing what had turned out to be a shade over an hour in the kayak.

Back at the hotel, Nicola and Rachel said they'd had a four-hour lesson, during which they both listened carefully, concentrated hard and consequently learnt the basics of surfing.

14 November 2009

My wife went away with our daughter for a few days, leaving me and Sam to hold the fort. We had takeaways three nights in a row. Tuesday he had sumo sushi, Wednesday he had crispy duck and pancakes, yum yum, Thursday he kept it real with cheeseburger and chips. I had chicken Caesar salad every night. Got to watch that figure.

We ate in front of the telly, laughing at the wrestling; great big grimacing men with enormous boobs bursting out of their leotards. On the Wednesday, Sam spilt some soy sauce on the sofa. Panic, kitchen roll, dishcloth, 'Do you think she'll notice?'

Each night after we'd eaten we'd mute the wrestling while I'd test him in advance of his exams. Bit of French vocab, bit of transatlantic slave trade, bit of the main factors governing the choice of a site for an agricultural settlement.

The maths I leave to my wife. Sam is only in his second year at secondary school, yet already I'm nudging up against the limits of my ability to decode the x, the y and the brackets.

Revision done, we'd then put a film on: *The Rock* with Sean Connery and Nicolas Cage on the Tuesday; *The Boat That Rocked* with Bill Nighy, Rhys Ifans et al. on the Wednesday; *Get Shorty* with John Travolta and Gene Hackman on the Thursday. Once the film was done, Sam would ask if there was time for a wrestle, an actual wrestle, before bed. I'd say no. He'd say please. I'd say OK.

In the domestic division of labour, along with geography homework, cleaning football boots and telling plausible lies to authority when required, wrestling falls within my area of responsibility.

We spread an old rug on the deck at the back and got going. The form is that I shuffle around on my knees acting all groggy while Sam pretends to hit me and shouts, 'Signature move,' 'Clothes line' and 'Finisher.' It's good fun. More so for him than for me.

Recently we've developed two moves of our own. In the first, he sits on my nose until I submit. We call that one Buttface. If my daughter watches us wrestle, which she sometimes does, a mixture of amusement, disgust and fascination on her face, Buttface is when she'll scream, 'Gross!' and run inside.

Our second move is called Tic Tac. Sam and I are rather proud of Tic Tac. In Tic Tac, I put several of the pellet-shaped mints in my mouth. Then we go through our usual preamble, me staggering, Sam strutting around, taunting, trash-talking, whipping up the imaginary crowd of howling rednecks over by the wisteria, etc., etc.

After several minutes of this, the drama climaxes with Sam shoving me face first into a garden chair. My job is then to enact a final collapse while simultaneously spitting out the Tic Tacs. They look a bit like teeth.

I lay there on the rug in the cold, 10 p.m., my mouth full of Tic Tac stickiness, several of the half-dissolved spat-out sweets pressing into my cheek, and I told Sam it was time for bed. I knew I should go upstairs pretty soon myself. And yet, as on the previous two nights, I stayed up till gone two. For no reason other than I could. Idiotic.

The alarm rang at 6.55 a.m. Sam has to be at his school bus stop by 7.50, and the bus stop is 1.62 miles from our house – I measured it on my bike. All week I'd been walking him there, walking home, walking to work, walking home from work, walking back to the bus stop to pick him up at 4.45 p.m., walking home again. Do it once, no bother. Do it four days in a row on five hours' sleep, it wears you down.

Usually, Sam's mother takes him in the car. And indeed, the car had been sitting out front all week, Nicola and Rachel had gone north on the train. There was nothing actually stopping me driving Sam to and from his bus each day just as Nicola does. Nothing, that is, except habit and a fear of crashing (I tend to crash cars quite frequently). Habit and fear are a powerful combination.

So, however, is exhaustion and a throbbing pain where a

six-stone twelve-year-old would-be grapple star has been jumping up and down for days on end.

So this Friday morning, I said, 'Hey, Sam, let's drive.'

I imagine if I'd offered him a double Scotch his expression wouldn't have been much different: primeval desire to accept plus certainty that no good would come of it plus curiosity plus anxiety over what would happen if his mother found out.

'OK,' he said slowly, 'do you think it'll be all right?'

We made it without incident. On the way we played Springsteen.

'What does Bruce mean,' asked Sam, 'when he says, "This gun's for hire"?'

'He means he needs a woman,' I said. 'Whenever men try to live without women, it's fun for a while, but it's best not to try it for too long.'

12 December 2009

Time to get Christmas out of its box. Well, three boxes, stuff accumulates over the years, stacked on a shelf in the garage. Tinsel, baubles, wreath for the front door, Father Christmas on a motorbike who sings 'Santa Claus Is Coming To Town' when you press his foot, usual drill. Plus not one, not two, but three miniature twiggy trees, cos they're really classy, aren't they, miniature twiggy trees?

We'll get the real tree tomorrow, Sunday. Go down to the flower market on Columbia Road, battle through the tourists, hand over thirty quid, worth it just to watch the tree go through the special netting machine, never fails to impress. Carry the captured tree to the car. Not enough room for me and Sam, we have to walk back. Rachel'll make a face at her brother as she drives off with her mum.

At home, I'll do the donkey work of manoeuvring the thing into position, holding it upright while it's secured, then be dismissed while more skilled hands do the decoration.

To be honest, I'm not that fussed. After the netting machine, my favourite part of the tree business is sawing the thing into bits on 5 January.

I start giving Christmas serious consideration around about now. If my daughter had her way, it would have taken over the house in early October. Every Sunday morning, she sets up her assembly line on the kitchen table, tongue clamped between her teeth in concentration, churning out sparkly pine cones, silver stars, painted cardboard cottages with tufts of cotton wool glued to the roof.

There's glitter all over the floor, room, family. I went to interview Paul McCartney a couple of weeks ago. When I got home, I realized I had gold spots stuck all over my face. Macca didn't say anything, bless him. Mind you, with hair that colour, he's not in a position to criticize.

Going back to the tree, sometimes I get called in to help with the fairy lights. Not the actual electrics, just accessing the higher branches. This year I won't even get to do that.

I've got this Anglepoise lamp on my desk, chrome, retro, ultra-cool, IMHO. The last time the bulb went, I rooted around under the stairs, found a spare 100-watt screw-in. It seemed OK. Didn't blow up. I was quite pleased with myself, a minor domestic task accomplished, like when you put the bins out.

A few days pass. My son's in my room, we're mucking about on the Mac. I keep a pair of headphones draped artfully on the arm of the Anglepoise, they've slipped down near the shade, my son points out, and oh look, they've started smoking. Smoking headphones, that's odd, I think. I do not connect the soon-to-be-on-fire headphones with the new bulb.

Then I notice that when I go to turn off the Anglepoise before bed each night, the switch is so hot that my thumb is getting singed. Again, I fail to connect the searing switch with the new bulb. Instead, I start wrapping my hankie around my fingers to turn the light off.

Ninety-nine per cent of the time I know I'm not thick. The other 1 per cent I think I might be.

One night recently, I'm sitting minding my own business when the bulb in the Anglepoise drops on to the desk and smashes, glass all over. I think: that's not supposed to happen, is it? I call in my wife, she calls in her cousin, Steve, who lives with us. With some pliers and a screwdriver we chip and yank a quantity of fused metal and melted plastic from the fitting.

There's a sticker on the shade. 'Maximum 25W,' it says.

'I'd never noticed that before,' I say.

Close one. My wife and daughter roll their eyes.

Cousin Steve, I notice, shoots me a funny look, as if to say: 'I knew he was useless, but is he really that useless?'

My son? He just looks delighted at the possibility of a fire.

Yeah, quite the joker, young Sam, shaping up well. When I'm in the loo, or better still, the shower, he finds it amusing to lurk about on the landing next to the light switch. He'll wait a while, biding his time, then he'll plunge me into darkness, cackle and run off. And he doesn't just think it's funny once, he thinks it's funny ten, twenty, thirty times, each one as good as the first time. And the thing is, I agree.

Not sure what any of this has got to do with Christmas, except the Anglepoise was a Christmas present, and also, obviously, at this time of year, the sun gone by three in the afternoon, the turning-the-light-off-when-Dad's-in-the-loo routine is particularly effective.

Also, the festive season is big on lights, isn't it? Lights on trees, lights on houses, lights along the high street, lights in the sky, leading the way east to little baby Jesus. And it's big on other shiny stuff, too. And family. And stupidity. So really, it all fits pretty well.

2 January 2010

Happy New Year, and the big news is I have acquired a personal trainer. Fearsomely fit, ruthless, merciless, pitiless, awesomely competitive and entirely self-appointed, she's called Rachel Crampton. Yes, in 2010, my ten-year-old daughter has taken it upon herself to get her daddy in shape. Like other personal trainers, her reign of terror involves exercise. Unlike other personal trainers, however, Rachel also sees it as part of her brief to shout at me whenever I approach the fridge.

You know how motivating other people used to be all about the stick rather than the carrot? And then gradually a consensus emerged that most of us respond better to encouragement, praise and reward than we do to sergeant-major-style ranting and raving? Well, my daughter isn't part of that consensus. Defiantly old school, she's like a PE teacher from about 1955.

Rachel gave herself the job following a distressing incident in Cheshire shortly before Christmas. By way of a long, looping detour on our return from Hull to London, the family had called in on our friends Karen and Peter, who live near Nantwich. Unfortunately, it was short notice and they had plans to go out for the evening. So off they went, leaving us at their house with their daughter, Loulou, eleven.

My friend, colleague and travelling companion John Angerson, trusty photographer, was also along for the ride. Karen and Peter didn't have enough room in their house for John, but they do have a shed, so he bunked down in there. The rest of us would go and visit him from time to time in order to make fun of him.

This winter, feeling the cold now he's turned forty, John's taken to wearing a body warmer (he calls it a gilet) and a flat woolly cap. I've managed to persuade the children that this combination makes him look like a coach driver, and I've also taught them to run up to him and shout things like, 'Twenny-minute comfort break, ladies! Don't mek me come and find yer!' in a northern accent. They don't know what they're saying or why they're saying it, but it keeps me amused.

Recently, John was able to get his own back. One night, I made the mistake of wearing a zip-up retro Adidas top to the pub.

'Bloody hell,' said John. 'It's Cloughie, come back to life.' He then taught the children to run up to me and shout things like, 'Get in that box, young man!', also in a northern accent, also with no idea what they were saying or why, only that it made Tufty John (they call him Tufty John) cackle with laughter. Fun and games, these long winter nights.

Anyway, there we all were in Cheshire. As well as a shed, Karen and Peter have a hot tub. Obviously, the tub is one of the many attractions of a stay up there in the leafy North West. All six of us, three adults, three kids, swiftly piled in. John took some bullying out of his shed, and indeed his flat cap and body warmer, but we wore him down. Padding across the patio, shivering in his pants, in he tubbed.

I, meanwhile, was having trouble staying still. Every time I got comfortable on the moulded plastic bench, I'd float off to a different part of the tub. Like a balloon. A fifteen-stone balloon. Wearing pants.

'Having trouble with your buoyancy?' asked my wife.

Karen and Peter's hot tub boasts a rather splendid fountain feature near the lip. Or so I was told; this was my debut in the tub, and I couldn't see any sign of a fountain.

'Mummy, why is the fountain not working?' asked Rachel, who had had the pleasure of tubbing here several times before.

My wife has this uncanny ability first to assess any given

problem and then, in an instant, conclude that I am to blame. 'It's the water level,' she said. 'It's higher than usual because Daddy's here. It's covering the outlet. The fountain is working, but it's underwater.'

My children are not about to miss an open goal when their mother lays one on like that.

'Oi, Fatty,' said my son. 'You're spoiling the fountain.'

'Yeah, you've got to get out, then we can have the fountain,' said my daughter.

'Yeah, Robert, get out,' said Loulou, joining the attack.

'Come on, Doughnut,' said John, his steam- and smile-wreathed face a picture of happiness. 'You're ruining it for the kids.'

'Who's Doughnut?' asked Sam.

I explained that, when I was at primary school in the early seventies, the other kids called me Doughnut, after the obese character in *Here Come the Double Deckers!*, a popular children's programme of the day. I had once confided this to John, and fair play to him for storing it up and using it to such deadly effect many years later. Naturally, the children now call me Doughnut at any opportunity.

Back in Cheshire, they forced me to stand up in the freezing cold, and Rachel decided it was time for her to take charge of my lifestyle. I'm quite fed up of it, actually.

9 January 2010

The current locus of the ongoing power struggle in my twenty-year relationship with my wife, thirty-three years if you count the thirteen years we knew each other before we started going out together, is the stove. Not the cooking stove, she won control over that years ago, and I didn't put up much of a fight, but the heating stove, the multi-fuel, the big metal thing in the living room.

If you're thinking thirty-three years sounds a long time for a couple in their mid-forties to have known each other, my wife and I met at school when we were eleven. My first memory of her is playing on the same side at table football in the youth club one Friday night in 1975. Even though she had the goalie and the defenders and I had the midfield and the attack, and even though I'd been to France and played *le baby-foot* and she hadn't, eleven-year-old Nicola tried to tell me what to do. It's been pretty much the same story ever since.

Back to the stove. I feel as if I've fought a desperate rearguard action all the way through the living room, surrendering ground on the sofa covering, the precise position of the table, the finish on the radiators when they went off to be dipped. And now I've got my back against the wall next to the stove and I've said OK, here is where I make my stand, this is my Alamo, my Rorke's Drift, my Thermopylae. So far, woman, but no further!

Because, come on, setting fire to stuff, that's man's work, isn't it? Surely? Still? Even in 2010? The chopping, the stacking, the bringing in from outside, the scrunching, the setting, the lighting, the prodding, the tending, the venting? That's our thing, isn't it? All that fire stuff? You can let me have this one, can't you? Just this one? Please?

Er, no, actually.

Did you know that the difference between the length of your ring finger and the length of your index finger is a reliable indicator of how much testosterone you were exposed to in the womb? Generally, in men, the ring finger is longer than the index. In women, the two fingers are usually of equal length.

My wife and I are exceptions. While my ring finger is marginally shorter than my index finger, Nicola's is a full centimetre longer. So, basically, she's a master of the universe and I am, in fact, a girl.

The surprise isn't that she likes cars and engineering and,

indeed, fires. Or that I love to gossip and drink Baileys. The surprise is we're both heterosexual.

The war over who was in charge of the stove started the day it was installed. Skirmishes erupted over the use of fire lighters (she's pro, I am viscerally opposed) and instant-lighting fire logs (again she's pro, I take a more traditionalist stance), and what else we should burn (anything that'll catch fire, I say, she is more cautious). After those initial encounters, we moved into a trench-warfare stage, occasional offensives punctuated by periods of uneasy truce.

Gradually, painfully, zones of supremacy have been established. Nicola buys the fuel. Bob gets it out of the car boot, mucks about with it in the garden, brings what is required indoors. Nicola arranges it around the stove. As for the actual burning, the rule is whoever lays and lights takes the lead role in fire maintenance through the evening. It works OK.

Except when it doesn't. Because even when she's lit the fire, I can't stop myself a-stokin' and a-pokin', a-fannin' and a-fiddlin'. And even when I've lit the fire, she can't stop herself telling me to keep it small, get myself under control, let it die down a bit, leave the damn thing alone.

Recently we took Nicola's parents out to dinner at Tate Modern. Prior to going out, Nicola and I had been arguing about the fire. The usual: I'd overdone it, what a waste, we're going out anyway, you're a pyromaniac nutter, etc., etc. Yeah yeah yeah, heard it all before.

Unbeknown to me, however, Nicola had allowed her desire to claim a victory in the stove war to overrule her intelligence, and done a very silly thing. Just before we'd gone out, she had removed one of the logs I'd put in the stove, *a log that was already alight*, and returned it to the wood basket. That's daft, right?

When we got to the Tate, Nicola said she had something to

tell me. It cost her dear, but she'd decided admitting a mistake was less bad than the house burning down. As happy as I have been in ages, I caught a cab (to a mercifully still intact) home, replaced the charred log on the fire and got the same cab back to the Tate for dinner.

'What was that all about?' asked the mystified cabbie.

I explained.

'Well, sorry it's cost you forty quid,' he commiserated.

'Are you kidding?' I said. 'Forty quid to be totally, unarguably, unanswerably right in a dispute with your wife? Have you any idea how rare that is? Cheap at twice the price.'

13 March 2010

I haven't written about Steve, my wife's cousin's son and our lodger, for a while. Any mention of Cousin Steve, as you can imagine, always goes down well among the extended family up north. Nicola's Uncle Dave (Steve's granddad) and his mates at the allotments lap it up. They've got the previous namechecks pinned on the wall of their hut, next to something about big aubergines. It's important to keep Uncle Dave sweet; he gives us free veg.

Steve is twenty-two and a postgraduate maths student. He's been in the spare room for more than a year, and I'm pleased to report that our humble home is better for having him in it. When he moves out, as he says he will when he gets a job this autumn, it'll be a blow. So I'm already formulating strategies to get him to stay.

As I am, incidentally, with the children. Their departures are years in the future, but it does no harm to plan ahead. I've never understood why parents moan that their kids haven't left home yet, or that they left and then came back. I'd be perfectly happy for Sam and Rachel to stay for ever, like Bobby and JR at

Southfork. That'd make me Jock, so we could hang a hideous great big portrait of me over the mantelpiece. Wearing a Stetson. Also, I could spy on Victoria Principal in the shower.

Sam once said he'd like to go to college in America when he was older.

'Sorry son, you're mistaken about that,' I said, squashing the idea as ruthlessly as when he'd said he'd buy a motorbike when he turned seventeen and I'd told him if he did I'd lie down in the road naked in front of it. Wacky emigration plans for tertiary education? I don't think so.

Fast-forward six years: 'Have you seen my passport, Dad?'

'Oh that? I burnt it.'

Going back to Steve, there are lots of reasons to want to keep him around. He's a good laff, a wingman, a buddy, someone to laugh at Steven Seagal and Bruce Willis movies with. We used to go out drinking; now we do weights and discuss what new gym equipment we're going to buy at the weekend. Steve watches the rugby with me too, doesn't seem to mind my blathering on about quick ball. And he gets up early and works hard and is thus a good role model to this landlord twice his age.

Plus, the children think Steve's great, so he soaks up a lot of their attention, leaving me free to loll around talking endlessly about secondary-school transfer with my wife. And naturally the children's maths has improved out of sight since Steve arrived. Not just theirs, mine too: square root of 625? Too easy, ask me another.

A further benefit is that a fifth person in the house forces the other four to be nicer to each other. You can't very well take the gloves off in a family punch-up if it'd embarrass nice young Cousin Steve sat doing his really hard sums by the fire, can you? Just when a domestic meltdown is threatening, a major ten-year-old – or indeed forty-five-year-old – tantrum about to blow, you remember you've got to mind your manners, not allow the full horrors of the nuclear family out into the open.

So Steve's presence is civilizing, and useful, and enjoyable. But naturally the main advantage of having him around is that he tips the gender balance in our favour. Pre-Steve, it was two against two, my wife and her young henchwoman versus me and the boy. And Sam and I are no match for those two – or indeed either one of them individually – when they're in full cry. We needed reinforcements.

Obviously in any set-piece confrontation Nicola and Rachel are still going to rip us to bits, Steve or no Steve. For example, I have a habit of kicking, rather than pushing, the fridge door shut. The two of them would object to that no matter how many of us chaps there were. But if the three of us lie low, maybe drift out to my room for a sly game of darts and a listen to Bon Jovi (Sam is going through a stadium-rock phase), at least there's safety in numbers when they track us down.

And just on a day-to-day level – the potential audience for bowel-related humour, for instance – three is a much bigger number than two.

The lad's still only twenty-two, though, so he's got a lot to learn. When my wife was away with the children recently, just Steve and me in the house, we had a serious leak (the rain was incessant) into the kitchen. This leak was not unrelated to my having failed, despite frequent requests from my wife, to unblock the gutter adjacent to where the water coursed in.

Still, no harm done, we cleared up the flood, Nicola need never have known. Except – touching innocence – Steve conscientiously reported the matter to her when she got back, not understanding swiftly enough why I was standing behind her making throat-cutting gestures and shaking my head vigorously. He apologized to me later. I told him that clearly his training was not yet nearly complete.

10 April 2010

We had not long arrived in the US when a proud smile lit up my daughter's face.

'This is the third time I've been to America,' she announced.

'That's right,' I said, 'and it's my twenty-first time.'

What sort of man is it that keeps count? And what sort of man is it that uses that count to best his eleven-year-old daughter?

Er, that'd be me.

'I've been to New York,' Rachel went on, not realizing what manner of competition she was getting herself into, 'and San Francisco and Los Angeles, and now we've been back to New York and we're going down to Florida. Will there be sharks in Florida?'

'Never mind about the sharks,' I said. 'Surely you want to talk about all the times I've been? To America.'

'I suppose so.'

'Well, make yourself comfortable.'

The first time I came to America, I explained, was in 1981, when I was seventeen. We flew to Seattle and ended up, via the Trans-Canadian Railway, in Boston, Connecticut and New York. And you're only eleven and already you've been three times and I'm struggling, not entirely successfully, to keep the envy out of my voice. Especially when, after that first trip, I didn't visit America again until I was twenty-seven and came with Mummy to New York for the weekend.

'For the weekend?' she said, shocked at the thought her decrepit parents could ever have been so indulgent, so cool, so young, as to consider flying seven hours to spend the weekend somewhere.

'Yeah,' I replied smugly. 'The weekend. Pretty radical, eh? Pretty, what is it you say, sick?'

'We don't say sick any more.'

'Oh, is sick lame?'

'We don't say lame any more either. It'd be really lame to say lame, if saying lame wasn't already lame, which it is which is why we don't say it.'

Whatever, I said. After that second visit, things started to hot up. Came to Washington in '93, San Francisco and Vegas in '94, LA to interview Rod, also in '94.

'Who's Rod?'

'Rod Stewart.'

'Who's Rod Stewart?'

'He's a singer. Quite famous.'

'Never heard of him.'

'Then it was John Prescott in New York.'

'Who's John Prescott?'

'Fat bloke. Laughing stock. Politician.'

'Never heard of him.'

'Then it was Andy McNab at the FBI academy in Virginia in '97.'

'Who's Andy McNab?'

'Soldier. Wrote a book about the Gulf War.'

'Never heard of him.'

At this point I have to admit I had crossed a line from not only trying to impress my daughter with the frequency of my trips across the Atlantic (a dismal enough tactic), but I was also – and this I think you'll agree is truly pathetic – trying to glorify myself with the nature of those visits, the equivalent of a business executive boasting that Daddy flew all the way to America for A Really Important Sales Conference. In my case, these work trips happened to involve interviewing famous people. But work trips is all they were. Plane, hotel, meeting, plane, report.

And besides, these people may have been, still may be, famous

. . . but not to Rachel. It wasn't as if I'd been hanging out with Hannah Montana or that smug Troy kid from *High School Musical*. Or someone in *Friends*. Prince, Jamie Oliver, R.E.M., Lennox Lewis, Michael Moore, P.J. O'Rourke . . . One popular cultural big hitter after another slipped by, each sufficiently celebrated for a newspaper to fly a reporter across an ocean to meet, each passing unrecognized by this particular eleven-year-old.

Fair enough, she did know who Bruce Springsteen was, but only because she's suffered the Boss on countless car journeys since she was a baby, and regards him as she would, say, the Queen, or perhaps God: someone whom she is perhaps beginning to hold in lower esteem than she knows she ought, someone also who is just there, part of the furniture.

As we moved into the modern era – Obama's inauguration, Usain Bolt, trips Rachel can remember me making – the value, such as it was, of this shameless bragging ebbed away.

'Do you know how many states you've been to?' I asked, tacking back towards brute geographical number crunching.

'California, New York . . . any others?'

'No, that's it. Two, I'm afraid. I've been to twelve.'

'That's not many,' she said. 'There are fifty states.'

'Yes, there are fifty states,' I agreed, 'and you're right, it's not as many as it should be. But I'm planning to bump up the total a lot in the next couple of weeks. West Virginia, the Carolinas, Tennessee, slip into northern Mississippi, Georgia, Florida. Should bag at least seven, maybe more if I can do something tricksy around Kentucky.'

'Mummy said you were up to something like that,' Rachel said guilelessly.

'Did she? What did she say?'

'She said that the three of us wanted to drive to Florida as quickly as possible to get in the sunshine, but we had to be careful because Daddy would try to drag us all over to boring battlefields and museums and across the borders of different states trying to visit as many as possible, just so he could say he'd been.'

'Really? She said that?'

'Yes.'

Foiled again.

10 July 2010

To the Cotswolds, a stunning midsummer day, the celebrated stone aglow, the hills rolling, the streams sparkling, the gravel drives of the barn conversions raked and levelled just so, the horse brasses winking in the snug, the sachets of Nescafé nestling in the wicker box next to the kettle with its special 'British hotel edition' flex nine inches long, the leading edge of the bathroom Andrex folded into a precise isosceles, the couple up from London as wedding guests checked in and lunched with plenty of time to spare.

But what's this? The first stirrings of trouble in paradise. The man, me, for it is I, suited and booted and good-to-go these many minutes past, jacket already discarded, collar already starting to chafe, trousers already starting to stick, huge pad of plaster and felt taped to his blister the previous evening by his friend Liz the Podiatrist starting to throb, the suggestion of perspiration beginning its long journey from his shoulder blades to his buttocks, need I go on – politely inquiring of his wife, for it is she, how much longer she's thinking it might be before she's possibly maybe perhaps, you know, sort of, ready to leave?

The wife replying in fairly short order, the man retreating, palms up in a universal gesture of peace.

Half an hour later, not yet panicked nor even nudging up

against anxious, but still, their cushion of a spare quarter-hour evaporating in the pounding haze of heat, the couple arrive at what their navigation system indicates is their destination, the woman, as ever, piloting the family Honda, the man in its passenger seat, his left thigh exposed to the merciless glare, his right pressed up against the gear stick, seeking out even that scant scintilla of shadow. He's bothered, he's boiling, he's bursting with fear and hatred over the possibility of being even ten seconds late for an appointment.

'Well, it's a church,' says the man, as the Honda slows and stops, 'and it's in Oxfordshire. But there's nobody here. It's deserted. You've brought us to the wrong place.'

'Would you get your leg off the gear stick?' says the woman. 'I need to turn the car round.'

She explains that the wedding invitation contains a postcode, but no street name for the church. Therefore, she had programmed the satnav with the postcode and, a reasonable guess, input the street name as Church Lane. And thus the computer had delivered up the Church Lane attached to that postcode, but it was the Church Lane housing St Mark's in Chipping Ringpiece, as opposed to the Church Lane accommodating St Matthew's in Little Bell End, if indeed such a Church Lane exists.

'Must have the same postcode,' shrugs the wife, smoothly nosing the car back in the direction they have come. 'There were some people at that pub back there. We'll stop and ask the way.'

The husband, predictably, reacts badly to these dread words, possibly the least welcome combination in the English language. 'I can't believe you've cocked this up,' he says.

A full-scale argument ensues.

She says (to summarize): 'I haven't cocked anything up. I told you this morning there was no address, but you weren't listening. I did my best. I booked the hotel. I looked up the route. I organized the wedding present. I found your suit this morning when you were in a panic, running up and down stairs in your pants. Who says I was in charge of finding the church as well? It was you that had the invitation. You could just as easily have taken responsibility for finding the church as me. Chris is your friend anyway, you see him practically every day at work. You could have said, at any point in the last three months, "Hey, Chris, what exactly is the address of the church?" Or you could have looked it up on Google like I did with the hotel. And now you're getting all angry just because you've got to ask somebody the way. And we're not even going to be late. We've got plenty of time.'

He says (to summarize): 'Why does it have to be so f***ing hot?'

The people in the pub car park, emerging from their lunch under an umbrella, are, as with British people everywhere when asked directions, helpful without being in any way hopeful of a successful conclusion.

'Oh, it's a long way,' they say, shaking their heads, calling for reinforcements. 'A very long way. Best go up to the main road and take it from there.'

It turns out we are a mere three miles off course. Crucially, however, our destination lies across the great divide of the A361, which in these parts seems to represent a barrier, more psychological than physical perhaps, as wide as the Mississippi.

Anyway, we arrive. Five minutes early. And the bride a fashionable fifteen minutes late. The first hymn is 'Amazing Grace', and a most wonderful day is had by all.

17 July 2010

Sam is away in France, Cousin Steve is away in Hull. I'm left on my own in London with two women, sometimes a lot more than two if they have their friends round. When that happens, I really don't stand a chance, eleven-year-old girls lurking round every corner, waiting to spring out and shove popcorn down the back of my shirt. Life turns into one long ambush.

Even with just the three of us it isn't easy. They sit there on the sofa, mother and daughter, the one a carbon copy of the other, watching bloody *Gok's Bloody Fashion Fix* and *Mary Queen of Bloody Shops*, dispatching me on endless errands.

'I meant to get some Diet Cokes, can you go over to the shop?'

'We haven't got any cash for Svetlana, can you go to the machine?'

'I've nothing for my packed lunch, can you go and buy some stuff?'

'The tyres on my bike are a bit flat, can you pump them up?'

'We're worried we haven't seen Tiger and Lucky for ages, can you go and find them?'

And so on.

Each time I complete one chore, they remember something else. I spend half the evening trudging to and from Mustafa's shop. One night I went back and forth four times.

'Oh, Robert,' Mustafa says, rolling his eyes theatrically, the shameless ham. 'What is The Nicola want now?'

It's significant, don't you think, that she gets that The in front of her name and I don't. Mustafa knows the score. Our domestic settlement used to upset Mustafa, in a Turkish sort of way. He used to shake his head sadly and ask, 'Why you always the bicycle, Robert? Why The Nicola always do the drive?' Now, he just grins.

I take whatever it is they've demanded back to their lair, hanging about in the doorway like a dog hoping for a pat, but instead they get tetchy because they've had to put Gok on pause, his silly grinning face frozen across the telly.

'Oh yeah, thanks,' Rachel will say as I hold up a bag of crisps, her fingers hovering over the remote, waiting for me to leave.

The first night Sam was away, the three of us went out for dinner, by way of a treat. When we got home, they put *Catwalk's Next Top Runway* or some such on the TV and sent me straight back out for orange squash. When I brought that back they said the restaurant had just phoned up to say Rachel had left her iTouch on the table.

'I said we would go and get it,' Nicola told me, not needing to define who 'we' meant in this context.

I am not, incidentally, entirely sure what an iTouch is. I think it's probably a phone because the waitress explained she had known who to call by going into the Contacts list, scrolling down to Mummy A and Mummy B and ringing the first one. Smart woman.

Rachel has only got the one mummy, by the way. Mummy A stands for Mummy Apple and Mummy B stands for Mummy BlackBerry, my wife being well supplied with communications devices.

A sore point at the moment, actually, communications devices. Unlike my wife, I make do with a bog-standard Nokia, or at least I did until Wednesday, when it spent ninety minutes on the warm cycle in the washing machine.

'There's a funny noise coming from the washing machine,' Nicola called out, 'and I think I've just seen your mobile going round and round.'

It was already late, but naturally Rachel, sensing the prospect of some humour at her father's expense, emerged from her bedroom to join in her mother's merriment.

'Perhaps we'll be able to dry it out,' I said.

But we couldn't, it was finished, dead and gone. Lovely and clean, though.

Interesting experiment, putting your mobile in the wash. It

was a couple of days before I got a replacement and, after an initial panic, I rather relished the freedom of being transported back a decade or more, back to that dim remembered age when you weren't being beeped and trilled and vibrated on a constant basis. Normally, I take my phone everywhere, even to the loo. But for two whole days, I went about my business phoneless and the world didn't come to an end.

Also, I lost all my numbers, every last one. Which is a bit of a pain, obviously, but also strangely cathartic, because sooner or later either people call you, in which case you get their number again, or they don't, in which case they can shove off, can't they?

The only downside of the phone incident is that my fastest times on Sea Sweeper have been erased. I'd spent years shaving milliseconds off those times, got down to one minute eleven seconds on expert, which I think is rather good, and now I'm having to start from scratch. Keeps me out of trouble, I suppose, while I wait for the boys to get back.

18 September 2010

I went for lunch with my pal Phill at Shoreditch House, a private members' club in east London favoured by media folk. Phill's a bit of a mover and shaker in media-land, so he's a member. I've never moved or shaken anything much, so I'm not.

All around us, deep in sofas artfully strewn over the reclaimed distressed flooring, lovely young people were tapping away on their laptops and palmtops and mobiles, writing, designing, brainstorming, networking, doing whatever exciting stuff it is that lovely young people do.

'Look at this, Phill,' I said, gesturing in what I took to be an expansive, wonders-of-the-modern-world fashion. 'This is the future, isn't it?'

'Yes, it is,' said Phill, who's much more up than I am on the impact new technology (as I still regard it) is having on the nation's working habits. 'And I believe it's been the future for quite some time.'

On my journey to work, at least for the first stretch in gentrifying Hackney, not so much around the Bengali cash 'n' carrys in the East End, it's the same story. Cafés chock-full of kids, tiptapping away, an entire workforce never going anywhere near anything as antiquated as an office, and yet all doing well. Well enough, certainly, to segue from the cafés to the bars around 5 p.m. and get on the lash.

I wrote last week how *The Times* is moving to a new office where I won't have my own room any more. Yes indeed, I am returning to the ranks, epaulettes torn off. I'm concerned, so I'm thinking, by way of a fallback, maybe I should seize the chance to embrace the new working style. Just chill with my Mac in a succession of venues, always movin' on, fluid, flexible and Facebooky, awash with coffee all day, awash with booze all evening, roll home drunk, ignore the kids and slope off to bed. It's an option, isn't it?

Facebook, that's another issue. My son has been lobbying hard to sign up. He's thirteen and says all his friends are on it, which possibly over the course of his long campaign has become almost true. My wife and I have resisted the pressure, and frankly I thought the party line was that we still were resisting it, but then this summer she changed her mind and promised Sam she would change mine, too.

Monday night is date night in my family. Cousin Steve babysits, Nicola and I go out to the bar and talk through what we think about various issues to do with the children. Well, she says what she thinks and then we decide that's what I think as well. Last Monday I sucked at my margarita through a straw and listened while Nicola explained in words of one syllable what Facebook is all about and why it's OK for Sam to be on it. The lovely young people at the adjoining table were most amused. Fair enough: Nicola must have sounded about seventy-three; I probably sounded about a hundred and two. And in any case, I'm told many lovely young people don't bother with Facebook any more. Too old hat.

'But I can't see the point of it,' I said, already having given in yet offering up token defiance. 'Why can't he just go out shop-lifting and commit minor acts of criminal damage like I did at his age?'

'We'd have loved Facebook when we were kids,' my wife said. 'It's harmless. Anyway,' she added, 'you've got your own page.'

'No, I haven't,' I said.

'Yes, you have,' she said. 'Someone's copied your Wikipedia entry and turned it into a Facebook page. I've seen it. Apparently three people want to be your friend.'

'Three? Isn't that humiliating?'

'Early days.'

My other great technological leap forward has been to acquire an Oyster card. I don't use the Tube or bus that often, but when I do, I always pay full whack, believing that Oyster cards can be used to track your movements, in the same way shops use loyalty cards to track your purchases. Obviously no freeborn Englishman could ever tolerate such surveillance.

Then a couple of months ago I happened to interview Boris Johnson. Boris told me I'd got it all wrong.

'No, no,' he said, fishing out his own card. 'They know *some-one* possessing this Oyster card has done such and such a journey. But they don't know *who* that someone is.'

'Really?'

'Yes!' shouted Boris. 'I'm with you completely on the civil liberties thing, but nothing on this card says it's me. Well, it says Mayor of London on the back, but they all say that.'

Thus am I dragged inch by inch into the new communications age.

13 November 2010

It's come on a lot, where we live, but it's still not safe for my son, thirteen, to hang about on the streets like I did when I was his age. Which presents a problem. I don't want him to be mugged or bullied, but neither do I want him to live out his teenage years indoors. So I've come up with the obvious solution: we hang about on the streets together, a bit like Richard Branson going on his son's gap year. Only less mortifying, I hope, for my boy than that must have been for Branson's.

Good job Sam and I like each other. Well, I like him. Not sure what he makes of me.

It's not so strange. The Apache took their sons off to sweat lodges in the desert, the Masai disappeared into the savannah to turn their boys into men, obnoxious New England Wasps in films buy their heirs country-club memberships and call girls. My east London variant on these ancient traditions is to skulk around the park, father and son, trying to give the lad a little moral and social instruction in between spouting nonsense at each other.

My wife and daughter settled in front of *Ugly Betty*, Sam and I zip up our hoodies and slip out the door.

'Good work getting your mum those flowers from the market earlier,' I tell him.

'Do you think she liked them?'

'Definitely.' A few steps in silence.

'Not so good to tell her you'd got them dirt cheap.'

'Really? Do you think so?'

'I know so.'

First stop, Mustafa's, where everyone's favourite Turkish

grocer offers us a sample of his homeland's most famous export. Not marijuana, Turkish delight. Not the gloop we get here, Mustafa explains, but the good stuff his mum sends from home.

'I thought you didn't like Turkish delight,' says Sam, through a mouthful of pink gunk, when we're back outside.

'Can't stand the stuff,' I say, swallowing hard. 'But it would have been rude to refuse.'

'Why would it have been rude?' he wants to know.

'You've got to imagine yourself in Mustafa's shoes,' I reply. 'He's here in a foreign country, he's grafting away, six in the morning till eleven at night, hard work, often boring, sometimes difficult. He gets some Turkish delight from his mum, it means a lot more to him than just sweets. It's a taste of family, childhood, home, full of eastern promise, who knows? If someone offers to share something that means so much to him, you'd better say yes.'

'What do you mean, full of eastern promise?'

'It was the slogan in an advert when I was younger, good-looking bloke dressed as a sheikh, slices chocolate in half with big sword, girl mightily impressed. Something like that. Your basic sex-sell.'

'Does slicing Turkish delight in half with a big sword work with girls in real life?'

'There are less melodramatic ways to a woman's heart.'

We proceed into the park and a discussion about how many motorbikes it would take to fill the area between the football pitch and the lido.

'Can I get a motorbike when I'm older?'

'No.'

'When I'm eighteen you can't stop me.'

'That's what you think. "Motorbikes and horses, that's what keeps us in business." Do you know who told me that?'

'Yes,' yawns Sam. 'The doctor at the hospital when you fell off that motorbike. You've told me a hundred times. I won't fall off my motorbike.'

'That's true, you won't. Because you won't have one.'

Swinging a right towards the railway, we come into an industrial area, scrap yards, lock-ups, factories, garages.

'Do you think any of these places are fronts for ruthless criminal enterprises?' asks Sam.

'Don't know about ruthless or enterprising,' I say. 'Criminal, yes, without a shadow of a doubt.'

Just then two girls, no more than twenty, twenty-one, approach us.

'Is this the way to Broadway Market?' one of them asks, sounding nervous – not, I regret to say, entirely without justification. As I said, this area, particularly this bit here by the railway, is not, despite the nearby market's renaissance as a popular socializing spot, as safe as one would like. I start to give directions, but it's complicated, directions always are; their attention wanders.

'We'll walk you if you like,' I offer. 'Is that OK?'

'No problem.'

Sam, chest visibly swelling, takes charge of the small talk as we form up. The girls get a potted history of the equipment in the children's playground, followed by a preview of the range of refreshment choices available to them once safely delivered.

'My dad and me like going to the cocktail bar sometimes,' Sam confides. 'He has a margarita and I have a lager shandy, half and half.'

'Like it, son,' I say on our way home. 'Put them at their ease, leaving me to scan for potential threats and pretend I've got a curly plastic wire in my ear. Excellent.'

And thus does the vital work of easing the lad's transition into the weird and wonderful world of men continue.

26 February 2011

I was in this restaurant in east London and the maître d' said, 'You write that column for *The Times*, I like it,' and I pouted and tossed my hair back and said, 'Why, thank you,' and he asked if I lived locally and I said yes indeedy doody. And then we talked about Giles Coren. And that, I thought, was that.

Then, a few minutes later, the waiter brought over a plate of langoustines.

'We didn't order these,' my wife and I said in unison, both of us, in the English way, moving instantly on to full alert for potential social embarrassment.

'Compliments of the chef,' said the waiter.

It took another long moment for the penny to drop. My oh my oh my, I thought: free prawns! Fame at last.

'For he that hath,' I am fond of quoting, and I did so again now as the maître d' smiled across the restaurant, 'to him shall be given; and he that hath not, from him shall be taken even that which he hath.'

'Nice prawns though,' said my wife.

This has happened a few times recently. Not gratuitous seafood, but meeting people I don't know who know me. Or know my face, at any rate. Nicola and I don't have paparazzi chasing us down the street shouting, 'Bob! Bob! Who's the mystery blonde?' although all in good time. Yet something has shifted.

In the days following the langoustine incident I pondered what might have brought about a situation in which (a tiny handful of) strangers know my face, a situation in which I appear to have hooked at least the top joint of one finger on to the lowest rung of the long ladder of celebrity.

'I know,' I said, struck by a flash of inspiration. 'Maybe I've got really good!'

Nah, I thought, can't be that.

I began to develop another hypothesis. Squirrelling myself away with my cuttings archives, the big books where I stick all this nonsense, I set out to prove it. And prove it I did. The evidence of the cuttings books is indisputable. I stand condemned out of my own *oeuvre*. Quite simply, I have turned into the most blatant camera-hogging media tart.

It is twenty years since I joined *The Times*. In the first fifteen of those years, corresponding to cuttings books one through eight, I had my picture published on twenty occasions. That's not counting the bylines that accompany these or other columns. I mean large pictures of me illustrating long features.

Thus, in my late twenties and early thirties, we had me parachuting, me abseiling, me boxing, me cycling, me microlighting, me clubbing in Reykjavik. And then in my late thirties and early forties, we had me cooking, me dressed as Santa Claus, me doing anger management, me on various family holidays. That sounds like a lot of pictures, but the truth is, these me-centred articles were infrequent. They appeared once or twice a year.

In the past four years, however, having studied cuttings books nine, ten and now into eleven, the cuttings books of shame, if you will, I can reveal that my photograph – again not counting picture bylines – has been published in *The Times* on no fewer than twenty-five occasions. That's every two months. That is more than many people who actually are famous. Rarity has been replaced by something approaching ubiquity.

In the past year, my photograph has been in *The Times* fully eleven times. Crampton trying to improve his public-speaking skills, Crampton stuck in Florida, Crampton on Prozac, Crampton failing to get a six-pack stomach, Crampton still on Prozac, Crampton coming off the booze, Crampton still on Prozac – Crampton's fat! Crampton's drunk! Crampton's mad! – and so on. It's now more normal for Crampton to write a piece accompanied by a picture of Crampton than one that isn't.

Some weeks, I spend hours in the studio. I know what a key light is. As I arrive half an hour late, photographer mates who used to value me as a fellow hack reach wearily for their gear and mutter about how Bob's gone over to the dark side. At the last session, I actually heard myself asking if Beth was available to do hair and make-up.

And yet the way I see it is this: we're in a marketplace here, right? Changing editorial tastes only reflect changing consumer tastes. When I started out, the confessional article was still terra incognita. Then, a few brave pioneers owned up to something embarrassing in print. The audience response – your response – was very positive. The frontier collapsed. And when it collapsed, a secondary wave of egomaniacs surged forward to stake our claim to fame. And our prawns.

So yes, reader, the inflation of my ravening vanity is all your fault. I haven't turned into a full-on monster quite yet. But no doubt I will. It can't hurt to get an excuse up and running.

26 March 2011

One of my most cherished fantasies is to learn to do something cool, to a high standard, in conditions of total secrecy, and then shock, amaze and impress the world, or at the very least my wife and children, with my new skill. I've dreamt of doing this with fluent Italian and/or Russian and/or Arabic, learning the saxophone and/or violin and/or piano, perfecting a swallow dive from the ten-metre board and/or a bridge and/or a cliff, doing tricks on my bike, ice skating backwards (or indeed, forwards) and so on.

Needless to say, the fantasy has always remained just that,

spiked on the jagged realities of lack of ability, lack of time, lack of discipline, lack of courage.

After I first went to Russia, and then when I saw the scene in *A Fish Called Wanda* where John Cleese seduces Jamie Lee Curtis by speaking Russian, I got as far as learning the Cyrillic alphabet. Hard work, though, and as it turned out, not even fancying Jamie Lee Curtis rotten was sufficient motivation to slog away night after night to master 'Hello comrade, where is the pharmacy?' or whatever.

This pattern has been on repeat as long as I can remember. Fantasy, burst of enthusiasm, obstacle, reality, failure. Guitar club at primary school? Complicated, fingers hurt. Maths O level at secondary school? Complicated, brain hurt. Football team at college? Tiring, feet hurt. Working through the classics in my twenties? Boring, eyes hurt. Scuba diving in my thirties? Frightening, ears hurt. Singing lessons a few years ago? Humiliating, pride hurt. And so on.

I keep trying, though, keep on keeping on. Even as the failures mount up, I haven't settled for being the person I currently am. The vogue nowadays is for acceptance, learning to love what you really are, all that Eastern passivity stuff. I say: no! I'm a northern European Protestant, striving is what we do. And this time, this year, the striving is going to work.

I'm attempting to acquire not one but two new skills at the moment. I mentioned the harmonica a while ago. That is progressing, after a fashion, a lesson a week, unless I cancel, which I usually do, for reasons of health, holiday, pressure of work, bone idleness, etc. Yet modest gains have been made. Sound is forthcoming. Correct notes have been stumbled across. My teacher, the super-talented, super-cool Philip Achille (check him out on YouTube, playing at the Albert Hall), is encouraging. 'It'll come,' says Philip, wincing as another ghastly wheeze blares out. 'Don't give up.'

Unlike the harmonica, my second task benefits from a modicum of natural ability. As an adolescent, in the brief window between losing weight and starting to smoke, a window when I briefly glimpsed the combination of agility and fitness, I became rather good at scaling trees, lamp posts, other people's property and so on. Good in the sense of understanding what to do, which I don't with music or foreign languages or indeed most other activities requiring physical dexterity or effort.

I am trying to rediscover and develop this ability at Mile End Climbing Wall in east London, a conveniently short ride up the towpath from my house. My pal Phill and I have had a couple of lessons. Nolan, our instructor, says we're not at all bad, considering Phill's dodgy shoulder, my fragile back, our combined age of ninety-two and our combined climbing age, as in experience, of something not unadjacent to zero.

I liked Nolan straight away. He laughed at my jokes. Mostly I liked him because he started climbing only six years ago and can now swarm up even the silliest overhang with gravity-defying grace. Looking up at Nolan, it is possible to imagine myself up there six years from now, fifty two(and a half)-year-old Spider Bob, young 'uns looking on thinking, blimey, that old guy can't play the mouth organ for toffee, but he's pretty useful on the wall, their girlfriends slipping me their number like Sienna Miller slips Daniel Craig her number in *Layer Cake*.

Maybe it'll happen. Not Sienna Miller giving me her number, that's unlikely – the climbing thing. For one thing, I love the kit. Tight boots, baggy trousers, harness with metal hanging off, no shirt, talcum powder all over your hands, it's basically the builder in the Diet Coke advert, secretaries gawping from the office block. Pretty sexy look, right? Maybe lose the talcum powder, though.

These things are about desire, in the end, aren't they? You've got to want the end enough to will the means. With the climbing, I think I do. When he first came to the climbing wall, Nolan says, he felt the overwhelming urge to master it. I felt the same way.

'Imagine how cool it'd be to be able to come in here and climb across the ceiling,' I said to Phill.

'With your wife and kids watching,' said Phill.

'Yeah,' I agreed in a dreamy voice, 'with your wife and kids watching.'

2 April 2011

I'm on stage doing the quiz I've been plugging relentlessly (and yet, I hope, tastefully) these past few weeks. And I'm rapidly developing a newfound respect for teachers, actors, project coordinator youth outreach community doo-dah types, anyone whose job involves engaging and managing an audience. Talk about stress.

Engaging is the easy part. My gags and questions have by and large been well received. So has the venue, the charming Wilton's Music Hall in east London. But now it's time for the answers and the participants are marking each other's papers. It's 9.30 p.m. Drink has been taken. Noise levels are rising. My job has become less about light entertainment and more about crowd control.

'When you say the answer to "How did Nelson get home from Trafalgar?" is "In a barrel of brandy,"' query the table of very nice *Times* readers to my left, 'would you accept just "A barrel" for a full mark?'

'Yes,' I say.

'No,' says my wife, seated to my right.

Yes, Nicola is present; she's written most of the quiz. And now, if I'm the Good Cop who offers a smoke and a plea bargain, Nicola has assumed the Bad Cop role, the one who stands behind the suspect and hisses into his ear about homosexual rape in prison.

'Just "A barrel" gets half a mark,' I announce.

'What did you say?' shouts someone further back.

'What about "A barrel of rum"?' asks my daughter.

Yes, my children are there, too. It's Rachel's twelfth birthday, by the by. Ensuring she has a good time has draped a thick extra layer of anxiety over her father, Quizmaster Very Ordinaire. But not as thick a layer as the one provided by not being able to remember whether Nelson really was brought back from Trafalgar in a barrel of brandy, or rum, or some other spirit and some other receptacle entirely. Nicola has triple-checked most of the answers. This is one of those she left to me.

There are 120 people in front of me. Readers, friends, colleagues, relatives, all mixed together in a titanic clash of cultures reminiscent of a wedding. I'm in a suit and smart shoes. Not only are the shoes tight and uncomfortable, they are also slippery. My freedom of movement constrained by the fear I could fall on my face, I have developed a cautious stage-mince, a mince that becomes more exaggerated as I plough through four pints of lager on top of no food.

Worse, my hair, I realize, is in drastic need of a wash and a cut. Far from the swept-back distinguished man-of-letters style I am attempting, the Crampton locks have sagged, greasy and exhausted, into the sort of lank centre parting sported by an aspirant fifteen-year-old heavy metallist. This gently sweating disaster looms large inside, as well as on top of, my head.

Victorian music halls were not designed for the stage to hear the stalls. Any comment or query from more than one row back – and there are many – is indecipherable. I am semi-blinded by two large spotlights. I can sense Wilton's staff circulating – benign, and yet moving towards an embrace of the notion that pretty damn soon might be the time for this *Times* joker to bring proceedings to a close.

'"A barrel of rum" also gets a half-mark,' I say to Rachel.

'What?'

'What did he say?'

'Speak up!'

'That's not fair,' shouts someone. 'Why should "A barrel of rum" get the same as just "A barrel"?'

'They're both wrong, anyway,' says my wife. 'They should get nothing.'

'*Exactement!*' I hear a familiar voice cry from my half-right. 'Nuzzink! Nuzzink! We give zem nuzzink!'

It's my friend Franck, known for reasons of nationality and eccentricity as the Crazy Frog. Crazy Frog, it turns out, has adopted a defiantly legalistic line in marking the adjacent table's answers. This adjacent table contains the features editor of this newspaper, plus her husband, her children and a man in a green bobble hat.

'We want half a mark!' shouts Green Bobble Hat.

'Nur, nur, nur,' says Crazy Frog, wagging his finger in classic Gallic fashion. 'Nuzzink. Zair-oh.'

'Give them half a mark, Franck,' I plead.

'What did he say?' calls someone.

My wife rolls her eyes. My daughter looks concerned. My son sniggers. 'Epic fail,' I hear him say.

Cousin Steve – yes, he's there, too – leans over and says something to Sam. Sam sniggers again.

'Robert!' calls a voice from further back, cutting through the rolling, rising babble. I recognize the voice as belonging to a stratospherically powerful News International executive. Shielding my eyes, I can see her, surrounded by a praetorian guard of suited-and-booted marketing boys.

'Er, yes?' I reply, my voice cracking.

'This Nelson business,' says the exec. 'What do you want to happen?'

What I want to happen, every fibre in my body is screaming at me to yell, is for everybody. To. Please. Shut. The. F***. Up.

On balance, I think it's best I didn't say that.

9 April 2011

I write from the epicentre of the whirlwind that is the Crampton family birthday season. Two children, one wife, all born within the same fortnight. What are the chances of that? About evens, I reckon, given what I've read about probability over the years. If you analyse the maths, everything that appears uncannily coincidental always turns out not to be.

Besides birthdays, Mother's Day is there in the mix, too. And Easter's floating about as well. Cards, flowers, presents, eggs, parties, meals out, special surprise treats, there's a lot to organize. It's a busy time. Expensive, too. Not that I resent it. Perish the thought.

When I say 'all born within the same fortnight', by the way, I don't mean literally 'all born within the same fortnight'. I mean 'all born within the same fortnight' if you travel backwards from Rachel's birth in 1999 to Sam's in 1997 to Nicola's in 1964. So, quite different fortnights. In the first instance. But now, always the same.

Enough of that. Obviously, my main concern at this very special time for my nearest and dearest is that my statistics do not suffer. My stats – for alcohol and food intake, walking, cycling, other exercise and sleeping – are very important to me. I write them down each day in my diary in different-coloured felt-tip pens. This is my way of exerting control over my environment. Or pretending to exert control.

As we all know, good stats are dependent on good routine. Thus, unless you are ultra-careful, any disruption to that routine (and three birthdays with attendant celebrations within a fortnight counts as a disruption) risks taking a wrecking ball to your stats.

Eternal vigilance is required to resist the fizzy wine, Iced Gems, Pringles and chocolate cake that present themselves under your nose. Also, my children (not so much my wife) being of an age to wake up despicably early on their big days, vital half-hours can be shaved off the land of nod. The prospective big loser, however, the weak link, the lame gazelle of the stats herd vulnerable to the ravening birthday beast, is exercise. Specifically: mileage.

Birthdays mean family trips – to restaurants, to parties, to friends – and family trips mean engines, as opposed to feet or pedals. Normally, I can go weeks without getting into a car. That may seem an unlikely claim, but I have arranged my life such that, in the usual course of events, barely any journey requires the use of any power I cannot supply myself. I have, in fact, become phobic about travelling by car, partly because the loss of independence is maddening, mostly because I hate the prospect of miles I could be walking or cycling slipping away, miles that should be in the historical record, shoring up the averages.

Apart from any – which is to say all – undesirable behaviour exhibited by our son that can be blamed on his father, transportation creates more aggravation in our house than any other subject. On longer journeys, it's all about departure time, routes, the satnav, map-reading, the usual stuff. Within the city, disputes flare over my wanting to walk or cycle somewhere while my wife wants to drive.

'I'll meet you there,' I say.

'Can't we just arrive somewhere together, for once?' she replies.

Anyway, I booked dinner for Nicola's birthday. The restaurant is maybe fifteen minutes' walk from home. I thought: with the walk there and the walk back, that's a solid two miles in the bag; plus other bits and bobs, that'll be four for the day, not great but acceptable given the constraints of the birthday season.

'Have you booked a cab?' Nicola asks.

'Eh? It's only ten minutes' walk.'

'More like twenty.'

'Twelve at most.'

'Whatever. I'm wearing heels.'

'You could wear trainers, then change at the restaurant.'

'I don't want to.'

'Oh, go on, you look nice in trainers.'

'No.'

Drat. Her birthday: nothing to be done.

Of course, the cab's late. I give them five minutes' grace, then call.

'It's a blue Sierra, mate, just pulling up now.'

'No, it's not.'

'Yeah, it's a blue Sierra.'

'No, I mean I'm standing outside my house and it's not here.'

Pause. Crackle. 'Two minutes away.'

Five minutes later the Sierra arrives. 'We could have walked there by now,' I point out.

'No, we couldn't. And I didn't want to.'

Nice meal. Bottle of wine. Ten thirty, we're ready to leave.

'Let's order a minicab,' says Nicola.

'What?'

'A minicab. I've still got my heels on and it's cold.'

'Let's go and hail a black cab on the Hackney Road.'

'There won't be one.'

'Yeah, there will, there's loads.'

'Oh all right, but I'm not walking.'

Twenty minutes later, my wife refusing to speak to me other than to reveal she has developed a blister on her toe, we arrive home. I'm not entirely sure the extra mile was worth it.

7 January 2012

One thing I miss over the holiday season is the office canteen. I miss it at the weekends, too, but then that's only for a bearable two days, not the week-long absence I must endure over the festive period. Even so, if the rest of the family is away at the weekend, I have been known – or rather, not known, because I've kept it a secret until now – to come into work on a Saturday or Sunday just to go to the canteen. Cheap, nutritious, quick: what's the shame in that?

Monday to Friday lunchtime, I'm up there bang on opening, loading up. 'I love coming to the canteen for lunch,' I sighed happily to Ben recently as we sat down with our plates heaped high, half the day's calories taken care of for £3.50. 'It's the second-best time of the day.'

Ben paused. 'OK,' he said, accepting his fate. 'What's your favourite time of day?'

'Getting into bed,' I replied.

Around this time of year, it's traditional to think about what you want to change in your life. I tend to do that, however, either in spring or at back-to-school time in early September. In these dark and dismal days, I find it preferable to count my blessings. And the pleasure of getting into bed every night is right up there.

We ought, as a species, to congratulate ourselves more often on our achievements. I don't just mean the Hadron Collider or eradicating smallpox or writing the Bible, but also the more humdrum successes we take for granted. And in that regard, bed

– the entire mattress-sheet-pillow-duvet configuration – is right up there.

It could all be very different. The chair, for instance, I don't think we've cracked that yet. Some chairs are great, most are OK, some are really quite bad. And when they are bad, chairs are useless. But with a bed, even a bad one will do a job for you.

And bed linen, that's come on leaps and bounds, just in my lifetime, my goodness. As a child, it was nylon pyjamas meets nylon sheets, fizzing zigzags of blue static arcing around the room like *Doctor Who*. Now, bed linen is impossibly soft and lovely, like something from a fairy tale, like something only princesses slept on just two generations ago.

We've got this duvet in two parts, a thick and a thin. Thin is summer duvet. Thick is spring and autumn duvet. And thick and thin press-studded together form winter duvet. Winter duvet is on duty at the moment, and it is utterly magnificent. The weight of it, the warmth, the comfort . . .

There are, I think, only three drawbacks.

First, obviously, getting out of bed, ever, becomes a super-humanly difficult thing to do. We've had to resort to this old-fashioned hatefully loud alarm we call Horror Alarm, as in, 'Did you set Horror?'

''Fraid so, yes.'

'I hate Horror.'

'So do I.'

Second, winter duvet makes fitting a clean duvet cover even hasslier than it usually is, especially when your role is to stand there, outstretched arms in agony, like a prisoner in a stress position, holding the duvet while your wife flicks the fresh cover on using some technique you don't understand but looks similar to that way women can take their bras off through their sleeve, which you don't understand either. And also resent bitterly.

And third, winter duvet makes me more prone to nightmares,

partly because of the weight, partly because I'm in bed so much longer the likelihood of a nightmare increases.

Then again, I've been having nightmares as long as I can remember: ghastly old Druids plodding up the stairs; police forces of several countries hunting me down for awful crimes I know I've done; turning up late for O-level maths, unprepared and naked from the waist down. The usual stuff. I'm not even particularly frightened by most of my library of nightmares any longer; they're like a scary film you've seen six times, terrifying at first, now merely unpleasant.

Mind you, I had a nightmare not long ago that was no fun at all. It starred Lloyd Cole . . . as a zombie! That's Lloyd Cole as in Lloyd Cole and the Commotions, Lloyd Cole as in two cracking albums in the eighties, Lloyd Cole as in used to look like Pierce Brosnan, now looks like Mike Gatting. In the nightmare, Lloyd Cole lumbered around in orthodox zombie fashion, stiff legs, arms outstretched, terrible neck wound, yet I'd get away just in time. But then the zombie Commotions turned up as well. That didn't end well.

Speaking of nightmares, our daughter recently appeared in our bedroom in the middle of the night.

'I had a nightmare someone tried to kidnap me,' I heard her explain to my wife, 'but it was OK, because you threatened them with a gun.'

'What was I doing, sweetheart?' I asked.

'You were hiding in the logbox with the cats,' said Rachel.

She tried to keep the contempt out of her voice, but I could tell she wasn't impressed.

18 February 2012

A couple of weeks ago my son asked how I was. A casual inquiry, he got more than he bargained for.

'Oh, not so bad,' I began, in the traditional fashion. 'Underslept, overworked, stressed, mild hangover, freezing cold 80 per cent of the day, niggle in left hip, strain in right knee, a stone possibly a stone and a half overweight, totally at war with my new phone, and your mother's just said the third-worst collection of words a man can ever hear. Apart from that, great.' Silence. 'Don't you want to know the worst words a man can hear?' I said.

'Go on then.'

'Well, since you ask, the worst are, "Stage four, three to six months at best." The second-worst are, "A minimum of thirty years without possibility of parole." And the third-worst are what your mother's just said: "I don't mind what we do for Valentine's Day, I'll leave it to you to arrange a nice surprise."'

At almost fifteen, Sam is old enough to know this called for an expression of world-weary male solidarity. Sadly, he is not yet quite old enough to know what form this expression should take.

'Never mind,' he said, giving it a go. 'It'll soon be half-term.'

'Good effort, son,' I said, ruffling his hair. 'But while the world of school trades in half-terms, the world of work takes no notice of them whatsoever.'

'Really?' he said, in the shocked tone teenagers use when they discover some fresh hell awaiting them in adult life.

'Yes, really,' I said. 'I haven't had a half-term since 1982. The occasional bank holiday, perhaps, but not many of them recently. Haven't you ever noticed?'

'No.'

He won't have noticed this half-term either, because he wasn't around. Nor was his sister. Rachel spent the break in the French Alps at her friend's family's ski chalet (Ray and Fiona, cheers for that, much obliged, come down to the holiday park in Kent any time you like), while Sam spent his holiday in Hull with his grandparents. Each to their own, eh? For my wife and me, the half-empty house felt like a taste of things to come. It is not a taste I particularly care for. As each of them departed on their respective journeys, I had to restrain myself from making a terrible scene in the road, clutching their ankles like a spurned lover in a film, 'No, no, please don't go, don't go!' and so forth.

Yes indeed. Like, I suspect, many fathers, when my children were smaller I was (how to put this politely?) more indifferent than I am now to any distance between us. I even, on occasion, welcomed such distance, although never for very long. As they have got bigger and more interesting, however, my default preference regarding their deployment is on either side of me, ideally at home, ideally occupied in a wholesome diversion that doesn't involve noise, a power supply or links to the outside world.

In my mind's eye, the fire is lit, the rugby is on the telly (the stuff about diversions not requiring a power supply, etc., does not apply to me) and I am on the sofa, left arm around my daughter, right arm cradling a shotgun to deal with any suitors unwise enough to call. My son is far enough away to give me a clear field of fire, yet near enough to be at my right hand in an instant. The children only stir either to ask me a general-knowledge question to which I instantly supply the answer or to bring me another drink. The spell of this tableau is otherwise only broken by my wife summoning us to the vast banquet she has prepared.

I do not feel under any pressure to revise this scenario simply because my children have entered adolescence. Nor will I feel the need to revise it ten, twenty, God willing, thirty years from now. It is they, inevitably, who will do the revising, it being one of the less amusing cosmic jokes that the amount of time a father wants to spend with his children increases in inverse proportion to the amount of time the child wants to spend with him.

If you draw a graph, with the desire for shared time up the

vertical axis (every waking minute at the top, absolutely zero at the bottom) and the child's age along the horizontal axis, and you plot two lines representing the father's desire and the child's desire respectively, you get something that looks a lot like a letter X, the diagonals intersecting, sharing a brief embrace if you will, somewhere around the age of eleven. And that age is now, for both of my children, a fading memory.

Time marches on.

19 May 2012

I went to my school reunion two Saturdays ago, a hotel on the outskirts of Hull, and when I woke up on the Sunday morning I had a nagging sense something had gone wrong the previous night. There was the throbbing ache behind my right eye, but that wasn't it. The bladder hovering between orange alert (high risk) and red (severe risk)? Hot flush? Parrot-cage mouth? No, none of them. But they were all in some way connected to whatever mistake I'd made . . . I went back to sleep.

Two hours later, wee situation now utterly critical, I shambled down to the loo. And that's where I realized what was bothering me about the reunion: I hadn't bought a round. My cheeks burnt up with shame.

Back in bed with a cup of tea, I pieced together my personal drink-buying history the night before. Arrive with Nicola and Nicola's dad, Reg. (Reg had been headmaster of one of the primary schools feeding the secondary school and thus been asked along.) Go to the bar. Pint for Reg, pint for me, vodka and tonic for Nicola. So far, so good.

Meet a few old schoolfriends. Nick, Andy Mac, Voakesy, chat chat, time for another one. Turns out these lads and others have set up a kitty. Fair dos; I'll stick to Reg and Nicola for the time being.

'Same again, Reg?'

'My round,' says Reg.

'I'll get them.'

'No, Robert, my round,' says Reg, more firmly.

Ritual complete, off he goes.

Talk to two chaps I used to know, David and Alastair. They aren't in the kitty.

'What are you drinking?'

'Pint of Stella, please.'

Track down Reg and Nicola. Reg is about to leave, Nicola'll have another vodka tonic. Proceed to the bar.

This is where things get complicated. The staff are slow, the queue is building, I estimate a five-, maybe even a ten-minute wait. Nothing worse, but nothing to be done. I prepare myself for the ordeal.

Hold on, Mark is ahead of me, he's getting served, he's seen me.

'What you having, Rob? I'll stick 'em on my round.'

'Nah,' I say. 'You're all right, I'm getting a few.'

He insists. I'm tempted. I crack. I tell Mark my order, offer a tenner by way of a contribution.

'Don't be daft.'

I take the drinks back.

'Cheers,' says David.

'Not me, mate. Mark bought them in the end.'

More chat. Jobs. Kids. Schools. Nottingham, where he is. London, where I am. The News International imbroglio. Thirsty work.

'My round,' says David.

'No, I'll get them.'

'You got the last one.'

'That was Mark.'

'Whatever.'

Off he goes.

And so it goes on. That damned kitty, every time I offer, they're all taken care of. Worse, after four or five, they don't care who's in the kitty and who isn't, so it's 'Clev's getting 'em in, Crammo. Do you want one?'

My resistance weakens. What am I going to do? Insist on buying my own? Or stand there yakking away like a girl while a succession of blokes brings me drinks, which is actually rather nice and convenient? I'm going to yak away like a girl, that's what. And I did.

Speaking of which, I did, of course, buy several drinks for my wife. And indeed for our mutual friend, Eman. And I suppose a southerner might argue this qualifies as buying a round. But a southerner would be wrong, because among northerners, if you're out in mixed company, women do not buy their own drinks or anybody else's, and therefore they are simply not part of the round-buying equation. It's not sexism, it's just the way it is.

Well, OK, it is sexism, but it's still the way it is.

In London perhaps, in special circumstances, such as if she will get served quicker, and provided any other men in our party are southerners and provided we're somewhere trendy and not in a traditional pub, not that there are many of them left, then Nicola might – I say might – go to the bar. But in Hull? Surrounded by Yorkshiremen? Unthinkable.

Put it this way: if there had been some horrible breakdown in drink-buying communication and Nicola or Eman had ended up queuing for the bar, as soon as any one of the lads in our group had seen it, even though some of them hadn't clapped eyes on either woman for thirty years, every one of us would have intervened to get the drink instead. I guarantee it. For Nicola or Eman to go to the bar would have cast shame on the entire group of men with them. Me doubly so, because I'm married to one of them.

So, no, buying Nicola and Eman drinks cannot alter the stark fact that I went out in Hull and failed to buy a round, words I can hardly bear to form in my own head, let alone commit to print. All I can do is apologize. And plead twenty-six years in the South by way of mitigation.

23 June 2012

It's Sod's Law: announce in advance you're going to do such and such, life turns around and smacks you in the face. Or the back, in my case. Or the sciatic nerve, to be really specific.

Absolutely no fun whatsoever, sciatica. Crippling pain in the lower back, then over one hip (the left, in my case), down the thigh, the shin and, worst of all, the heel. Tricky things, heels. I could barely walk for days, hobbling around, Frankie Howerd, ooo me back and so forth.

The upshot was, despite being due to join the Olympic torch a week ago, in Gateshead, I only actually caught up with the relay in York on Wednesday. Hence my long-delayed and much trumpeted (by me, at any rate) entry into the multimedia revolution was put off by a further four days. Grovelling apologies to anyone looking out for the promised tweets and whatnot in that period. You won't have found any, because there weren't any. I let you down. But only because my sciatic nerve let me down. Useless lump of gristle.

I didn't know it was sciatica. I thought I'd done my back playing tennis. But then my friend Liz came round and diagnosed it straight off. The doctor agreed. So did the physio. So did the internet. When I read the symptoms, I realized I've had it for years. Up until then, I thought I just did my back in a couple of times a year and that was what life was like; you went around moaning about it for a few days until the pain wore off.

In other words, the classic male reaction to illness or injury: ignorance, whingeing, fatalism dressed up as heroism and an absolute refusal to do anything to address the problem.

Anyway, funny I mentioned tennis, this being that time of year when we all go crazy for the sport. I thought I'd get in training early for this Wimbledon, get the drop on everyone else. The drop shot indeed. Hah hah. Hence arranging the game of tennis where I thought I'd done my back.

Well, not so much a game, more of a lesson. With Fabian, who is from Cameroon, bulging with muscle and diamond earrings. My kids think Fabian's the coolest guy they've ever met.

'But he's got a fold-up bike!' I say.

'Fabian's cool enough to get away with it,' they reply.

'He speaks like Inspector Clouseau!'

'Yeah, but that makes him even more cool.'

'He's got that silly basket for picking up all the balls!'

'We like the basket. It's clever, the way he doesn't have to bend down.'

'But he does a double-handed backhand!' I shout in exasperation.

'What's wrong with a double-handed backhand?'

'It's a form of cheating, brought in by baseline specialists such as Jimmy Connors and Chris Evert in the seventies. John McEnroe and Martina Navratilova didn't do double-handed backhands and neither do I.'

Pause.

'Who are all these people you're talking about?'

Sigh. Time marches on; what you still regard as vaguely contemporary actually became ancient history a long time ago. The grass-court game of my youth is fading away.

Hard courts, that's what's done it. Take the drop shot I mentioned: you can't do drop shots on hard courts; the ball bounces too high. Same with lobs. Same with serve and volley off the frame over the fence. All going or gone. Now you just whack it from somewhere up by your ears. Probably just as well. Much less running around.

Before the sciatica intervened, Fabian said I was progressing quite well. Reasonable forehand, not too much racket abuse, high-quality grunting on serve. We played a short game, tie-break rules, first to seven. He won 7–0. Fair enough, he's twenty years younger and a professional tennis coach. Damned ball just kept coming back.

One thing I've noticed: the standard of tennis (not my own, but in general) that you see on public courts is vastly improved.

Twenty years ago, most casual players were dreadful. Now, you see some high-quality hitting. I suppose people are fitter. Plus, the success of Tim Henman and Andy Murray must have had an impact. I always feel sorry for Henman and Murray. They're portrayed as classic British losers, but the fact is they are (or were) exceptionally good.

My wife also thinks Fabian's cool.

'They took some railings away from the pavement by the tennis court,' she told me breathlessly, 'and Fabian noticed a lot of kids on bikes were going straight out into the road because they were used to stopping at the railings, and then he saw the mayor walking through the park and told him about the railings, and the council put them back.'

'So,' I said, 'as well as being ultra-cool and smoking hot and really good at tennis, now you're saying he should get some sort of medal for saving countless small children's lives as well?'

And she said, 'Yes.'

7 July 2012

Crowds. Litter. Standing up for long periods. Queuing. Flashing lights. Loud music. Mass hysteria. Fandom. Banners. Marijuana. Being frisked by morose men wearing paramilitary uniforms. Drinking expensive warm beer out of a plastic beaker. Being ordered to 'Make more noise!' by twenty-one-year-old multi-millionaires singing about how money's not important.

Yes indeed, much of what I dislike the most form key components of your typical music festival. Which is why I don't go to them.

I'm trying to think of things I don't like doing that don't generally feature at a festival. Long-haul economy class, there's no real call for that. Eating liquorice, that's not integral. Interviewing Andie MacDowell, at least she's not likely to turn up. Small mercies, etc.

Still, the children have been clamouring to go to one, and they're not quite old enough to go unchaperoned, so I got some tickets to Radio 1's Hackney Weekend, a couple of miles from our house.

Off we all went on the Saturday, a nice wholesome family day out, listening to Jay-Z going on about niggahs and bitches. And then off again on Sunday, another nice wholesome family day out, listening to Rihanna going on about shagging. S&M shagging, mostly.

Obviously, the children tried to ditch us the instant we were through Security.

'We're going to see Rizzle Kicks.'

'OK, I'll come too, who did you say they were? The Grizzle Dicks?'

'No, Rizzle Kicks.'

'Rizla Pricks?'

'They're called Rizzle Kicks. They're really famous.'

'Oh, the Tickling Sticks, that's nice. I didn't know Ken Dodd was going to be here. I like Ken Dodd.'

'Who's Ken Dodd?'

'A comedian with a feather duster.'

'Please go away.'

The odd tragic ageing muso aside, I was the oldest person there by some distance. Well, my wife's five months older than me but she looks younger than her age, whereas I don't, so she doesn't count.

I interviewed David Bailey a few weeks ago.

'How old are you?' he asked.

'Forty-seven.'

'Yeah, I thought about fifty,' he said. Cheers, Dave! Set me up nicely for the summer, that did.

'On a scale of one to ten,' I said to my wife, 'one being the ultimate thrill and ten being catatonic, how bored are you?'

'Six,' she said. 'You?'

'Remember that TV series in the seventies, *The Water Margin*? Japanese? Badly dubbed? Lots of decapitation?'

'Yes.'

'I've been thinking how all these banners stuck in the ground here are exactly like the ones the guys on horseback used to carry in the opening credits to *The Water Margin*.'

'I see.'

I set myself up in the media enclosure (free coffee, not too noisy), scribbling in my notebook while all these young online types hunched over their laptops muttering about doublers and combo updates and barrel distortion. I spent fifteen minutes trying to persuade my daughter that the Ford Focus parked backstage belonged to Beyoncé.

'I've decided to view myself as the elder statesman of the press tent,' I said to Nicola, about 10.30 on the Saturday night, taking a break from Jay-Z shouting about being the best rapper in the world, yadda yadda yadda.

'And at least we've got somewhere to sit down inside,' she said, yawning.

Walking home, we got soaked.

Just not my scene, I'm afraid. I don't dislike festivals because I'm forty-seven. I didn't like them when I was seventeen – I just hadn't worked up the courage to admit it. I went to Glastonbury in 1983, never felt the need to return. I went to the Futurama all-nighter at Queen's Hall, Leeds, in 1980. U2, Siouxsie and the Banshees, Echo & the Bunnymen. Very tiring. I went to Rock Against Racism in Victoria Park, 1978. The Clash and Buzzcocks. Willing it to end.

Oh yeah, I've served my time. I went to the Style Council in Brockwell Park, Brixton, 1983. Unforgiving Jam fans hated the new soul sound and the way Weller had draped a pink jumper casually over his shoulders. They started chucking bottles so he stormed off after only two tracks. Of course, I pretended to be outraged like everyone else. Secretly, I was thinking: excellent, might make the earlier train home.

The only festival I remember with affection was the Specials at Roundhay Park in Leeds, 1981. Not because of the music, although I do like the Specials, but because some National Front bastards turned up and there was quite a decent fight. Good fun, that was.

I was generally more interested in the politics than the music. I must have been the only sixteen-year-old at an Anti-Nazi League or CND rally in 1980 waiting for the Jam to pipe down so I could listen to Tony Benn.

Next day, back for more. Jessie J. Florence + the Machine. Tinie Tempah. I like Tinie Tempah. Even so, when he tells everyone to 'Put ya hands in the air!' I say, 'No, Tempah, don't want to.'

A small act of rebellion. About as political as these things get nowadays.

8 September 2012

Finding ourselves unexpectedly home alone for a day or two, my wife and I decide to go for a bike ride together, something I don't think we've done since 1978, when we were both fourteen years old. The children get older and more independent, Nicola and I revert to doing what we did when we were children ourselves. Perhaps next weekend we can find a disco in a Scout hut to go to.

It never ceases to intrigue people, incidentally, to discover my wife and I were at school together. 'That's sweet,' they say.

And then Nicola always pre-empts their next question, with rather too much alacrity for my comfort, with her familiar mantra, 'We were just friends then nothing more than that we weren't boyfriend and girlfriend we went out with other people before during and after university we only got together when we were twenty-seven.'

'Twenty-five,' I say.

Anyway, bike-wise, not a great deal has changed since 1978. As in 1978, Nicola's on a Shopper, three-speed, small wheels, basket on the front. As in 1978, Nicola determines the destination, route, speed and duration of the outing. And, as in 1978, I make sure to do a fair bit of nonchalant no-hands, in the hope this might impress her sufficiently to merit a snog.

Nothing doing.

Over the past twenty years, adding up the number of miles I have cycled in and around east London, I'd guess that my total stands at around forty thousand. Nicola, meanwhile, a very occasional cyclist, has put in no more than a few dozen miles.

Perhaps surprising, then, that she should assume such total

command of proceedings? Er, no, not surprising at all, not to anyone familiar with the, ahem, robust leadership qualities of my wife. The one surprise, indeed, is that Nicola never actually tells me what gear I ought to be in (gear as in sprocket, not gear as in attire), as she does on the rare occasions I am permitted to drive the car. I'm sure, if the joint bike rides become a regular event, such instructions will be issued in due course.

Presented with a range of unfolding choices, this way or that way, here or there, my wife will assess the situation and form an opinion as to the best course of action.

Of course we all do this, all the time. But Nicola does it out loud. 'Let's go down here,' she'll say. Or, 'Look at that over there,' or, 'Let's lock the bikes up here and go into that café there.'

My approach is similar in most respects. I'll proceed, taking in my surroundings, noting something of interest, assessing possible options, in much the same way, as far as I can know, that Nicola does. But I don't say anything. Or barely anything. A grunt, perhaps. An 'OK by me.' My process is almost entirely silent. I hoard opinions. Nicola divulges them, instantly and constantly.

To generalize wildly, but possibly not that wildly, this different approach is not just specific to Nicola and me, but to many women and men. She says I'm secretive, I say she's bossy.

'Don't tell me what to do all the time,' I say.

'I don't know what you want; I'm not a mind-reader,' says Nicola.

Sound familiar?

Why, women may wonder, are men so secretive so much of the time? Why can't they just come out and say what they're thinking and then it can be debated and a way forward found? That, women say, is how they find solutions to problems. They put a view out there, they take in other views, other facts, they modify their initial view. It's a never-ending process.

I'll tell you why men keep their mouths shut, and it's not because whatever is under discussion is too trivial, or beneath us, or our minds are on more important matters. And it's not because we're not good at talking about our feelings. Gigantic red herring, that one. It's because deep down, we want, when we speak, to deliver ourselves not just of a mere opinion, but an absolute definitive unanswerable judgement. And we don't know what that is.

And even – the tragedy deepens – even if we did, we know it would sound ridiculous. So we say nothing.

We want to be God. Or at least, king.

Or at least, chief. Or at least, wise.

When I pronounce on whether we go left or right on the bike ride, I want it to be a speech, a lecture, a sermon, whole, consummate, final, carved in marble, with footnotes. But I also know that is very silly. And I also know she might disagree. So I say, hey, I don't mind. But what seems all groovy and chilled springs from a deeply authoritarian impulse.

Men want to be bossy, but come over all consensual. Women want to be consensual, but come over all bossy. That's what my wife told me to conclude, in any event.

19 January 2013

So I'm at work last Wednesday and – ping – I get a text from my daughter. She's in a stand-off with her mother over some hockey kit left at school. Nicola has told her that she, Rachel, has got to go to retrieve the kit the next day, even though Rachel has the day off because the school is busy hosting entrance exams. Rachel thinks her mother is being unreasonable. Her text is an attempt to canvass support for when the argument resumes.

I ignore the text and phone Nicola. Gotta stick together,

haven't you, as parents? Otherwise they'll just walk all over you.

Nicola sighs. 'Let's talk about it when you get in,' she says.

Big Daddy Bob makes his way home. A chilly evening on the bike, and yet our hero is comforted by the warm glow that soon-to-be-dispensed patriarchal duty provides.

Rachel is watching TV in the front room. I wouldn't want to use the word 'sulk', so let's say instead that my daughter's expression betrays a degree of unhappiness concerning her recent past and immediate future. Nicola is reading in the back room. Sam is lurking in the kitchen, scenting an opportunity to make capital from his sister's discomfort.

Initial assessment completed, Big Daddy Bob opens a beer and tucks into his tea. First things first.

Both of our children, incidentally, have recently mentioned their friends' confusion over the fact that they, Sam and Rachel, refer to their evening meal as their tea, as opposed to their dinner, or, God forbid, their s*pp*r.

'Why do we call tea tea?' they ask us.

'Because that's what it is,' we tell them.

'But is it?' they say.

'Listen,' we tell them. 'Tea was good enough for us and it's good enough for you.'

My wife briefs me on the hockey kit dispute. Rachel has started attending a hockey club on Thursday evenings. She has been bought a new stick, gumshield (or mouthguard, as they are now called) and boots. These items are all at school. Nicola has been telling Rachel for days to bring them home. Yet hockey club is tomorrow night and Rachel has the day off school!

Still with me? Nicola has told Rachel she must get the bus to school in the morning as per usual and retrieve the kit. Rachel is refusing to go. Nicola is insistent, partly because Rachel needs the gear, partly because it'll teach her a lesson. What do I think?

I agree, I say. Absolutely. One hundred per cent. Let's get the little madam in here and I'll tell her what's what.

Rachel is summoned. Sam darts in behind her, grinning expectantly. I order him upstairs, he protests, I stand firm, he goes. Lining Rachel up in front of me, trying my very best to look stern, I hand down the parental verdict.

Rachel protests. No, I say, you're going and that's that. But I've got the day off, says Rachel. Hard luck, I tell her. But I can use my old stick, she argues, and some other trainers, and I don't really need a mouthguard because we're only doing skills and drills not matchplay and it won't matter just one time. I say: er . . . OK, that sounds reasonable.

I add – in a majestically authoritative touch, I think you'll agree – 'Now go and watch the telly!'

Nicola advances.

'That went well,' I say, attempting to lighten the mood.

She isn't having it. 'You really are pathetic,' she says, launching into a dissection of my failure, stretching back close on fourteen years, to ever successfully discipline my daughter. The words 'wrapped', 'around' and 'her little finger' are employed.

'I'm just trying to reach a compromise,' I wail, reaching for the classic cry of the indulgent father down the ages.

Upstairs, downstairs, the debate continues. Over time, Nicola relents on the boots and the stick; her sticking point is the mouthguard.

'The one thing the woman at the hockey club said was, "Make sure she brings a mouthguard."'

'I don't need it,' insists Rachel.

'You played hockey for years without a mouthguard,' I remind Nicola.

'Yeah, and I got hit in the face and all my teeth were loose afterwards,' she responds.

Long story short, I volunteer to take Rachel to JD Sports in the morning and buy another damned mouthguard.

'They won't have one,' predicts Nicola.

And guess what? When Rachel and I ring up at 9 a.m., Nicola is proved right. Adidas, Sports Direct, the Nike shop at Westfield, they don't have any mouthguards either. Neither, Lord have mercy, does the sainted John Lewis.

'I suppose I'll have to go to school,' says Rachel, all resigned and forlorn.

Nonsense, I tell her, and duck off into the garage. Where, after a long search, I unearth a wrinkled, deformed, frankly utterly minging gumshield I used to wear for boxing. We soak it in boiling water and it sort of fits.

Wait till your father gets home, eh? Not quite the threat it once was.

23 February 2013

So, last Wednesday, ten days ago, my wife and I go out for a Valentine's Day dinner.

Not on the Thursday, you will note, which was actual Valentine's Day, because that would have involved me phoning up the restaurant three weeks previously, which is when Nicola first suggested I should. As it was, I had hoped for the best and left it to the Monday three days prior to the big night. Mistake.

My report of that call went something like this: 'Nicola, I've got good news and bad news. The bad news is, our favourite restaurant is fully booked for Thursday night. The good news is, I have managed to get us a table elsewhere, somewhat later than customary, but it could be romantic sitting down to dinner at 11 p.m., like the Spanish. And this place is quite local. It's an Indian on Brick Lane.'

The upshot was I called our preferred venue back and secured a table at a normal time on the Wednesday, Valentine's Day minus one.

So in we go, maître d', fake smile, sir and madam, can I take your coats, all that awkward stuff. 'And your bag, sir?' he asks, eyebrows raised.

'No, you're all right, I'll keep it with me,' I tell him, clutching my rucksack protectively to my chest, aware of my dormant northern accent springing into life, as it always seems to in high-end settings. Some sort of pre-emptive positioning against accusations of turning into a soft southern sell-out, no doubt. I realize when I said, 'No, you're all right,' to the maître d', I'd very nearly put 'pal' on the end.

'You didn't really have to bring that with you, did you?' says Nicola as we are led to the table.

'Please,' I say, 'we've talked about this before: don't slag off my bag.'

'I just think sometimes you could come out without your rucksack,' she says. 'It'd be good for you, liberating.'

'I don't want to be liberated from my bag,' I reply, hugging it ever tighter.

Ah-ha, here's the menu. We study it, then listen politely to the waitress as she describes the soupe du jour, the plat du jour, the poisson du jour, the colour of the bog roll in the lavatory du jour, all manner of detail.

We pretend to think it all over, faking the weighing up of options as might a proper gourmet, and then, after a suitable interval, we both order steak.

Nicola and I may hold robustly opposing views on a number of issues – the desirability of taking many of your belongings to a restaurant in a rucksack, for example – but in the matter of scoffing red meat on a night out, we are as one. Medium rare. With loads of chips. And a salad you don't eat.

Chat. Glass of wine. More chat. More wine. A little light eavesdropping on the conversations either side and then, voilà, the starters arrive. I appear to have ordered mushrooms on toast. Fair enough, tuck that away in short order, dive in for bread and butter slice number six. All good.

It being a special occasion – and it also being utterly freezing outside – I resist the urge to go for a cigarette between courses. Good call, as it turns out: the service is prompt, here comes a French fella bearing a mound of beef. Teeth starting to twitch, I only just succeed in allowing Nicola first dibs. What a gent.

But, twenty minutes later, what manner of outrage is this? For the first time in a long shared history of carnivorous greed, the Almond–Crampton pairing (not to put Nicola's name first feels like misleading my public) appears to have suffered an ignominious portion-related defeat. Illness? A heavy lunch? Too much bread? Surely not an attack of self-restraint? However confused the excuse, the evidence is clear: three hefty slices of cow, in plain view, uneaten. Stone cold they may be, hefty and delicious they nevertheless remain. And yet there they lie for all to see.

Nicola reacts in a mature fashion. 'I'm full up,' she says.

'So am I,' I say. 'But that doesn't matter, I'm going to eat it anyway.'

'Don't be silly,' she says. 'They brought a lot. It's fine to leave a bit.'

'No, it isn't.'

'Yes, it is. I often leave some food on my plate.'

'Yeah,' I say. 'And then I always eat what you've left.'

'Well, this time you don't have to.'

'OK,' I say, after a little sulk. 'I won't have it now, I'll take it with me.'

'That'll be embarrassing.'

'I know.' I nod grimly. 'But I can't have it said I couldn't finish a steak. And anyway, there was an £8 supplementary charge.'

A waiter hovers.

'Can I ask a favour?' I say. 'I'd like to take this beef home for my dog. He's massive.'

Pretending you own a dog to disguise your failure to see off a plate of meat? Doesn't get much more beta male than that.

23 March 2013

If I had to rank the members of my immediate family (and for present purposes, I do) in terms of their will to win, their need to come top, I'd go: Rachel; Nicola; me; Sam. That ranking – of ambition, if not always of attainment – holds true for sport, games, exams, map-reading, who makes the best toast . . . Pretty much everything.

Drilling down into the data, as we ultra-modern, twenty-first-century types like to say, I'd have to admit that Rachel, Nicola and myself are not separated by much. My wife and I are competitive people. Our killer instinct may have been blunted somewhat by age and experience – but not by a great deal.

From an early age, it was apparent our daughter had inherited a double dose of the same urge to dominate.

Even as a baby, Rachel would sniff out a challenge and take it on. Around nine months old, fed up with nightly confinement to her cot, she simply smashed her way out. We found her asleep on the floor in the morning, exhausted by the effort, the struts designed to contain her buckled, bent, broken, beaten.

Sam, by contrast, has always tended to go with the flow. When he was about nine, at a school sports day, he spent what was supposed to be the sprint jogging in an outside lane, chatting to other pupils and parents he had spotted in the crowd. The desirability of victory, even the concept of victory, didn't appear to register.

That's the setting, the context, the story our family tells itself and others.

And yet, human beings are complicated creatures, not readily subject to neat summaries. Sam, for instance, has decided that, while almost all sport is irrelevant to his self-image, he wants to be good at pool. The balls and baize, the pockets and potting, the cue and, er . . . um . . . coin – the coin, the one you put in the slot, which then jams so that you have to ask the scary landlady for a refund – these matters have become important to him.

When he first played, a few years ago, Sam's every shot was a calamity in waiting: the ball to a bystander's face, the ragged trench dug in the baize, the careless cue tip to his own eye, each was a mere heartbeat away. Since then, he's got a lot better. Over our week in Finland, we played a fair bit of pool in the hotel. He won a few frames, neither of us missed many sitters, we didn't let ourselves or our country down.

Just as importantly, the contests were conducted in a sportsmanlike manner. Play to win, sure. But observe the rules, no special pleading, respect your opponent, shake hands at the end. That's the way I was taught by my dad; that's the way my son has been taught by his. All fine and dandy.

Until Nicola and Rachel turned up.

'Go away,' said Sam.

'Yeah,' I said, 'you're only here to cause trouble.'

'Don't be like that,' said Nicola.

'We want to play you at doubles,' said Rachel. 'And we're going to win.'

Reluctantly, knowing no good would come of it but seeing no way out, Sam and I agreed.

Many moons ago, in the mid-nineties, pre-children, Nicola and I would play pool. In those days, we were well matched, i.e., both consistently mediocre. Over the ensuing years, however, while I have managed the odd cheeky session here and there, Nicola, I was not remotely sorry to note, had let her pool standards slide. Rachel? Quick learner, Rachel, yet still, the girl's barely ever held a cue. Sam and I cruised into an early lead.

Which, of course, is when they started ridiculing us for taking it too seriously. Which meant, on the subsequent numerous occasions when one of them potted the wrong ball, or failed to hit any ball at all, Sam and I felt obliged to waive our right to a free shot. This leniency meant they eventually caught us up. Before long, like Dennis Taylor against Steve Davis in 1985, it was all down to the black.

I missed; Nicola didn't.

At which point, mother and daughter went wild in righteous feminist celebration – cheering, whooping, gyrating, go girl-fren', all that stuff, worse than a rabble on daytime TV. After several minutes, they skipped off arm in arm across the hotel lobby like Morecambe and Wise at the end of their show.

'It's all right, Sammy,' I said after a while. 'They've gone now.'

'So,' Sam said, fighting back his rage. 'They force us to play. They make fun of us for playing properly. We let them off loads of foul shots, they win, they pretend they've won a real game.'

'Excellent recap,' I agreed.

'But it's not fair,' he muttered.

'No, son,' I replied, 'and neither is life, so get used to it. Anyway, we still should have won. We had our chances; we didn't take them. Next time, we will. Now rack 'em up.'

11 May 2013

My wife and I went up to Hereford for our friend Floyd's fiftieth. The children stayed in London, Cousin Steve in charge. They were invited, but these days, at sixteen and fourteen, they don't always – or, in fact, ever – want to socialize with us. Still, never mind, Sam and Rachel's absence gave me and Nicola the chance to resurrect old unresolved tensions and argue bitterly about the route. It was just like old times.

The satnav on our Honda broke several years ago, an inconvenience to Nicola when I am asleep, slumped to her left, face creased by the seatbelt. But no great loss when I am awake, because obviously I always know which way to go. Not for nothing am I known – admittedly exclusively by myself – as the Human Compass. Tell me two points on these islands, or most of western Europe come to that, and I'll tell you the optimal way between them, swiftly, concisely, correctly. Don't need a satnav, don't need a map, don't need any input from the driver, damn sure don't need to stop and – the horror – ask for directions, as Nicola occasionally suggests.

Maybe it's nature – a wisp of DNA encoding the *AA Road Atlas of Great Britain*, with annual revisions, buried deep in the Bobbly brain. Or maybe it's nurture – my parents were both geography teachers after all; I've been around globes and maps, charts and street plans all my life. Or maybe it's a bit of both, I don't know. I prefer to see my ability always to know the correct route without reference to any navigational aids whatsoever as simply a gift, a mystery best left unexamined.

Nicola doesn't have quite the same confidence in the gift as I do. Sometimes I suspect she doesn't believe in the gift at all, and instead thinks I merely suffer from the classic male aversion to ever consulting a map in a car. She doesn't accept the argument that 'the only map I need' – taps right temple smugly – 'is right in here'. She hasn't any patience with 'and besides, a map is only a representation; what really counts is sensing the lie of the land'. She is not impressed with the analogy of a Red Indian tracker, leaping from his pony to sniff the trail. She just says, 'Please look at the atlas or we'll go wrong.'

This matter of my direction-finding skills is one of the few remaining active battlefields in our marriage. After fifteen years, most have fallen silent. Either I've won (accompanying her to Ikea, say, or rather, not accompanying her to Ikea), or an uneasy truce is maintained (my smoking), or Nicola's will has prevailed (everything else). On wanting to be regarded as the Human Compass, however, I have held out. Something to do with defending the Crampton family's geographical honour, no doubt.

And thus I am ashamed to report, as the Honda noses through Cheltenham at 10 mph when it should be zipping along a ring road around Gloucester at 60 mph, that Nicola can chalk up another victory, some kink in the Human Compass having not long before caused it to recommend turning in precisely the opposite direction to the one required. For the next twenty minutes our vehicle is gripped by an icy silence I imagine would be familiar to couples the world over.

As we enter the wilds of the Wye, the madness of the Marches, the going becomes bitty and bendy. No doubt the locals hereabouts employ all manner of wily bootlegging *Dukes of Hazzard*-style short cuts, Bo and Luke vaulting the General Lee over the creek while Daisy Duke distracts Sheriff Rosco with her notorious cut-off shorts, etc. But for these incomers, the navigator's claim to an instinctive route-divining sixth sense in ashes, the map must be consulted.

Which is, dutifully, defeatedly, what I do. The atmosphere thaws, the Cheltenham debacle recedes in the rear-view mirror. An apology is offered, one or two pleasantries exchanged. Still half an hour from Floyd's house, it looks as if relations will be repaired in time.

But hold on, what's this? Nicola says it isn't helpful for me to inform her of a turn-off a few seconds before she must take it. She needs more warning, and ideally more information.

'What sort of information?'

She says it would be useful to know up to a mile or so before a turn, and what landmarks might precede it, and what road numbers and place names were likely to be included on the relevant sign.

'Oh, for God's sake, Nicola,' I snort. 'We're not in a bloody rally.'

'It helps when you're driving to know what's coming up,' she says.

'Well, I wouldn't know about that because you never let me drive.'

'I thought we were supposed to be being nice to each other?'

And so on, the happy couple heading off into the west, swiftly lost to sight in the fold of a hill.

25 May 2013

Floyd in Hereford one week, Karen in Cheshire the next: those fiftieth-birthday parties are coming so thick and fast I'm beginning to suspect our old friend, a gap in the space–time continuum – as so often opens up, with calamitous consequences, in *Doctor Who* – may be in play. Certainly something's not right. It isn't five minutes since every bash we went to was a fortieth.

I know that youngsters – one minute knee-high, the next hulking around the place – seem to have twice as many birthdays as grown-ups, yet I find that life also accelerates in middle age. Next August it'll be my turn to clock up the half-century. Doesn't bear thinking about.

Karen is my wife's best friend. They've been mates since they were at university thirty years ago. When Nicola and I started going out.

I noticed she was always ready, willing and able, first flush of romance notwithstanding, to tear herself from my arms for a lengthy phone call with her pal.

Well, I say 'lengthy'; others might prefer 'epic'. Or perhaps 'interminable'.

I thought, hold on, who is this Karen character who gets asked for advice every time my girlfriend has a decision to make? Should I be jealous?

No, I swiftly accepted, I should not. Karen's counsel was far superior to anything I might offer. Measured, sensible, morally correct, on any issue ranging from a change of job to a choice of curtains (assuming there is a moral aspect to curtains, which there may well be), Karen was out of my league.

I also worked out that if Nicola was busy nattering away to Karen, she wasn't giving me any grief.

Karen's a Manc. She may have grown up in Clitheroe or some such place, and her family allegiance may well be to Blackburn Rovers, and she may now reside not far from Tarporley, a full forty-five minutes from Manchester proper, but all that is by the by. As far as I'm concerned, the evidence is clear. Karen is a Manc and after many years living in the South, she has now gone back home to Mancland.

No problem with that. I only mention it following a question my daughter asked on the way to Cheshire. Three hours in, I had recently woken from a long sleep. Sam was still unconscious. Rachel had enjoyed the sort of crafty doze she later denies because she views sleeping in the car as a sign of weakness. Nicola, who barely requires any sleep in a bed, let alone a car, was of course driving.

'If you could choose to live anywhere,' Rachel piped up from the back seat, 'anywhere at all, where would it be?'

Now, to you, this may seem no more than an entertaining way to kill ten minutes on the road. For me and Nicola, however, answering such an apparently frivolous question is not something we can treat lightly.

Why? Because as northerners living in the South we are aware that the issue of where we would prefer to be is governed by a strict convention. For reasons of family ties, sentiment, regional solidarity, quality of life and, not least, the price of property, we are supposed to say – the rules clearly state – that we are only down here among the shandy drinkers for the money.

Thus, when challenged, you must say emphatically that if it weren't for the work, you'd be back up the M1 in a heartbeat.

I've heard myself saying as much – to northerners, to avoid an argument, and to southerners, to start one.

But it's not true. Not for us, anyhow. Nicola and I lived in Hull for many years, we left, we don't want to live there again, no offence. Even if I didn't have to be in London for work – and these days, I don't, not really – I'd still want to be here. It's the most thrilling place on the planet.

Sorry to break ranks, but I can't see why a northerner who has stayed in the North, when invited to fantasize in a similar way, is allowed to say 'Andalusia' or 'California' or 'Provence' or any of the other usual suspects, while I have to say 'Hull'.

Then again, I couldn't contemplate a move to anywhere exotic, either. Partly because paradise has a habit of turning sour, or at least dull, and partly because I used up so much energy getting myself from Hull to London I haven't enough left for onward movement. So, no, you can keep your Tuscanys and your Umbrias, your Manhattans and your Malibus. It turned out my horizon extended as far as Hackney – but no further.

Naturally, 'We're happy where we are' – being neither an expression of salty northern loyalty nor exciting globetrotting wanderlust – was hardly the answer Rachel wanted to hear. By the time I'd finished explaining why it was, nonetheless, the God's honest truth, she had fallen back to sleep.

15 June 2013

Unlike many parents, my wife and I take a hard line on helping the children with their homework. Sure, we'll give them a few pointers, a few hints, some general tips on what is required. But beyond that, we both take the old-school view that it's their task, not ours, and that for us to get too involved with the causes of the English Civil War or irregular French verbs or x plus blinking y would invalidate the whole process. This principled stance is, you will appreciate, not always a popular one. Especially at 8 p.m. on a Sunday.

Exams, however, in which both our children are currently embroiled, they're different. Doing their homework for them? That doesn't serve any useful purpose, long term. Helping them prepare for an exam, however? That is a legitimate exploitation of familial resources. They've still got to sit the damn thing themselves, right?

My wife and I – and not just us, but our parents, a majority of our siblings and cousins and most of our friends and colleagues – prospered in large part as a result of an ability to do well in exams. It'd be weird if we didn't seek to hand this ability on. I once had a friend who complained that her boyfriend's family only valued 'golf, cars and money'. I sympathized – it's a bleak combination – but I would still defend the right of that family to give their nearest and dearest a head start in matters relating to, well, golf, cars and money, should the need ever arise. Only natural, isn't it?

In short, if my son comes to me and says, 'Help me write this history essay,' I say, 'Sorry Sam, can't do it.'

Yet if he comes to me and says, 'Help me revise for this history exam,' I say, 'Sure thing, son. When's good for you?'

As regards the detail, Nicola and I divide – not entirely equitably, as will be seen – our intellectual efforts. As indicated,

I cover history. She does geography, French, Latin, art, maths and physics. English throws up a dilemma.

On the one hand, I write for a living. On the other, Nicola's got an English degree, more patience, more time, greater pedagogical skill, first-class concentration, a better appreciation of what is required and far superior grammar. Oh, and she's also almost always sober, whereas often I am not.

Not that much of a dilemma then, all things considered. Cousin Steve is drafted in to advise on tricky maths and physics when it turns complicated and nasty, as physics is wont to do. And Cousin Steve's equally clever pal Zara is on hand for chemistry and biology and to explain such maths as Steve has travelled too far down Geek Street to be able to convert into words. And that's the syllabus covered, by and large. Except Rachel's Mandarin. The girl's on her own for Mandarin. Ni hao!

Strange, you might think, that a journalist would not be the go-to parent for advice on English. The fact is, though, that the prose style required by this trade wins no favours from exam boards. We're all about clarity and compression. English exams reward the opposite. Newspapers take the view that when people open their mouths, they don't do so to exclaim, explain, declaim or proclaim something, but to say it. What examiners see as range, I regard as verbosity. Best to keep well away.

My reductionist tendencies also create problems when I try to help out with history. History essays require competing arguments to be rehearsed, due respect paid to different schools of thought, interwoven chains of causation scrutinized. Whatever else it may be, the assumption goes, history is most definitely a very complicated business. Trouble is, the older I get, the more I come to believe that history isn't complicated at all.

What, in your view, were the chief causes of the American Civil War?

'Southern racists.'

Explain the growth of the civil rights movement in post-war America.

'Southern racists again.'

Analyse the political, diplomatic, social and economic factors behind the outbreak of war in 1914.

'Germans wanted to take over Europe; had to be stopped.'

Analyse the political, diplomatic, social and economic factors behind the outbreak of war in 1939.

'Germans still wanted to take over Europe; had to be stopped again.'

Summarize the main reasons leading to the end of the Cold War and the subsequent collapse of the Soviet Union.

'Communism doesn't work.'

And so on.

Naturally my children, schooled in the methodology of a bit of this, a bit of that, six of one, half a dozen of the other, regard my pronouncements as embarrassingly unsophisticated.

'You're supposed to know about history,' they moan.

'I do know,' I tell them. 'The great Dolly Parton likes to say, "It takes a lot of money to look this cheap." Well, it also takes a lot of study to say something simple. You'll thank me when you're older.'

22 June 2013

Friday night, having an end-of-week drink with my colleague Hilary, obviously I ask what the weekend holds for her.

'Girlie stuff,' she says. 'Shopping, a pedicure. Nothing exciting, but at least on Monday morning I'll have very pretty toenails, which is more than you can say.'

'Don't be too sure about that,' I tell her. 'My friend Liz the podiatrist is coming over with her clippers tonight.'

And not before time.

Although we've known each other since we were eleven-year-old kids in suburban Hull, my wife and I didn't get together until we were twenty-five and both living in London. Always slower off the mark than Nicola, I had been in the capital for only a few months, whereas she'd been here for four years. Given that, I can't deny it surprised me when, in the early weeks of our relationship, Nicola announced we'd be heading back up north the following weekend because she needed a haircut.

'You still get your hair cut in Hull?'

'Yes, Simon does it, has done for ages.'

'But you've lived in London four years.'

'That's right.'

'And Hull is almost two hundred miles away.'

'Yes.'

'And you get your hair cut, what, every three months or so?'

'Yes. It's a very personal thing, hair. I like the way Simon does it.'

That routine went on for quite a few years, only coming to an end when Simon the hairdresser emigrated to Melbourne, an even more inconveniently long way from London than is Hull.

I have to say that, at the time, I thought Nicola's loyalty a little excessive. Now, however, an older and wiser man, I can totally understand the desire, in certain vital areas of personal grooming, to stick to what you know. Except while with Nicola the vital area was hair, with me it's toenails.

Martyr to my toenails, I am. Thick, curly, hungrily ingrowing given even the sniff of a chance, keeping these horrible mis-shapen horns in order is not so much a cosmetic procedure, more a mechanical task, one best performed with the sort of implements carried around by military doctors in the nine-teenth century. Having said that, provided I went to see Liz at her practice in Islington every couple of months, expansion could be sufficiently controlled to avoid anything truly disgusting occurring.

But then a year ago Liz moved to Khartoum. And thus a vital strut in the Bob support edifice was booted way off into the eastern Sahara desert. Now, Khartoum isn't as far as Melbourne. But flying to the Sudan six times a year to have my toenails cut is an indulgence beyond my means. Yet no way was I about to let anyone else loose in this most sensitive region. For a while, with Liz coming back to London now and then, I struggled along, the unusually cold weather helping my cause, because toenails, like hair, grow much quicker when it's warm. But then, having returned to Sudan after Christmas, Liz didn't come back for more than five months. After which my toes were not a pretty sight. Words such as 'red', 'inflamed', 'bulbous' and 'very f***ing painful' were starting to be employed.

A Sunday night in mid-June. My house. Liz, back on UK soil for less than twenty-four hours, glasses propped up on her forehead, studies the problem she had known would be landing in her lap around about now. Nicola has fetched the desk lamp from my study, the better to illuminate proceedings. Surgical spirit, kitchen roll and various medieval tools are to hand. The children safely quarantined in another room, watching TV, shielded from the horror. No place for kids.

'This,' Liz announces, 'is going to hurt.'

The patient, in his mind's eye John Wayne stretched flat on the kitchen table in a remote farmhouse way out west in about 1860, a paraffin lamp swinging from a beam, the only anaesthetic – the only antiseptic as well – a splash of bourbon, the bullet not life-threatening but nonetheless in urgent need of removal by the exceptionally attractive young frontierswoman in the figure-hugging checked shirt and jeans, nods in recognition of the prognosis.

'Let's get on with it,' he grunts, beads of sweat springing out on his forehead.

Liz goes to work. Pain – proper pain – immediately ensues. Nicola, making what sound a lot like gagging noises, gets up and leaves the room.

A test of manhood for the ages, this. Nerve-endings fanning out like tentacles across the centuries, snaking over the rocks of Thermopylae, the valleys of Balaclava, the mud of Passchendaele, the gorse of Tumbledown, the grit and gravel of Helmand. To wriggle and to writhe, to wince and to whimper? Or to suck it up in silence? Primitive situation, two stark options, this one or that one, hero or coward, good or bad. A definitive moment. Which are you going to choose?

'Oh, do shut up, Bob,' says Liz, 'I've had seven-year-olds make less noise than you.'

3 August 2013

To get to my family's holiday home in south-west France, you take a series of back roads of gradually dwindling width, and then, for the last quarter-mile or so, you turn on to a more or less paved track, winding lazily up a slope to the house. To your right is a plum orchard; to your left, the sunflower and wheat fields unroll in a Van Gogh haze to the horizon. In the middle distance, three miles away, the local bastide shimmers on a hill.

There are more dramatic views in the world, more spectacular, more engaging, but for sheer pastoral prettiness, few can rival this one. If you're fortunate, you may spot one of the deer that roam the nearby wood. Or you may run into Jean-Luc, surely the most handsome plum farmer in all of France. In the absence of either sighting, however, when I drive up that track, I simply remind myself that I am a very, very lucky boy indeed.

A bastide, incidentally, is a fortified medieval town or village, not a Gascon corruption of the English word meaning an illegitimate, unpleasant or unforgiving individual.

I'd also like to mention that the way Americans pronounce 'Van Gogh' as 'Van Go' is really, really silly and ought to stop.

And yet, though I have surveyed this idyll on countless occasions over two decades, a tiny niggle of irritation compromises my good spirits. The niggle arises from the existence of a second way – a covert, clandestine, cross-country way – to access the house. And while I have walked this route many times, I have never driven it. Why? My wife won't let me.

This other route follows a rutted, boggy, overgrown path through a thick and ancient wood. I say path, it's as much a tunnel as a path, dark as night in places, branches reaching out from side to side and above and below, until eventually the trees peter out and there, as in a fairy tale, stands our house. How utterly thrilling is that?

'Let's drive back through the wood,' I've been saying to Nicola, every year for twenty years.

'No,' Nicola has been replying for just as long. 'You need a quad bike or a 4x4 for that path. In an ordinary car, you'd get stuck.'

'Oh come on, gotta take a risk now and again.'

'It's not a risk, it's a 100 per cent certainty you'd get stuck.'

'Don't be boring.'

'I'm being practical.'

Well, on this last trip, I lost patience with practical. Returning to the house in the Volvo, Sam and Rachel and Rachel's friend Rionach in the car but, crucially, with Nicola elsewhere, I swing, in what I imagine is a rakish, devil-may-care manner, off the road and into the forest. The children, who've been lobbying to go Back Way, as they call it, since they were old enough to talk, are beside themselves in the back seat, setting up a loud chant of 'Back Way! Back Way! Back Way!'

The going is good, progress slow but steady, sunlight piercing the foliage, a wide selection of God's creatures chirping and scuffling and scurrying in the undergrowth. I feel happy beyond reason. Not just happy, but vital, vigorous, virile. And vibrant. And, er, yeah, vivid, that's another one. And vivacious. But not verdant, because then I'd be all covered in grass and shrubs and whatnot, and that is not the case.

'Hah!' I shout. 'All these years, Nicola, you said it couldn't be done, and here I am doing it, taking on the challenge, meeting the challenge, laughing merrily in the face of the challenge, an outlaw in the woods, footloose and free in my, er, Volvo.'

The children giggle nervously, awareness perhaps dawning that this is not a harmlessly eccentric jaunt, more an instalment in a confusing, long-running and not entirely healthy marital psychodrama.

The path narrows. The ruts deepen. Dry earth gives way to squelching mud. The back-seat chant quietens and dies.

'Maybe we should turn round,' says Sam.

'Nonsense.' Another ten yards. Volvo tilting drunkenly one way then the other, speed below an arthritic crawl, the so-called path now merely a series of trenches and holes filled with slime.

'We can't go any further,' says Rachel.

Wipe sweat out of eyes. Grit teeth. Hunch over wheel. 'Yes. We. Bloody. Well. Can.'

No, we bloody well can't. Huge lurch to the right, car settles at crazy angle, left-side wheels barely in contact with the ground, right-side wheels half-buried in a bog. Mild panic. Stamp right foot down as hard as possible.

Impressive gouts of mud. Distinctive aroma of burning rubber. Wheels now three-quarters buried in bog.

'This,' I announce, 'has the makings of what is known as a f***ing disaster. Get out and push.'

Thirty seconds of revving later and nothing has changed, except the bog-bound wheels are now totally submerged and the children are coated in mud.

'Ah well,' I sigh, suddenly exhausted, 'you'd better go and tell your mother.'

To be continued . . .

10 August 2013

So, to recap: last week's cliffhanger left me standing next to my Volvo, a Volvo firmly wedged in a boggy pothole on a forest track in France. The children, covered in mud following a failed clutch attempt at liberation, have trudged off to fetch my wife from our house a few hundred yards away. I can't pretend to be much looking forward to her arrival.

Over the previous twenty years, the occasions on which Nicola has told me on no account ever to try driving along this track probably number more than one hundred. Something tells me she will be reminding me of this advice in the very near future. Like a condemned man walking to the gallows, I look around at the beauty of the woods, turn my face to the sky for a final time, inhale deeply.

I hear her before I see her. Thirty or so yards ahead of the immobilized car, the track takes a sharp turn to the right. Beyond that turn, a voice is growing louder. Most of the words begin with an F. Others include 'idiot', 'pathetic' and 'loser'. And now she's in view – small, shapely, terrifying – picking her way swiftly through the ruts and bumps, the children, plus Cousin Steve, trailing miserably behind.

Best not to dwell on the next ten minutes. I am, of course, eviscerated. As is, less predictably, my daughter.

'I didn't expect anything more from him,' Nicola tells Rachel. 'But I expected more from you' – an interesting insight into my wife's opinion of her husband. Announcing she will have nothing to do with any efforts to recover the car, Nicola departs. Once she's safely out of sight, Cousin Steve offers me a consoling pat on the shoulder.

'We need some help,' I announce. 'I'll go and talk to the farmer.'

'Do you want me to come with you?' asks Steve.

I look at Steve, taking in the ponytail, the Harry Potter specs, the goatee, the sunburnt arms similar in colour to the bright red vest and shorts, the crappy John Lennon tattoo, the flip-flops. What goes down well in Shoreditch, I decide, might not play so well in the ultra-conservative back-of-beyond French countryside.

'No,' I say to Steve. 'You stay here. I'll take Rachel.'

Rachel and I plod up to the farmer's house. A boy of about five comes to the door, surveying us shyly through the glass.

'Est-ce que il papa dans la maison?' I shout. The kid shakes his head – not surprising, I realize, as I've just asked him, partially in Italian, if the Pope is in the house.

A seven-year-old girl appears, big eyes wide and fearful. Rachel smiles at her and she smiles back. Bringing Rachel instead of Steve, I reflect, is the first decent decision I've made so far today. Now a woman joins the gathering on the other side of the door. She is also uncertain. Finally, in what I can't help noticing is a classic demonstration of the type of traditional patriarchal set-up I have not enjoyed for so much as one solitary second of my family life, Thierry the farmer materializes and opens the door.

'Ah, bonjour monsieur,' I say, flapping my hands in what I hope is a reassuringly Gallic fashion. 'Ma voiture est dans le forêt. Dans la boîte.' Thierry lifts an eyebrow. I have just told him my car is in the forest. In the box. Still, he latches on quickly enough, and moments later we're climbing into the rather exciting cab of the massive pick-up truck parked in the drive.

Steve emerges from behind a tree. 'Il y a Steve. C'est ma cousine,' I say, as in, 'There is Steve. It is my (female) cousin.' Thierry nods in understanding.

'Can I get in as well?' says Steve.

'No,' I tell him. We trundle off towards the woods, Steve following on foot.

It's all pretty straightforward after that. Thierry reverses the pick-up down the track. He's friendly enough, and God knows I'm grateful to the man, but it's not entirely necessary, to my mind, for him to tell me three times in the space of two hundred yards that driving an ordinary car on this terrain is not advisable because, well, you can get stuck. Mate, I feel like saying, you're starting to sound like my wife. Still, that's the French for you.

When we round the corner and he spots the Volvo in his mirror, Thierry actually says, 'Oh là là.' I fish a tow rope from the boot of the Volvo, Steve tries to make a contribution by jamming a few twigs under the tyres, Thierry does a bit of shrugging and lip-pursing, Rachel tells Steve to stand aside, Thierry hauls us to solid ground, I dispatch Rachel to fetch him a couple of bottles of wine.

'All sorted,' I tell Nicola, trying to sound all efficient.

The bollocking resumes, however, and continues for some time.

7 September 2013

We've had a house guest the past month or so – Zara, twenty-five, a friend of Cousin Steve's since they were both about fifteen. They met while attending the same maths camp, which is a summer school for children who are really good at maths. I like to remind Steve and Zara quite frequently about maths camp, except I call it 'math camp', in a wacky American accent. What a hilarious fellow I am.

Zara's in what used to be Steve's room – indeed, two years after he moved out of it, it is still known as The Steve Room. Like most young people, she seems to exist on pizza and chocolate without being an ounce overweight. She has a lot of showers, too. Always showering, youngsters. My son spends much of his life under falling water. She's slotted right into our family dynamic, has Zara. That is, she takes Nicola seriously and makes fun of me.

Zara shares my appreciation of the romantic comedy genre. And, like me, and indeed my daughter, who has watched *27 Dresses* well over twenty-seven times, Zara is more than happy to see a film she has seen many times before. Happier, in fact, because there's none of the stress of not knowing what's going to happen. I hate not knowing what's going to happen. When I start a book, I look at the last page first to make sure everything's going to be all right in the end.

And also like me and Rachel, Zara has incredibly low stand ards, rom-com-wise. If Katherine Heigl or Cameron Diaz or John Cusack or Hugh Grant are in it, it's going to be good. Zara admires pretty much Jennifer Aniston's entire output, although she did admit *Along Came Polly* was a rare blip.

I recommended *Chalet Girl*. Within three hours, Zara had rented it, watched it and pronounced it brilliant.

So these past few weeks the DVD and movie channel have taken a hammering. We've established our preferred spots. Nicola sits at one end of the sofa in charge of the remote controls (we seem to require four to go from turning the telly on to actually activating a DVD). I'm at the other end of the sofa. Rachel is in the middle. Zara has her own chair to my right. Sam is upstairs on his PlayStation.

We might have some snacks on the go.

One night – I think it was for *Love Actually* – Zara bought jam tarts from Mustafa's. A bottle of wine might get involved. Everyone's in pyjamas. The whole business really is highly agreeable.

Except for a couple of issues. First, good manners dictate that I have to call for the pause button every half-hour or so, mutter that I'm just nipping into my office 'to check my emails', then dash into the garden to discharge a volley of suppressed wind loud enough to rattle the windows. After a few nights of this, Zara told me she could hear the farting through the wall anyway.

The second issue: much as I enjoy (indeed, in general, prefer) female company, I also know that a ratio of three women to one man is only ever heading one way – pretty soon, they're going to gang up on you. We were watching *13 Going on 30* when Nicola hit pause and announced that the kid in the film was the spitting image of me when I was thirteen. Not the good-looking, popular athletic kid, the fat nerdy kid with the useless hair.

'Were you chubby as a child, then?' asked Zara.

'I wasn't just chubby,' I said through a mouthful of some cake or other, 'I was proper fat. My nickname at primary school was Doughnut after the obese kid in *Here Come the Double Deckers!* Bit before your time, I suppose, *Double Deckers*.'

'Yeah,' she agreed. 'But the name Doughnut pretty much paints the picture.'

Inevitably, Zara then had to be brought up to speed on how, when we were teenagers, I fancied Nicola, pursued her, kept inventing reasons for her to come round to my house, including letting her cut my hair and redecorate my bedroom, neither task accomplished especially well, and yet despite everything, she only (worst words in the English language coming up) 'liked me as a friend'.

Nicola, Zara and – disappointingly, I have to say – Rachel had a good old giggle over that, all girls together, hah hah hah. All the while the fat face and lank hair of my doppelgänger stared miserably out from the frozen screen.

Much later that night, everyone else in bed, feeling peckish, I surveyed the contents of the fridge. There wasn't a great deal in there, but there was enough, because someone had thoughtfully prepared herself a rather inviting ham and cheese sandwich by way of a packed lunch for work tomorrow. A packed lunch she was now not going to enjoy.

12 October 2013

I'd been badgering him for years, and finally, a few weeks ago, Cousin Steve took my advice and bought himself a bicycle. And, in the spirit of youth (Steve is twenty-five), he has been lecturing me ever since on the merits of the bicycle as a convenient means of urban transportation. They're quick, Steve says, and efficient, and cheap, and healthy, and did I realize that, while on a bike, you retain control over your journey in a way that in a car or on public transport you don't?

I smile indulgently and congratulate the lad on his good judgement.

I wouldn't wish to suggest Steve is in any way daft. He is, rest assured, a seriously clever chap. And yet, occasionally, inevitably, Steve betrays his tender age in the fashion described above, that is by announcing what he presumes is a major discovery – a major discovery which is not, in fact, even a minor discovery. Or any sort of discovery at all. Once – admittedly a good few years ago, when he was still in his teens – Steve informed me, in the course of a single conversation, that 1) Elvis Presley was 'really talented', 2) high-altitude mountain climbing was 'incredibly dangerous', and 3) Adolf Hitler was 'an utter s***'.

Blimey. Who knew?

Anyway, Steve got his bike and all was well. And then, abruptly, all was not well, because Steve's new bike got stolen. Outside Tesco in Hackney. Locked up, broad daylight, popped in for less than five minutes, the usual scenario – but no less shocking for all that.

'When something you own gets nicked,' Steve fulminated, 'it's bloody annoying.'

Words of wisdom there, mate, I replied. Couldn't have put it better myself.

Steve's friend Luke kindly loaned him a bike that he (Luke) temporarily had no need of. In the way of surplus bicycles, the tyres were flat, the chain dry, the saddle required adjustment. Steve asked if he could pop round to use my toolkit. He also said he might need advice on how best to employ such tools as were in the toolkit. I said, Steve, come on over.

If you need to repair something, and you ask for my help, you're in trouble.

All the more so given that the 'toolkit' in which Steve seemed to be investing such faith comprises, in splendid entirety, one spanner and one pump. And the pump – smart, snazzy, no doubt a design classic, yet utterly baffling – I can't get to work. God knows I've tried.

I do have another pump – an old-school, fire-and-forget, idiot-proof pump – and thus a pump, which, while creaky (and indeed squeaky, not to mention leaky – although not, to be fair, cheeky, freaky or peaky), I do know how to operate. But I've lost it.

Steve arrived. He wheeled the Luke bike in and set about pretending to know what he was doing. I thought, hey, that looks fun, my own wheels could do with some attention, maybe I should pretend to know what I'm doing as well? Maybe we could make a day of it, put some Springsteen on, get a sexy workshop vibe going here in the back garden. Or 'back yard', I should say. Or 'out back', even.

Whatever. Point is, it'd be me 'n' Steve, just two regular guys fixin' things up real nice, quite possibly while wearing our workin' pants, talkin' 'bout the old days and, er, gettin' our spanners out. And such like.

I'll have some of that. Hell yes.

Half an hour later my wife, son and daughter came back from the shops. I happened, at the moment they walked in, to be emerging from the garden shed carrying a toolkit. Not the joke toolkit that belongs to me, the one previously mentioned, but the proper ass-kicking macho toolkit my wife fetches when she has to mend stuff. My family looked at me, and they looked at the toolkit – and then they all burst out laughing.

Not that I was doing anything overtly amusing. The mere fact of having a toolkit in my hand was sufficient cause for hilarity. This is the sort of mockery I have to put up with.

Then they looked at the Luke bike, and my bike, both partially dismantled among a mess of nuts and bolts, washers and brackets, pins, posts, pedals, pads, parts and . . . er . . . other loosely bicycle-related items beginning with P . . . and they burst out laughing again. Panniers would count, I suppose. Except neither Steve nor I have any panniers, and it wouldn't do for me to start bending the truth for comic effect. Can't have that.

'Let me guess,' said my wife. 'You've taken your bike apart, and you can't work out how to put it together again?'

'That pretty much covers it.'

'You should have laid out all the bits in the order you took them off.'

'I realize that now,' I said, 'but please, spare me the lecture. Here's your toolkit. Will you get my bike back in one piece?'

So she did.

2 November 2013

My son, sixteen, has left school and started at catering college. Or rather, as my wife says we must call it, cookery school. Whichever, six weeks in, Sam is thriving in the world of the pot and the pan. He seems to be doing well, if the food I wolf down when he brings it home is anything to go by. The one problem so far, now that he has one foot firmly in the big wide world, is that half-term holidays have become a thing of the past. He wasn't happy about this.

'Son,' I told him, 'suck it up.'

As fatherly advice goes, 'suck it up' obviously lacks a little finesse. Then again, sometimes – quite often, in fact – 'suck it up' is all a dad can say. And all a dad should say.

Sam's indignation was compounded by the fact that his sister, fourteen, not only continues to enjoy the pleasures of the mid-term break, but this year, for some reason, that break lasted fully a fortnight.

Off Rachel went on a combined hockey and netball tour to Jersey, as you do. And, seizing the opportunity, off similarly went Nicola, my wife, for some R&R in Cornwall with her pal. Which left, once the smoke had cleared, the young trainee chef home alone in the care of his equally vacationless father.

What fun we had.

It wasn't as if I let the lad run wild. Fair play, I take a lighter touch on the parental tiller than does my wife – but still, I'm no pushover. And anyway, he's a sensible boy; it was as much a case of him keeping me in line as the other way around. Between us, I like to think Sam and I observed at least rudimentary standards of decorum and discipline. We slept. We washed. We dressed. We ate. We fed the cats. We kept the house heated, secured and unburnt-down. We didn't smash anything.

The fabric of respectable middle-class life was – just about

– maintained. And yet, in the context of the, ahem, rather more structured way our household operates when its full comple- ment is in residence, I can't deny Sam and I allowed a degree of laxity to creep into our domestic routine. I say 'laxity'; some might argue the word 'squalor' would be more accurate.

The concepts of 'the mealtime' and 'the bedtime' were swiftly emptied of any descriptive power. Takeaways charged to the fore: Italian; Indian; Thai; Chinese – a balanced diet if ever I saw it. Bin bags accumulated. As did, alongside, a pile of those pizza boxes, foil containers and other packaging that for one reason or another we hadn't yet got round to putting in a bin bag. The dishwasher took a well earned break. Once efficiently stripped of its contents, so did the fridge. Likewise such TV channels as concern themselves with interior design, makeovers or high-school comedies were left untroubled.

Celebrities, historical figures, cultural icons, local characters, foreigners, friends, certain absent family members, all were luxuriously mocked, without even once anybody spoiling the party by asking, 'Why do you two have to make fun of every- body all the time?' or any wet-blanket nonsense of that ilk.

Duvets lay unsmoothed, pillows unplumped, curtains undrawn, post unopened, floors unswept, stubble unshaved, flatulence unsuppressed, profanities uncensored, cleaning products unmolested, generalizations undisputed, *The Archers* unheard, idiocies unchallenged, live and exclusive coverage of the Champions League uninterrupted. Apart from by the adverts. Which we ridiculed.

All this, for four days straight. Heaven.

And then – as it always has, always does, always will – the day of reckoning arrived. Rachel was coming back from Jersey on the Saturday. Due respect to my daughter, but Saturday was not the day of reckoning. Nicola was to return on the Thursday, her ETA threatened for mid-afternoon. Thus, for Sam and me, both required to be out of the house early doors Thursday morning and not home again until late, the day of reckoning fell on Wednesday. Wednesday evening. After we'd scoffed our Chinese and caught the second half of Man Utd vs Real Sociedad, naturally.

Horizontal on the sofa, I released a huge burp.

'Sam,' I said, as the echoes died away, 'I'll make you a deal.'

'What deal?' he asked, promptly matching his father's eructation for both volume and duration, if not, perhaps, body – although that will come with time.

'Well, son,' I replied, 'we've got to have a bit of a tidy-up. Let's be honest, we've done nothing for days. The house is a mess. Agreed?'

'Oh yeah,' he said, 'total disgrace.'

'So we need to get busy. The deal is, if you handle the kitchen, I'll do everywhere else.'

He weighed up the offer. Accepted it.

'Excellent,' I said. 'Let's get cracking. Nice burp by the way.'

'Thanks.'

A frenzy of activity ensued, the like of which has rarely been seen.

I'm confident we got away with it.

14 December 2013

Remember *Witness*, that film about Harrison Ford hiding out with the Amish? Of course you do! The signature scene in *Witness*, you will also recall, is the one in which the whole Amish community comes together to build a barn. This 'barn-raising scene' has become famous. It is still cited by American politicians keen to illustrate the virtue of collective action.

Last weekend I participated in a barn-raising scene of my own.

At this time of year – every year, but especially this year, what with all this windiness going on – my garden is beset by huge quantities of fallen leaves. Brown/green, flat/curly, wet/dry, newly expired/largely decomposed – will I ever, I start to wonder, be free of all these f***ing leaves? I'm out there, rain or shine, brushing, scooping, bagging – and next morning, another load has landed, rustling and drifting and swirling this way and that.

Now some might say that trying to stay leaf-free throughout the autumn is a waste of time. And fair enough, in the grand scheme of things, compared with damp, or frost, or badgers, or mad axemen escaped from Broadmoor, leaves don't present much of a threat to people or property. Plus, when they turn on the style – red, gold, orange and whatnot – leaves can look nice. So why not wait – this school of thought suggests – until every last leaf has fallen, and clear them up then?

Or even, not clear them up. Not in the winter. Not the following spring. Not ever. Which is the attitude most people here in hipster Hackney adopt. Leaf clearance – prompt or delayed – is seen as the sort of embarrassing bourgeois affliction from which many local residents are fleeing.

I'm not having it. After much study, my settled opinion is that embarrassing bourgeois afflictions are precisely what stand between civilization and anarchy. It's unswept leaves one minute, complete social breakdown the next. What starts out as minor domestic lethargy ends with a total loss of moral fibre. Before you know it, you've lost your job and you're lying around in bed all day injecting drugs.

I believe in the dignity of labour. I take pride in a job well done. I don't want my wife and children slipping over on skiddy leaf detritus. Also, when I see one value system smugly prevailing over another, my instinct is to back the underdog. If I lived in a spotless suburban avenue, I'd make sure my house looked like a slum: peeling paint, broken windows, knackered mattresses in the front garden, the works.

Even so, it can be a right pain, keeping up appearances. Another storm-force gale having swept the nation overnight, a man wakes yet again to survey the nullification of yesterday's toil, and may on occasion be forgiven an anguished sigh, a stirring of despair, a contorted face raised to the heavens, a plea to his God to explain why He has forsaken him, leaf inundation-wise. In such circumstances, a man needs help.

Thus we return to the business of barn-raising.

I can't pretend the whole neighbourhood pitched in. Nor even that the whole family made an effort – my son and daughter both tend to remember urgent homework assignments when drudge work is required. But Cousin Steve showed up, as did Nicola, as did I, and the three of us set to, all mucking in, none of that gender division like they had in *Witness*. Nicola didn't once, for instance, smile shyly and hand me a glass of lemonade in a subservient manner while wearing a bonnet.

What a formidable troika we proved to be: the Lenin, Trotsky and Stalin of an, ahem, sweeping revolution. (I'm obviously Lenin; Nicola's even more obviously Stalin.) An hour later, we may not have constructed a brand-new country, or even a large agricultural storage facility in rural Pennsylvania, but you could have eaten your dinner off that lawn. A warm glow of shared achievement suffused each comrade.

Suffused Stalin and Trotsky at any rate. Old Lenin felt strangely out of sorts.

Why? Because over the years I had convinced myself that leaf collection was not mere mindless toil, but rather required special skills – special skills I alone had developed. And now Nicola and Steve's participation had exposed this belief as the tragic delusion it always was. There is no skill, none whatsoever, I was forced to conclude, involved in putting leaves into a bin liner. Someone doing it for the first time can be every bit as efficient as someone doing it for the thousandth time.

I also knew, with the leaf job done and dusted, that Nicola would find me something else to do – something that did require a modicum of skill, something fiddly, something at which I would fail. This, she duly did: the old fitting-a-clean-cover-on-the-duvet nightmare.

I fastened two press studs while she did eight.

1 March 2014

Assessing, as is my duty, the impact of the columnar output – the body of work, the *oeuvre*, if you will – I cannot deny that, of my recent efforts, two were appreciated more than all the others combined. Those being the one in which, despite my wife's warnings, I got the car stuck on a muddy track in France, and the one in which, my wife and daughter away from home, my son and I lived like utter slobs for a few days.

Can you see a pattern emerging? I certainly can. Husband and wife caricatures – I tell you, they're comedy gold. And thus I present the tale of what happened when Nicola went away (again) and Bob decided to hand-wash his socks.

Thanks to thirty years of smoking, my circulation isn't what it ought to be. And when you've got poor circulation, your feet feel it first. So sockwear is important to me. Woolly, cashmere, cotton, Lycra-mix – I can boast an impressive collection. Sadly, after a day (possibly longer) in close proximity to my feet, these socks need washing. By hand. And although Nicola covers all the family's other laundry requirements, she's made clear that soaking and squidging her husband's minging hosiery is not her responsibility.

Women, eh?

Obviously, I wait until I haven't got any clean socks left. Then I fish out the least crusty pair and recycle them. Then the second least crusty pair, and so on – eventually, however, I sigh and fetch the special Bob dirty-sock bag and decant the whole scrunched-up cheesy stash into a washing-up bowl full of warm water and detergent. Then I leave it to soak for an hour. Or two hours. Or three hours. Or, as regards the most recent load, with Nicola not around to hurry things along, forty-eight hours.

Yep, that bowl sat there, on the draining board next to the kitchen sink, for two long days, fermenting away, the water turning first grey, then brown, then black, the surface bubbling energetically like some potion in a mad professor's laboratory. Besides the socks, I'd also tipped in a jockstrap I wear when boxing with my son. I don't know what precise chemistry the jockstrap was adding to the mix – nothing good, I suspect. Not the sweet perfume of fresh-cut flowers, that's for sure.

You'll recall that last summer we had a house guest staying with us for a couple of months – Zara, twenty-six, a friend of Cousin Steve's, and now a friend of ours, too. Well . . . Zara's back. She's in the spare bedroom, on the ground floor overlooking the back garden.

Having spent a day or so presumably hoping that the disgusting bowlful of farting socks next to the sink would disappear, young Zara had had enough. 'I'm begging you,' she said to me. 'Please do something about THAT!'

Blimey. One bossy woman was enough, then Rachel came along and there were two, and now, bugger me, here's another.

Of course I did as I was told.

I'll pass over the cleaning and rinsing process. I can't say I enjoyed it. No one would.

As for the drying, I decided that if I rigged up a washing line in the garden, just outside Zara's bedroom window as it happens, not only would my socks get dry, they'd get dry in a folksy, authentic, free-range, organic kinda fashion. Also, I calculated that an improvised washing line would win me points for being all practical and problem-solving and whatnot.

Plus, when I went to Belize on an adventure holiday in 1989, the organizers had told me to bring a length of something called paracord. Paracord is a sort of thin rope the army makes much use of, and back in 1989 I thought it was just about the coolest thing outside actual weaponry I'd ever seen. Post-Belize, this paracord, ten yards of the stuff, has been hanging looped up in the garage. Try as I might, in twenty-five years, I've never been able to find a use for the stuff. Until now.

Starting at the drainpipe, across to the scaffolding pole which props up the roof, over to the chain suspending the punchbag, I slung that paracord every which way. I put in various knots – slip knots, possibly, or reef knots, or hitch knots, or wind-it-round-a-bit-and-hope-it-holds knots – and then I lovingly draped two dozen not perhaps wholly clean but not as revolting as they had been socks along its length. And one item of male athletic support.

Wind and gravity are marvellous things. All I had to do was go along the line every so often squeezing the bottoms, oo-er missus, and let nature take its course. Unless, of course, a force greater than either wind or gravity, greater even than nature itself, intervened.

'Get rid of it,' Nicola commanded, within about twelve seconds of entering the house. 'Zara's got a jockstrap in her face.'

Which is not a sentence you hear every day.

Foiled again.

22 March 2014

Up until the age of about fifteen, I was a self-confident (some would say arrogant), opinionated (some would say overbearing), incautious (some would say idiotic) extrovert (some would say shameless exhibitionist). And then, beaten down by sexual rejection, mockery, the first intimations of intellectual fallibility – and not forgetting old-fashioned violence suffered at the fists of larger boys who failed to find me entertaining – my personality changed.

Retreating into my shell, for a decade or so I became, if not exactly shy, then certainly a great deal more fearful. Having never been prey to either self-consciousness or self-doubt, I was, for a number of years, constrained by both. Not paralysed, not crippled, yet nonetheless a shadow of the boisterous, limelight-loving child I had once been.

You could argue this withdrawal came as a necessary and welcome correction to an insufferably egotistical manner. On balance, however, I'd say it sucked.

At twenty-five, in 1990, I started going out with the woman to whom I am now married. And at that point, not coincidentally, the era of tortured introspection, timidity and failure (or imagined failure) began to draw to a close. I was slowly able to regain a measure of the assertiveness (now happily shorn of the juvenile gobbiness) that had marked my childhood.

If this potted psychological biography comes across as outrageous navel-gazing, that's because it is, even by the exalted standards of this column. And yet my story will, I suspect, be nonetheless familiar to many young men – and to their partners, if they were lucky enough to find one.

Since I've been with Nicola, I've enjoyed a quarter-century – my second quarter-century; here's hoping for a third and, who knows, maybe a fraction of a fourth, too – of steady progress. Thanks in large part to her counsel, encouragement, optimism, terrifying self-assurance and, of course, sheer bossiness, virtually all of the obstacles to personal happiness have been dismantled or surmounted. Some of these barriers Nicola dispatched swiftly; others have taken longer to overcome. Under her guidance, I ditched bitterness, blame and self-pity. I no longer despise people for no reason – they have to provide one. Other things being equal, I'm a friendly, welcoming chap. I fulfil almost all of my professional, social and familial obligations. I am able to choose, nurture and cherish friends. I take exercise, go on holiday, pay my mortgage, maintain a reasonable level of personal hygiene. I'd like to think I have even developed at least some basic competence as regards sexual relations.

In wider company, I have learnt to converse with strangers without becoming offended, sullen, argumentative, cruel or aggressive. I can allow other people to have their say without viewing it as an affront. What's more, I can now allow myself to have my say without assuming (as I did during the risk-averse years of my youth) that anyone in earshot will loathe me. And if they do, I now recognize that's their problem, not mine. Last but by no means least, after much coaxing, I am able to dance with other people present. I wouldn't go so far as to say I enjoy dancing – and nobody else enjoys me dancing either. But if the occasion demands, I'll do it. And as and when I do, I do it not just to please Nicola, but because I've finally accepted the truth of the statement that, hey, chill out, what the hell, nobody gives a stuff about technique if you're having a good time.

A bit like the sex, really.

And yet one ancient inhibition remains very firmly in place. It's no accident that this inhibition is among the few also felt by my wife. Yes indeed, I speak for both of us when I say that karaoke is just not our thing. Far from being one of the many modes of expression my wife is keen for me to explore, she thinks I should stay as far away from microphones as she does.

The karaoke started up at a party we attended two Saturdays ago. I'd say about half of the sixty or so guests gave it a go. Some were good, a few were sensational, most were OK. The worse someone was, the louder the cheers. It was a friendly crowd. In the spirit of the evening, the decent, convivial, life-embracing thing to do was clearly to cast dignity aside and join in the fun.

In the way of things, people kept urging us to have a go – 'Come on, you can't be that bad,' and so on. Nicola and I explained that in fact we were that bad, and any effort we made would be met not by comradely applause, but embarrassed coughing and urgent trips to the loo. They still kept at it, though.

So we quietly left the karaoke room, collared a couple of like-minded souls, found a quiet corner and discussed the pros and cons of Scottish independence.

29 March 2014

Last Saturday, my family did something we haven't done for ages and went shopping together, just the four of us, all nice and nuclear. We got in the car, drove a few miles, parked up, patronized a selection of outlets, had lunch, drove home. With the children now fifteen and almost seventeen, busy with their sporting or social or simply solitary staying-in-their-room commitments, such outings have become rare.

The expedition also felt, for me at least, unusual, unfamiliar, even a little unsettling. I don't get in the car very often. I don't get to the shops very often. I don't, in point of fact, get out very often. Except to go to Hull, obviously. And, every so often, Scandinavia. Sitting there in the passenger seat, equal parts anxious and excited, nervous and nostalgic, I felt like a geriatric uncle being treated by his dutiful nieces (and nephew). A tartan rug spread over my increasingly twinge-plagued knees would have completed the picture perfectly.

'Ooo, well I never, that place wasn't there before, was it?' I heard myself saying. And, 'Ooo, I must say, it's all changed around here, hasn't it?' And, 'Ooo, careful, I think the light's about to go red.' And so on and so forth. I'd have gone with, 'Eee, dear, this were all green fields when I were a lad,' except the area of east London in question has been thoroughly urbanized since 1850. And I didn't grow up here, anyway.

The catalyst for the trip was the imminence of my wife's fiftieth birthday. To mark such an occasion, offerings – minor, perhaps, from the children; major, most definitely, from me – were required. Thus, on arrival at our chosen retail hunting ground, we split up – for which, from Sam and Rachel, petrified that they might bump into one of their friends, much thanks. The two of them hastened off. Nicola and I, meanwhile, sought out the nearest jeweller's.

Of course we did. Because, y'know, hey, when it really matters, when push comes to shove, when it's a big deal, it's gotta be a nice bit of tomfoolery, right? Thirtieth birthday, engage-ment, wedding, first child, second child, fortieth birthday, now fiftieth – every time I've ummed and aahed for ages, and then ended up going bling anyway.

For Nicola's fortieth, I bought her a fancy watch. She loves it. Ten years on, trying to keep it simple, the two of us standing there squinting at the window display, I asked her if she'd like another one.

'Another what?'

Another watch.

'But I've got a watch.'

Yeah, but how about another one, of the, er, exact same make as, er, that one you like so much? You could wear it on the other wrist – belt and braces. Punctuality is very important . . .

She opted for a ring instead.

Just as we were finalizing the deal, the lady serving us, having inspected Nicola's fingers at some length, caught sight of mine.

'You might want to do something about that,' she said.

What?

'That.'

I looked down at my left hand. The flesh on either side of my wedding ring was swollen so badly my finger looked like one of those balloon dachshunds beloved of children's entertainers.

'Doesn't it hurt?' asked Nicola.

Now that you mention it, I said, yeah, it does.

'But you hadn't noticed it?'

I had to admit I had not.

The jeweller and Nicola caught each other's eye. No words were exchanged – the meaning of their expressions was, however, crystal clear.

Nicola: 'Useless, isn't he?'

Jeweller: 'Most certainly. But don't worry, mine is too.'

At that point we were interrupted by the arrival of Sam and Rachel. Sam had bought himself some variety of ultra-oily cake, so that the bag it came in had accumulated a sump of grease in the bottom, a sump Sam proceeded absent-mindedly to tip all over the floor, then tread in and perform a comedy slide, arms flailing. A two-minute time-out while we mopped up with tissues and told our son to wait outside. A cameo appearance.

The jeweller would not be distracted. 'It'll have to come off,' she announced.

'Isn't that a bit drastic?' I squeaked.

'Not your finger,' said Nicola. 'Your ring.'

'There's no way it'll fit over that swelling,' I said.

'We'll cut it off,' said the jeweller.

'No, you won't,' I said. 'This ring belonged to my granddad. I'd rather lose the finger.'

Nicola told me not to be so melodramatic and explained the ring could be repaired and resized, good as new.

A chap called Marty emerged from a back room. Marty was

carrying a sinister-looking tool, a combination of pliers and circular saw, a miniature version of the contraption that so nearly put a premature end to James Bond's skirt-chasing career in *Goldfinger*. Snip, snip, scrape, scrape, off it came. Blessed relief.

Quite a crowd gathered to watch.

'Somehow, it always ends up being about you, doesn't it?' said my wife.

26 April 2014

The recent shopping expedition having restored a measure of my self-confidence (after a long period of nerve-losing, near-total isolation) in my dealings with the outside world, last Saturday I felt emboldened to venture forth again. And guess what? That's right: hilarious consequences ensued once more.

I'm telling you, it's a world of wonder out there. A. World. Of. Wonder.

Friday night, Nicola and I went to the cinema. Twin buckets of popcorn and Coke secured, she made straight for Screen 4.

'Hold on,' I said. 'What about our tickets?'

'Just doing them now,' Nicola replied, tilting her mobile towards the relevant usher, a suspiciously handsome young man who, even as we spoke, was zapping my wife's smartphone in – to my mind – an overly familiar fashion.

'Eeeh, dear,' I said, hastening to interpose myself. 'What will they think of next?'

Next day, Saturday morning, I was at my desk doing some admin, feeling all efficient, when Nicola came in to see what I was up to.

'I'm doing these invoices,' I said, eager for approval. 'They asked,' I went on, 'whether I wanted a bank transfer or a cheque.

Obviously' – snort of derision – 'I said I'd prefer a cheque.'
Silence.

'Bank transfers are much more convenient,' said Nicola.

That shook me.

'Are they?' I said. 'I thought we liked cheques. Personally, I—'

'Hardly anybody,' Nicola cut in, 'uses cheques any more.'

'Really?'

'Really.'

'But I love cheques,' I said. 'Not as good as cash obviously, but the next best thing.'

'Hardly anybody uses cash any more either,' she said.

Later that same day, Nicola told me I needed to get some new shoes. By which she meant proper shoes – as opposed to the Crocs, Birkenstocks and trainers that have served me so well (although not all at the same time) for the past decade. She said it was time for me to re-enter the world of normal footwear.

We – she – parked on a meter opposite the shoe shop. Then, instead of searching for one-pound coins as she normally would, she extracted her debit card and began to dial a number on her mobile, a mobile that seemed somehow to be connected to the speakers in the car.

'Who are you calling?' I asked. 'I thought we were supposed to be buying shoes.'

Nicola gestured for me to be quiet. So I was.

'I'm paying for the parking,' Nicola – her business transacted – explained.

'Eh? How?'

'By my card, on my phone.'

'Eh? Since when?'

'Since quite a while. I hardly ever pay for parking with coins any more.'

'Don't you?'

'No.'

'Nicola,' I said, 'what's going on?'

'What's going on, darling,' she replied, 'is the modern world. And it's leaving you behind.'

We went into the shoe shop.

'What size are you?' asked Nicola, starting to scan the racks.

'Nine,' I said, 'maybe nine and a half since I got so fat and my feet splayed out.'

'What's that in a European size?' she asked.

For a long moment, I thought I'd heard her wrong.

Realizing I'd heard her right, starting to process the implications of the question, I sensed my ears ringing, my vision blurring, my breathing labouring, my feet struggling for balance on the floor of the shoe shop.

My own wife, gone over to the dark side!

Because, you know, hey, I'm not unreasonable. I know change is inevitable, change is (occasionally) acceptable, change is (once in a while) laudable, and so on and so forth . . . but dammit I've known this girl since she was a girl! Since she was eleven years old! Since I was eleven years old! In 1975! She's Hull through and through. Her dad's had a season ticket at City since Attlee was prime minister, her Uncle Dave's got an allotment, they play dominoes every Wednesday in the British Legion . . . and now she wants to know what my shoe size might be in a metric measure.

You think you know someone, and then they come out with something, and you realize one human being can never know another human being at all. Not truly know them.

Still, I wasn't about to give up on my wife without a fight.

'How the hell,' I said, my voice a low snarl, 'should I know what my European' – I made sure to ladle the word 'European' with extra lashings of contempt – 'shoe size is? And what do I care anyway?'

'I tend to think in metric sizes nowadays,' said Nicola breezily, not sounding even the teensiest bit ashamed of herself.

'Oh do you,' I hissed.

'Yes, I do,' she said.

A stand-off. My wife looked at me. I looked at my wife. It felt like a pivotal moment – for her, for me, for the future of the two of us together.

'I'm a forty-three,' I muttered. 'A forty-four at a push.'

10 May 2014

I went over to France for a few days recently. Nicola and Rachel came too – Sammy, who doesn't get much holiday time at catering college, couldn't make it.

'Never mind, son,' I commiserated the night before we flew. 'You're a workin' man these days.'

'What, like Springsteen?' he said, his face brightening.

'Yeah, just like Bruce,' I told him.

We left the workin' man in the combined care of Zara the Lodger, Zara's boyfriend Andrew, Cousin Steve, Steve's girlfriend Abby, Barry the Painter, Svetlana the Cleaner and our pals Ben and Natalie.

Always a dangerous business, getting isolated with my wife and daughter. They rarely fail to take advantage, and this trip proved no exception. All my faults and foibles, my flaws and frailties, my failings and fallibilities were subject to relentless mockery. When Sam's around, he soaks up much of the punishment. In his absence, the twin cannon swivel on to me.

They blasted my weight. (Rachel: 'If you launched your own clothing range, you should call it O-Bese.') They pounded my near inability to drive. (The Volvo stuck on the woodland track incident from last summer was rehashed.) That led on to an attack on my execrable French, my having informed the local farmer, in the hope of securing a tow, that ma voiture was en casse dans une boîte – broken in a box – in the forest.

'I can't believe you learnt French for eight years at school,' said Rachel.

'Nine years,' I corrected.

They unloaded on my new tendency to clap my kneecaps and grunt, 'Eee dear,' when I get out of a chair.

'You're turning into Grandma,' warned Rachel, who at just fifteen perhaps does not fully appreciate the destructively emasculating effect on a man in being compared to his infirm eighty-one-year-old mother.

Or maybe she appreciates it only too well. Any concerns for my male sensibilities were certainly absent from her gleeful recitation of the famous nightmare – the Logbox Nightmare as it is known – that Rachel had when she was about ten.

I have to admit the Logbox Nightmare still hurts. Call a man overweight. Call him impractical. Call him, despite nearly a decade of instruction in a foreign language (and upwards of fifty visits to where that language is spoken), an irredeemable monoglot. Call him guilty, even, of developing traits in common with his mum. But please, don't accuse him of hiding in a box while his home and family are in danger.

After all, the first three charges are, in fairness, true. As for the fourth – well, I am, undeniably and unapologetically, related to my mother. But hiding in a box? That ain't fair. Hell, I worked in Northern Ireland when it was still kicking off. I did a stint in Bosnia, back in the day. I went to Iraq when stuff was exploding. I have walked through the shadow of the valley of death, yes indeedy doody. Psalm 23? A constant companion, mate. Constant companion.

Mind you: fear no evil? I don't think so. Quaking, each and every time.

My wife and daughter's most concentrated fire, however, was

directed neither at my appearance nor behaviour nor personality, but rather at my choice of hand luggage. Ryanair has a new
policy whereby it allows you to take your suitcase into the cabin
as carry-on. This policy is, by the by, a disaster: the overhead
lockers are already filled to bursting after only half the passengers
have boarded. It won't last. Yet as things stand, you're also
allowed one other small bag – thus, my regular backpack being
too big, I'd selected an old canvas satchel-slash-briefcase
instead.

My wife and daughter thought this briefcase was the funniest
thing they'd ever seen.

'Oooo, are you going to a Very Important Meeting?'

'Have you got to make a Big Pitch for a new account?'

'Will you be doing PowerPoint?'

And so on.

One night we were chatting about this and that, and Nicola
mentioned to Rachel that, back when he was about eighteen, her
dad (me, not my future father-in-law) had a job selling Betterware
cleaning products door-to-door. My daughter was captivated by
the thought of her useless father trying to flog oven scourers and
window spray to the housewives of suburban Hull. She then
swiftly developed the idea that I was actually still a Betterware
salesman and that's why I had the briefcase, to house my samples
as I made my big push to expand into south-west France.

The next night, at dinner, I needed my diary and delved into
my bag. The two of them had secretly filled it with dishcloths, tea
towels, a nailbrush and a couple of attachments off a Hoover.

My, how they laughed.

28 June 2014

With my mum in and out of hospital these past several weeks,
I've been pinging up and down, down and up, London King's

Cross to Hull station, your next and final stop, where this service will terminate. The buffet car is now closed but, hey, you're already off your faces on lukewarm cans of John Smith's, so never mind. On behalf of your on-board team today of myself, Kerry, along with Tracey and Lisa and your driver, Dave, I'd like to thank you for travelling with us. We hope to see you again in the very near future.

And so you shall, Kerry.

Sorry, did I write 'Hull station' just now? Oh my goodness, I believe I did. A slip of the keyboard, I'm afraid; please accept my humble apologies. What I meant to type, of course, was 'Hull Paragon Interchange', which is what we have to call the new, sexily rebranded rail and bus terminals nowadays. Even though they both look an awful lot like the old, most definitely unsexy rail and bus stations that have stood in the exact same places for more than forty years, and probably much longer.

On my most recent trip, my wife came with me. The two of us juggling hospital visits with the need to rejig the layout of my mum's house, I was struck by the way Nicola and I divvied up the tasks. Basically, if a job involves things (as in gear, kit, inanimate objects, etc.), then Nicola handles it. Whereas if a job majors on people (liaising, encouraging, conciliating, etc.), I tend to step forward.

Such a division of labour is, you will note, the precise opposite of the time-honoured male/female split. If the situation calls for the application of what have come to be termed the 'soft skills' of negotiation and persuasion and so forth, I take charge. If a new blind needs fitting in my mum's downstairs loo, then, whoa, watch out, because here comes the missus and she's holding a great big hammer.

In which circumstances, my job is to hang around limply in case she needs handing a pair of pliers or a larger screwdriver, not forgetting acting as ballast to the stepladder. My usefulness, I have to say, is limited.

'Can you pass me the bradawl?' she asked during one manoeuvre.

'What's a bradawl?' I replied.

And yet, while the law that Nicola does stuff and I do people almost always applies, a couple of exceptions do arise. The first is, if the people I'm supposed to be dealing with are trades-men (plumbers, decorators, joiners, etc.) as opposed to healthcare professionals (doctors, nurses, therapists, social workers, etc.), then Nicola takes over. And if the things Nicola is supposed to be dealing with are, for want of a better word, heavy, then I get involved.

You've got to recognize your limitations. You can have all the soft skills in the world, but if you fundamentally don't under-stand what is meant by 'supporting wall' or 'mains supply' or 'circuit spur' or 'waste fall', your participation in any dialogue incorporating those words is null and void. Similarly, however much you may desire to shift that sofa – and believe me, my wife's desire to shift that sofa without any assistance is so power-ful as to verge on the maniacal – if the muscle ain't there, a surfeit of spirit, commendable as it may be, will not suffice.

In short: when my interactions with people get technical, Nicola steps in; when her interactions with objects get rudi-mentary, I do likewise. Thus, although I am regularly exposed and embarrassed – not to mention excoriated and even, on occasion, when live electricity comes into play, endangered – I am not wholly emasculated. Mostly emasculated, yes. But not wholly. I am, when all is said and done, bringing perhaps half a testicle's worth of traditional male attributes to the party. Namely, my upper arms have a greater circumference than do my wife's. Which isn't much to shout about, really, given Nicola is eight stone and five feet nothing.

Eight stone and five feet nothing that is, nonetheless, capable of punching terrifyingly well above her weight as regards expressing exasperation with her husband's shortcomings in the practical-skills department. And as we know, those short-comings are legion. The brawn I may – but not, I fear, for much longer – still possess. The brains? Never been there.

'How do you propose to get this chair through this doorway?' I'll grunt, taking the not-inconsiderable strain.

'Pivot it back towards you,' she'll say, 'then over that way, rotate it, shuffle round a bit, go vertical and then it'll fit, no problem.'

'I'm sorry,' I respond. 'I simply cannot begin to imagine or picture or visualize or comprehend in any way, shape or form anything you've just said.'

She sighs.

I shove the bastard chair through the gap any old how.

5 July 2014

Shocking news! My eagerly awaited tennis comeback has been derailed. Slammed into the buffers. Stopped in its tracks. Shunted into a siding. At any rate chugging along at 15 mph somewhere between Grantham and Newark, well behind schedule, engineering works on the line, planned or thrillingly spontaneous, no one cares.

I've got a nagging calf strain in my left leg. I can hit the ball, but the movement of old just isn't there – and we all know how much my game relies on speed around the court. It rather looks as if, in common with the rest of the population, my interest in tennis will conclude for the summer at the end of the first week of July.

Still, I can always organize a comeback in another sport instead. Or can I? Football? Cricket? Rugby? God knows, the offers I receive to emerge from retirement for one last hurrah are that lucrative, they're embarrassing. I'm talking silly money. Even so, I'm not truly tempted. Besides, nagging calf strains are as debilitating on the pitch as they are on the court.

Same goes for the treadmill we've got at home. My wife hired it two months ago to get us all in shape for the summer. Sam's used it half a dozen times, Rachel twice, Nicola and I not at all. It's worked out about a tenner a mile so far. And if I wasn't pounding the conveyor belt before the nagging calf strain, I'm hardly going to start pounding it now, am I?

I could just stick to lying on my back lifting weights. Bulked-up Bob: built like a bouncer; unable to move. That cardio's gotta come from somewhere. Nothing for it, I'm going to have to start swimming again. Nicola's been on at me for ages to do just that.

'But I get self-conscious,' I tell her. 'Not to mention cold and wet and short of breath and mildly panicked and tired and hungry and itchy from the chlorine and quite possibly damp as well.'

'You're a good swimmer,' she says.

'Will you let me keep my trunks and goggles in my office?' I ask.

'Maybe,' Nicola replies. Which for her, I have to tell you, represents a major concession (albeit a concession she probably won't actually make, but let's put that to one side), because the whole keeping-some-clothes-in-my-office issue has become a significant source of conflict between us.

I like to keep certain items – sportswear, smart wear, grubbing-around-in-the-garden wear, cold-weather wear, warm-weather wear, emergency underpants, spare hankies, etc. – strewn on the floor around my office for ease of access. Nicola says I should keep my clothes in our bedroom as she does.

Women, eh? I'll never work out what makes them tick.

I say, don't be unreasonable. She says – huh! – that she's not being unreasonable, says that it's perfectly normal (given the presence of the usual drawers, cupboards, shelves, etc., in the bedroom) for a husband to house his clothing in the same vicinity as his wife's. Says, moreover, that my failure to do so symbolizes some subconscious desire to remain apart from the rest of the family, from the children, from her.

I say, come on, Nicola, don't be daft, it's purely about convenience, don't make such a thing out of it, it's not a big deal.

She says, OK, if it's not such a big deal, you won't mind just doing what I want then, will you, darling?

I say, drat. Walked into that one.

Then she says, while it may be convenient for me to keep sports kit in my room, it's only in the sense of my not having to walk up three flights of stairs to fetch that kit from the bedroom.

Exactly, I say.

But climbing stairs, Nicola then says, is a superb – and indeed highly convenient – form of exercise itself.

Drat again. Walked into that one as well.

Swears by the health benefits of stairs, does Nicola.

As a battle zone, it's always been bubbling along nicely, this clothes-in-room dispute. But a bit like, say, Kashmir, or Cyprus, or Korea, hostilities have generally stayed, if not exactly cold, at least tepid, and certainly rarely hot. Casualties thus far remain mercifully light. Sabre rattling, brinkmanship, diplomatic incidents, sullen stand-offs, aggressive manoeuvring close to the front line, even the occasional probing skirmish – yes, all of those. Tracksuit trousers – and jeans, and shorts, and indeed swimming trunks – summarily snatched and removed upstairs? Yes. The same items all successfully retrieved and returned to base? Yes again. But all-out escalation, mobilization, attack, carnage? Not as yet.

But it's coming. I know it is. Last week, we had a tug of war so brutal – 'It's going!' 'It's staying!' – we almost tore a T shirt in two.

No way to behave, is it, all things considered?

26 July 2014

Back on holiday in France, scene of by far and away my most popular article last year, the one about taking the car down a forest track against my wife's express instructions and then getting hopelessly stuck and having to be towed out by a French farmer. My goodness, how people love that story. It's all they ever want to talk to me about. I feel like a band who've made ten albums but all anybody wants to hear is that one signature hit from years ago. 'Bad Moon Rising', perhaps. Or 'Paranoid'. Or 'Sweet Home Alabama'. Yes indeed, I'm the Lynyrd Skynyrd of the whimsical column world. Except Robert Crampton is easier to spell.

So be it. Here's another France-based, car-themed, me-bungling-Nicola-triumphing effort. First rule of entertainment: always give your audience what it wants.

It's not as funny as the last one, mind.

Regular readers will know that in my family, my wife Nicola handles all car-related matters. That is, maintaining, fuelling, certificating – and of course driving – the family Honda falls entirely to her. In the normal course of events in London, and in fact anywhere else in the UK, I can go weeks without even getting into the car. On those occasions when I do gain entry, I am afforded (and that grudgingly) no more than under-sufferance, passenger-only status. No feet on dashboard. No wriggling about. No gestures, rude, polite or neutral, to other road users. No suggestions regarding speed, route, temperature control or choice of entertainment. And definitely no smoking.

Not even in really bad traffic jams on the Euston Road.

'I remember going from Zeebrugge to Bordeaux,' I tell Nicola. 'Summer of 1973. Hillman Hunter, windows shut tight, both parents chugging John Player Specials all the way. Didn't do me any harm.'

She remains unmoved. I break off into a prolonged coughing fit.

The restriction that bothers me most, however, is the one that ensures the exclusivity of Radio 4. If I lived out my remaining span without once more hearing, 'Now it's time for *The Archers*,' or, 'Hello and welcome to *Money Box*,' I wouldn't complain. I would, in fact, quietly clench my fists in profound celebration each and every day. Those rubrics, unfortunately, and others equally familiar, form part of the soundtrack to my wife's life, especially that significant part of her life she spends behind the wheel of a car. It is not a soundtrack she is willing to suspend for my benefit. Retuning strictly forbidden.

Here in France, though – here I get my chance. There's a car here, an old Volvo (still going strong even after being hauled out of a boggy hole at forty-five degrees with hilarious columnar consequences last summer), on which my historical claim is greater than Nicola's, it belonging to my parents. Not only am I allowed in this Volvo on a regular basis, sometimes she even lets me drive it.

And when I do, boy, you'd better believe I let rip. Windows down. Fag on the go. Correct racing line selected and taken. Abuse hurled at passing plum farmers. Radio pumping out soul classics on *Night Fever* – or Nart Feevaaire as the DJ puts it – on RFM. And if Nart Feevaaire isn't on, French radio can always be relied on for a bit of Queen. I get to do the hand-clap bit on 'Radio Ga Ga' and everything. What's not to like? The tiny sliver of my personality that hankers after turning into Jeremy Clarkson is, for a fortnight each year, satisfied.

Provided Nicola isn't in the Volvo anyway. When she is on board, notwithstanding my continued presence at the controls, the atmosphere lacks a little of the macho, cavalier, devil-may-care quality described above. No fag, no hand-clap thing, no badinage with fellow motorists. And most certainly no adherence to the racing line – otherwise known as driving on the wrong side of the road – while cornering.

Rather, our progress through the back roads of the delightful Lot-et-Garonne countryside resembles nothing so much as that of a rally driver, his co-driver beside him issuing a constant stream of instructions regarding gear changes, braking, acceleration, indicators, windscreen wiper speed, headlamp setting, potential (frankly, largely imagined) upcoming hazards and the like. Albeit a very slow rally driver. And albeit a very bossy, not to say brutally critical co-driver. A co-driver who also appoints herself in charge of heating, audio, checking the wing mirrors every three seconds and deciding when, where and how to park at journey's end. To be honest, such is Nicola's domination, she might as well be steering the damned car as well.

As I write, I have in 10 days thus far covered 143 miles at the wheel of the Volvo: 17 with my wife not present; the remaining 126 under conditions as outlined in the preceding paragraph. *Top Gear* it ain't.

8 November 2014

Just to be clear, 95 per cent of the emails and letters I get from readers are a pleasure to receive. Which is to say, nineteen out of every twenty people who take the trouble to communicate to me their thoughts on this column are complimentary about it. Having tried your patience for so long, such indications of appreciation delight me more with each passing year. Thank you, one and all.

Cursed as I am, however, with an unduly pessimistic nature, my fate is to discard the 95 per cent nice and obsess instead over the 4 per cent nasty. Apart from anything else, the nasties are often screamingly funny.

Who could fail to thrill to 'Please stop your whining effeminate drivel,' 'I always knew you were a w***er, Crampton,' or 'f*** off pouf'? Not forgetting, of course, the peerless 'How come you get paid to write this s***?' surely the *sine qua non* of out-of-a-clear-blue-sky abuse.

Before anyone belonging to that 4 per cent starts going all vitriolic about my arithmetic, I am aware that 95 and 4 make 99, not 100. And it's that last 1 per cent that I want to focus on today: namely, the one in a hundred correspondents who doesn't like what I write here yet refrains from not liking me. Guys and girls, this one's for you. I appreciate your restraint.

One complaint that I get more and more frequently comes in the form of an objection to the fundamental premise of this column (the clue to which is in the title). Such critics accuse me of perpetuating pernicious myths about men – that we're egotistical, idiotic, useless, etc. They say that Beta Male's ceaseless inventorizing of his shortcomings panders to a dangerous stereotype of male incompetence. They say that making myself the fall guy, week in, week out, is a disservice to my gender.

To which I say, there's a reason that men getting it wrong (from Chaucer to Carry On films, saucy seaside postcards to the bar-room banter set to be exchanged this very night) is such a comedy staple. And the reason is: we do. Get it wrong, that is. Often. While trying to get it right. And have done since the dawn of time – just look at Fred Flintstone, for goodness' sake.

Obviously women get stuff wrong as well. (Although in twenty-five years, now that I think about it, I can't recall my wife ever having got anything wrong at all. Ever. Just as I cannot recall ever having won a single, solitary argument with her.) But generally speaking, the gap between a man's reach and his grasp is larger than a woman's.

Once deep into middle age, it is a rare chap whose soul does not contain a large space between what he wants to be and what he is, between his imagined future and his actual present. Denying the prevalence of such a space in most of our lives is like denying you're going a bit thin on top or getting paunchy around the middle: comforting, perhaps. But untrue.

That said, obviously, I choose to emphasize the gap – the chasm – between my own fantasy and reality, play up the frequent failures, play down the slightly less frequent successes. Failure is funny, success isn't.

Last weekend, for instance, we had a bonfire in the garden at my mum's house in France. Nothing went wrong with it. The nearby hedge didn't catch alight. Jean-Luc's plum orchard just beyond the property line was not razed to the ground because I'd overdone the size or the accelerant and created a raging inferno. I hadn't. It was a sensible, medium-sized bonfire.

The large number of fallen conkers I'd cleared off the lawn and tipped into the blaze did not explode in the heat and come fizzing out at us like bullets. The children cooked up some Mars-bar-stuffed bananas in tinfoil in the embers and I did not try to steal a bite, then burn my mouth, swear, hop around in pain and get busted by Nicola.

Never much liked Mars bars, actually. Or bananas. Especially thermonuclear bananas.

Nor did I slip on a discarded banana skin, fall down an open manhole, tread on a rake, allow a grand piano to slide down a staircase or whack my son on the head by spinning around while holding a ladder horizontally.

The bonfire, in fact, commenced, conflagrated and concluded according to plan. A perfectly agreeable low-key family affair – flames suitably stared into, garden detritus suitably incinerated, ash suitably damped, your perfectly non-incompetent, non-irresponsible, non-pyromaniac columnist employing a hosepipe for the purpose – a hosepipe that he had prudently made sure was close by for the duration of the blaze. Just to be on the safe side.

All in all, a successful bonfire. Not a hapless failure or idiotic mishap in sight. Not a lot of laughs either, I'm sure you'll agree. The normal tomfoolery will resume next week.

22 November 2014

Highly unlikely I know, but just in case you missed last Saturday's edition of the paper, you should be aware that, in addition to my usual offering in this space, I was also featured in the *Weekend* section, writing about having Botox. A month previously my boss had asked if I'd undergo this increasingly popular anti-ageing treatment. I had said yes. As I always do. What a tart I have turned out to be. Last week I delivered my verdict on the experience.

There you go. If you weren't already, you are now fully up to speed.

Except . . . you're not! Because in that report a week ago, there was one salient fact I failed to mention. That is to say, I craftily held back a crucial piece of information for the exclusive enjoyment of devotees of this page. It is this: before having Botox, and in the weeks after having Botox, I neglected to tell my wife about having Botox. I finally told her last Friday night, with publication the following morning about to make discovery inevitable.

For a month, therefore, I didn't say a word. Kept it quiet – a private matter, just between me and the gatepost. And the Botox doctor. OK, so we're married to each other and all, but that shouldn't stop a man conducting a little personal business, should it? Doing a few deals? Bit of this, bit of that? Bobbin' and weavin', duckin' and divin'? Going to see a man about a dog? Or about having fifteen injections in your face? I don't have to share every last thing with the woman, do I? Know what I'm saying?

Of course you do: the easy course of action was to lie my head off. So I did.

Like any normal wife, Nicola asks me what I've been doing, what I've been working on, what commitments I've got coming up and so forth. And like any normal husband, I rarely answer any such questions with complete honesty. I don't exactly lie, to be fair. Not often, anyway. But I am secretive about many things, including some things there is absolutely no reason to be secretive about.

Sound familiar, ladies?

As with a lot of lies, the Botox fib started out by accident. Almost by accident, anyway. The morning I was due to do it, Nicola and I had a bit of a row. The details aren't relevant; the upshot was that, leaving the house in a huff and a hurry, I neglected to mention where I was going. I'm a busy man, I believe my thinking went at the time, I can't be doing with this bickering, I'll rise above it, crack on, nip up west on the Tube and get a dose of Botox. You know the drill.

It's not much of an excuse, I agree. I could have told Nicola the night before the needles went in, or the night after the needles went in, or any of the thirty-odd nights that passed between the needles going in and the no-place-to-hide necessity of eventual confession.

Which, once I had told her, was pretty much what Nicola said. 'It's not the bloody Botox,' she said. 'It's the lying that upsets me.'

How many times have we heard that, guys? OK, maybe not that precise form of words relating to prolonged deception over clandestine anti-ageing treatment, but over some other transgression? It's the same in politics. It's rarely the initial offence that brings you down; it's the attempted cover-up. Like with Nixon and Watergate.

'Why didn't you tell me?' asked Nicola.

'I thought you'd stop me doing it,' I said.

'Why would I have stopped you?'

'Because you would have.'

'What have I ever stopped you doing?' Nicola asked.

I had a long think. 'Parachuting,' I said eventually. 'You stopped me going parachuting twenty years ago, and er, that's why I, er, didn't tell you about the Botox.'

Nicola gave me a withering look. 'Do you seriously believe that?'

'Not really,' I admitted.

'You're doing your usual thing of trying to confuse the issue,' said Nicola. 'The fact is, you lied. You shouldn't have. If you just apologize, and mean it, with no qualifications or excuses, we can move on.'

Which is more or less what then happened. We summoned the children.

'I've had Botox,' I said. 'Sorry for not telling you before.'

'Did it hurt?' asked Rachel.

'Nothing hurts your daddy, sweetheart,' I said. 'You know that.'

Reading the article in question, Nicola was, to my total absence of surprise, critical. Not critical of the treatment (she thought the guy had done an excellent job, considering the depth and extent of my wrinkles) – but critical of me.

'So this doctor told you to lose weight and stop smoking, did he?' she said, scanning the page.

'Oh, they all say that,' I said.

'Not that you're particularly familiar with the concept,' Nicola sighed, 'but they all say it because it's the truth.'

14 February 2015

Another week, another survey, another unprovoked kick in the nuts for my home town. They just keep on coming. This time, some visitors to some website or other have voted Hull 'the least romantic destination' in the country. I know, I know, it shocked me too, on this day of all days. I can only assume the respondents are motivated by jealousy. Either that, or they've never actually set foot in the Venice (Barcelona? Athens? Istanbul?) of the North.

You want romance? I'll give you romance. A Friday night in the autumn of 1977. A disco, down there in the Scout hut on the corner of Redland Drive and Beverley Road, just along from Willerby Square, you know where I mean. Thirteen years old, suitably attired in my best powder-blue flares and polyester C&A shirt, I am Rockin' All Over The World in the company of the not especially desirable yet bracingly ardent Michelle Taylor. Michelle (imagine the thrill!) is in the third year, one above me. As befits an older woman, Michelle knows what she wants.

And what Michelle wants, I discover (as this elementally emancipated young lady propels me out into the refreshing November night), is some quality snogging time with this lucky boy, your future columnist. Shoving me across the Scout-hut car park and up against a fence, Michelle issues her instructions. By standing on tiptoe (she is a good head taller), tilting my head forty-five degrees and dilating my, ahem, oral cavity ('Pretend you're at the dentist') to its maximum extent (imagine two sink plungers pressed violently together), I manage to comply with Michelle's demands.

She tastes of chips. Having had a bag earlier myself, I'm guessing I do, too. The Quo? An amorous and sophisticated partner? Bonus flavours of deep-fried-potato residue? How can you get any more romantic than that?

I'll tell you how. Move forward four years to the autumn of 1981, the first term of the upper sixth. Our hero, an August baby, has not long turned seventeen. Some of his peers, however, are registering fully eighteen years alive. These landmarks are celebrated in a succession of catastrophic house parties in the suburbs and villages to the west of Hull, Soft Cell's 'Tainted Love' providing the soundtrack to each gatecrashing, kitchen-wrecking, carpet-ruining, crockery-smashing, garden-trampling, dad-fuming, mum-despairing disaster.

One of these gatherings, incidentally, I shall always associate with the delicate gambit offered by one (uninvited) guest as he lurched through the front door.

'Now then,' boomed Steve Wilson, a slightly older and infinitely rougher young man than most of us present, 'any birds here up for a poke?'

See how my maligned city is steeped in the language of love?

At a similar event I inveigled myself into the spare bedroom with a young lady. Matters were proceeding nicely until the unexpected return of the host's parents in the early hours necessitated my immediate departure via the bedroom window. A painful exit, I'm afraid – and yet, surely, also rather dashing: snagging your scrotum on a window latch before dropping ten feet into a flower bed and hobbling away home has a certain cavalier quality about it, after all.

A few months later, the smell of the fish docks blowing in off the Humber, I found myself in town, first to clean out my building society account and then over to Ratner's to buy an engagement ring. I chose a nice sparkler, if I say so myself – seventy-five quid, reduced from ninety-nine. Which was a very keen price, I'm sure you'll agree, even back in 1982, for two alleged diamonds flanking an alleged sapphire.

Four months further down the line, 'Come On Eileen' at number one, the wedding was off.

Of course, the girl I really wanted to be with, the woman I am with, the woman I'll be taking out tonight, was in those days immune to my charm. Nicola and I were friends, but only friends. As we advanced through our teens, I'd tried everything to win Nicola over, but she wasn't impressed by fighting, smoking or shoplifting and I couldn't do wheelies on my bike.

My next move? Obviously I took her to see an amateur-dramatic production of Bertolt Brecht's *The Caucasian Chalk Circle* at Cottingham Civic Hall. And also a protest meeting about cruise missiles at Bevin House, the local headquarters of the Transport and General Workers' Union. And then a municipal reception at the town hall in Bradford. How could a girl resist all that? You may well ask. Fact is, I had to wait the best part of another decade before she saw the light.

Fall in love with a girl at thirteen, hang about another thirteen years until she falls in love with you. If that isn't romantic, I don't know what is.

14 March 2015

So, Saturday evening, 6.30-ish, and your columnist is walking the short distance from his house to the local cinema. His wife and children are with him. Their intention is to catch the early showing of *The Second Best Exotic Delightfully Middle-class Marigold Hotel*. After which, bathed in a warm glow of exemplary British thespian talent, the plan is to meet up with Cousin Steve for dinner. Tea. Supper. Whatever. No drama. An innocent family outing. Home in time for *Match of the Day*.

And here we are, almost there – temporarily stalled, however, as we await the chance safely to cross a busy road. The man now coming towards us shows no such caution. Marching straight into the road, forcing a bus driver to slam on his brakes, this chap, while almost certainly under the influence of his chemical of choice, does not present as a tragi-comic lurching drunk. Rather, his manner is purposeful, assertive and – it swiftly transpires – aggressive.

Arriving at our side of the road, finding my wife ever so slightly in his path, this character gives Nicola a vigorous shove. Thus can your world change. In an instant.

'Whoa, hold on,' says Nicola.

Her assailant grunts. I cannot, I'm afraid, recall his words. I'm way too busy squaring up to the fella to focus on the detail.

Now hold on, Bob. Brawling in the street? Not exactly dignified, that, is it? At your age? Your kids in tow? Surely, in the immortal words of Danny Glover in *Lethal Weapon*, you are 'too old for this s***'? And what with you an (allegedly) respectable columnist for *The Times* of London?

Moreover, while this weirdo has, in the eyes of the law, most definitely assaulted your good lady wife, he has employed no more (nor less) than a push. A violent push, perhaps, but still only a push just the same. And a push, although obviously despicable, does not on balance constitute a clear and present danger to your nearest and dearest.

Besides which, Bob, other factors must be considered. This nutter is younger and (I know it's a cliché but it happens to be true) bigger than you. He is, given his behaviour, reckless, dis-inhibited and possessed of a complete disregard for commonly accepted standards of decorum. He is probably much better versed in the dark arts of street fighting than yourself. He may well be armed. Last but not least, he is quite likely off his bonce on some substance or other.

All in all, the sensible response is to usher your family rapidly in the opposite direction, away from all this unseemliness and towards the comforting embrace of Judi Dench and Maggie Smith. Not forgetting Bill Nighy and Celia Imrie.

You all enjoy the film, and later you tell the story; you shrug;

you sigh; you observe that in this life one is suffered sometimes to encounter a number of deeply unpleasant people; you put it down to experience and move on. In other words, in the classic idiom of the Saturday night fracas: leave it, mate, he ain't worth it.

Whatever. I whacked the bastard anyway. Whacked him to the best of my ability, at any rate. Which isn't saying much. I am, I have to admit, only averagely good at fighting. Not hopeless, not much cop either. No Floyd Mayweather, that's for sure. Assessing my record – going way back to the school gates, the rugby pitch, the initial chaos of first attending pubs and clubs and parties – I emerge as no more than a willing, barely competent journeyman. Won a few, drawn a few, lost a few.

With regard to this occasion, I get in a couple of blows. While not especially effectual, let alone conclusive, my flailings at least come as a surprise (judging by his gratifying 'ouff' of alarm) to a man clearly accustomed to bullying strangers at will. Score one for Battlin' Bob.

My opponent, unfortunately, soon recovers his poise, defends himself (which is fair enough) and seeks, not entirely unsuccessfully, to gain the upper hand (also fair enough, under the circumstances we now find ourselves in). We grapple and scuffle for a spell. He connects with an elbow, an elbow which I later discover has cut my forehead and given me a black eye. I hang in there as best I can.

We run out of steam, separate, Nicola intervenes – and the two of us tacitly agree, in the way of these things, to call a halt to the stupidity. My family and I go one way; he goes the other. I hope and trust I never clap eyes on the guy again.

Even as these events are unfolding, I identify two consolations. One is: this may well be a long way short of desirable, Bob old son, but at least Nicola will give you some credit. The second is: this nonsense has got to be worth a minimum of two columns. And look, one of those consolations has come to pass.

21 March 2015

First, a recap. Saturday, early evening, the family is walking to the cinema. A fellow pedestrian – male, thirties, not obviously either sane or sober – approaches, draws near, gives Nicola a hefty and unprovoked shove. I attack him. This character and I exchange blows. I sustain a black eye and a cut to the forehead. I hope I inflicted similar damage on him.

After the initial flurry, we grapple awhile, inconclusively, run out of puff, separate, recover – and by and by become aware of Nicola's firmly expressed instructions to stop this nonsense right now. My wife's opinion tending to have a salutary effect on the behaviour of even the most aggressive personalities, we comply. And so – he going one way, we going the other – does the actual action end. The aftermath, however – the aggravation, the accusations, the argument, the analysis – all of that is only just beginning. To be honest, even now, a fortnight later, it hasn't stopped.

I can't deny I've been surprised by Nicola's reaction. She is usually a strong advocate of taking a firm stand. Truth is, I thought she'd be pleased. Delighted. Frankly, even as the guy's elbow crunched into my face, I was too busy compiling a list of the sexual demands I would now be able to call in to be much bothered by the pain. When I say aftermath, obviously what I really mean is bollocking. One of the biggest, wide-ranging, long-lasting bollockings she's ever given me. And that's saying something.

It started straight away. Within minutes – milliseconds – of the cessation of physical hostilities, hostilities of another infinitely more wounding variety opened up.

You lost your temper, Nicola said. You overreacted. You made an unpleasant situation much worse. Yes, the guy shoved me, but he wasn't threatening me. You didn't need to protect me. You got it wrong. I can't believe you did that.

That was all within the first hundred yards. Only another hundred to the cinema, but she wasn't finished yet, not by any means. In doing what you did, Nicola continued, you put not only yourself but all of us in potentially much greater danger than we were. You wouldn't want Sam to behave like that in similar circumstances. The guy was clearly a nutter. You didn't appreciate how far gone he was. He wasn't all there. He could have had a knife or anything. In fact, she concluded, he probably did have a knife.

'Well, he had a bottle in his bag,' said Sam. 'I saw him reaching for it.'

Cheers for that, son. Thanks a million.

There you go, said Nicola, triumphantly. You (she went on) completely lost it. There was no need to do what you did. The world is full of unreasonable people. Sometimes you intervene; sometimes you say something; sometimes you don't. You draw a line, you make a judgement. In this case, the correct decision was to just walk away.

Rachel – silent up until that point – sniffled her agreement.

'Are you all right, sweetheart?' I asked. My daughter nodded, clearly upset, as well she might be. 'Nothing to worry about, babe,' I said, putting my arm around her, thinking first things first, got to signal to the kids everything's going to be OK. Thinking the main thing is to reassure them, put on a brave front, be a good father.

Thinking also, oh s***, they all reckon I called that wrong. Thinking, damn, three against one? I may be in trouble here. Thinking, maybe I should chase back down the road, catch up with the loony guy, see if I can get him on my side.

We arrived at the cinema, bought our popcorn, watched our film, me dabbing away at my injuries with a swiftly – and gratifyingly – bloodied hankie. Walking home afterwards, Nicola resumed her critique.

We're not living in the Stone Age, Robert. We're not eighteen, Robert. I don't need you to defend my honour, Robert. I don't require you to make these grand gestures, Robert. I'd much rather you got over this ridiculous obsession with your pride and move on, Robert. For God's sake, we're fifty years old, Robert. Plenty more where that came from, too. Bang bang. Ouch ouch.

And yet, hammer away as she might, I'm still not persuaded. Which is to say, whatever physical risks were inherent in my actual reaction must be balanced against the emotional corrosion – shame, humiliation, self-hatred – of my adopting her preferred reaction. Got to take the long view sometimes, haven't you? Got to be able to live with yourself.

11 April 2015

Today's effort is my 665th offering in this space. I mention this figure because I once saw a guy – in the Florida Keys, if I'm not mistaken – wearing a T-shirt emblazoned with the very same number. And underneath that number was written 'the neighbour of the beast', which is why such an apparently trivial observation stuck in my mind. Blimey, I thought, '665, the neighbour of the beast' – that's seriously witty, that is. I wish I'd come up with it. While at the same time noting that houses rarely number consecutively. Then again, sometimes they do. And besides, '665, the neighbour of the beast' is nigh-on unimprovable. It wouldn't work with either 664 or 668, more accurate as either may be.

So that's that off my chest.

Speaking of my chest, it's getting bigger.

On account of my having finally – roughly twenty-five years since they first became commonly available, affordable and more or less acceptable – set aside my residual prejudices and engaged the services of a personal trainer. Sapan, he's called. Total star, this fella. Sorting me right out, he is. And in the nick of time.

Obviously it was Nicola who located Sapan, contacted Sapan, encouraged – not to say entreated, not to say exhorted, not to say, in the final analysis, forced – me to see Sapan. It helped that Sapan's gym is about a hundred yards, maybe not even that, from our front door. In an arch under the railway, as it happens. Eeeh, when we first lived here, those arches were all lock-ups for gangsters. Or if not gangsters, then definitely borderline Arthur Daley types. With raggedy-arsed urchins cavorting in the streets outside. And so on.

That's what I drone on about to young Sapan, anyhow, by way of delaying his next exhausting command.

When I say my chest is getting bigger, that is not precisely true. It is, in fact, a total lie, because my chest is getting smaller. But in a good way. Not exactly in a sinewy, lithe, lean (and yet manfully rippling) Poldarkian way. Not yet anyway. But certainly a less fat way, which is a start. Give it time. Sapan and I have only been acquainted for a month. Star, he may be; magician, he is not.

Going back to those 'residual prejudices', what I mean by that is my all but extinct, and yet occasionally farting up to the surface, antipathy towards certain trends, habits and inanimate objects that came into existence, or at least prominence, in what was deemed to be the selfish, materialistic era of the late eighties and early nineties. Employing a personal trainer, for sure – but also owning a mobile phone and/or a Filofax, drinking imported lager and/or sparkling water, driving a Golf GTi and/or a

Peugeot 205, living in a gated community, and so on and so forth.

Readers under (and most over) forty will surely – and rightly – find it hard to believe that any of that stuff used to stir the blood. But take it from me, however daft it may sound – and yes, it now sounds pretty damn daft, I agree – sanguinary agitation did indeed occur. Within my veins, at any rate. I delayed getting a mobile phone, for instance, for several years after they had become close to a necessity, because I thought such a device might contaminate me in some way. Some unspecified, ill-defined and – now that I think about it – in fact utterly non-existent way.

What a dick.

And while we're about it, what a hypocrite, too. Back in 1990, my then girlfriend, my now wife, was making her living (and mine too, to be honest) in the big bad City of London. Nicola had the hot hatch, the gym membership, the mobile (to use the term loosely, it was actually bloody enormous) phone, the works. She was packing some pretty impressive shoulder pads too, as I recall.

Pretty sexy gear, to be fair. I wonder if she's still got any of that clobber kicking around at the back of the wardrobe . . .

And when that February Nicola suggested we should go skiing, generously offering to foot the bill (while politely not pointing out to her new boyfriend he was in no position to foot so much as a day trip to Skeggy), did that boyfriend refuse? Or did he get bang on the piste, mine's a large glühwein, ta very much?

All water under the bridge, right? Here and now in the spring of 2015, the salient point is that the boyfriend, now an older and wiser – and yet blurrier around the edges – husband and father, has acquired a personal trainer. A personal trainer to whose instructions – as regards squatting and stretching, pulsing and pushing, lifting and lunging, kettle-belling and . . . er . . . concentrating on the core – he is thus far, to his considerable surprise, succumbing three times each week. Weirdly, it seems to be working.

Frankly, I'm waiting for something to go wrong.

2 May 2015

Today is my wedding anniversary. Yes indeed, Nicola and I tied the knot on this very day in 1998. At St Bride's Church, Fleet Street. Reception at the Barbican. Salmon mousse, rubber chicken, raspberry pavlova.

Seventeen glorious years. Plus two years of engagement before that. Plus six years of cohabitation, coupledom and what I suppose must be called courtship, all the way back to the spring of 1990, when we first started going steady, to use another tragically outmoded phrase. That's twenty-five years ago.

Half my life. Half hers, too.

That's not counting the thirteen years prior to 1990, when Nicola and I were, frustratingly (to me at least), 'just good friends'. Thirty-eight years: never mind 50 per cent of our lives, that's close on 80. It goes without saying that it don't seem a day too long.

When we meet people for the first time, incidentally, as and when this detail of us having gone to the same school comes up, it is always a source of fascination and delight. 'Aaaah,' is the invariable response. 'Childhood sweethearts. How romantic.'

At which point I smile coyly while Nicola explains, in some detail, with some urgency, that we were only ever friends, we didn't hook up properly until we were twenty-five, we both in fact had several other significant (as well as insignificant, but nonetheless enjoyable) relationships in the interim. Which, while true, tends to rather spoil the moment.

It's not as unusual as you might think, by the by, even in this age of social media, dating apps and globalized doo-be-doo, to end up with someone whom you first met at school. Or still less, first met at college. Tinder, Grindr, Shag-me-now.com or whatever notwithstanding, a majority of us will (I'm sure I read this somewhere recently) already have our eventual life partner's number in our contacts list before we reach our twenty-fifth birthday.

Just thought I'd throw that out there for your consideration.

Blimey, I dunno: smokin' hot dating tips. What a service I provide.

Moving on (while swiftly referring back to the timeline described above), no doubt you'll be wanting to know why, after six years together, and having decided to take the plunge, Nicola and I then dilly-dallied for fully two further years before walking down the aisle.

Well, thanks for asking, because, as it happens, thereby hangs a tale. I got round to popping the question around June of '96. We were in the kitchen, as I recall, when I muttered something vague about how maybe it was, er, about time, we, er, y'know, got married, what d'you reckon?

Smooth, eh? And they say romance is dead.

In any event, Nicola accepted my proposal. A day or two later, we found ourselves in the great city of Manchester. We had a spare half-hour, went shopping, bought the ring in a jeweller's off Deansgate. Excellent progress. Before, during and after that excursion up north, we relayed the happy news to our nearest and dearest. No date set as yet, we said, but probably next spring. Cue much rejoicing.

A few days down the line found the newly affianced couple making preparations for their holiday in southern France. Back then we owned a vintage (1974, chrome bumpers, round wheel arches, total design classic if you care about these things) MG Midget. The plan was to drive down to Folkestone, take the tunnel to Calais, put the car on the motorail overnight to Brive, proceed in style to our destination.

'I'll do everything,' Nicola told me. 'You just make sure there's enough petrol in the car.'

You see where this is heading? Long story short, I failed (obviously) to fill the tank. I thought I'd got away with it but, no, the car ground to a halt at the precise moment of guiding it on to the train. We had to be shoved aside to receive an emergency top-up. Humiliation. Nicola was not at all happy.

But, hey, it all worked out OK. We made our motorail connection. We repaired to our cabin. A cabin in which, anxious to make amends, I immediately began plying my intended with some hastily acquired champagne. Rather a lot of champagne. One thing led to another. Caution was thrown to the wind. You can guess the rest.

Later that summer, Nicola announced there was no way she was getting married in a maternity dress. Hence the delay. Hence seventeen as opposed to eighteen years of wedded bliss. Hence me having to provide, according to the numerous websites I have consulted, a gift comprising furniture (as opposed to porcelain), amethysts (as opposed to garnets) and a bouquet of red carnations (as opposed to a non-specific one; Wikipedia isn't clear on the matter).

Better get busy.

23 January 2016

Today, 23 January, is my mum's birthday. And will, of course, for ever remain so, despite her no longer being around to celebrate it. She would have turned eighty-three – except a month ago, two nights before Christmas, at 11 p.m. in Hull Royal Infirmary, she died. We had the funeral ten days ago. Thus after fifty-five years of marriage, and five years of widowhood, my mum is now reunited with my dad.

Almost reunited, anyway – their graves are about fifteen feet apart. We thought the old man would appreciate a little bit of distance. He always liked his own space. Besides, by the time my mum got around to booking her own patch of East Yorkshire clay a year or so after her husband's death, the adjacent couple of plots to his had already been taken. Never mind. They were both always open to meeting new people. It was part of their charm.

Because he had served as a member of the European parliament, my dad qualified for a formal obituary here in *The Times*. Not wanting my mum to miss out on a similar appreciation, I thought I'd present, this week and next, begging your indulgence, an unofficial tribute. It's a version of the eulogy I gave at the service. Plus a few other things I had meant to say but (under the pressure of the occasion and suffering from a chronic lack of sleep, having stayed up ridiculously late the previous night swapping stories with my cousin George) I simply forgot to mention.

The condolence cards I got following my mum's death tended to use the same phrases. 'Force of nature', 'strong-willed', 'formidable' and 'highly persuasive' all made several appearances. So did various versions of the sentiment 'Your mum was always very kind and generous to me . . . whatever anyone else might say.' A telling postscript, that, you will agree.

Whereas my dad was liked by one and all, political opponents included, my mum was a woman, I am sure you have already inferred, who divided opinion. It was quite possible the seventy or so mourners – top turnout, happy with that – included a number of traumatized Tory councillors making doubly sure Margaret Crampton really was dead. As with that other infinitely more famous yet probably no more frightening politician called Margaret, my mum was not a woman to leave you in any doubt of her views on anything.

Which could, obviously, be socially mortifying for her

adolescent sons. Fact is, however, like Thatcher on the best way to run an economy, on her chosen subjects – feminism, environmental protection, apartheid – my mum was ahead of her time and absolutely correct. There was a time when these causes were considered outlandish, their champions mocked and pilloried. She stuck at it regardless.

She was, in short, someone who you were very glad was on your side. And I was in no doubt she was on my side, in a life-affirming, life-defining way. But for my mum's encouragement, ambition and, on occasion frankly, abuse and aggression, for instance, I wouldn't have gone to Oxford University. And if I hadn't gone to Oxford University, I would not in all likelihood be sitting here at this desk writing this now.

A desk that is located, with gratifying symmetry, a mere few hundred yards from where, on this day in 1933, my mum came into the world, in Bermondsey, south London. My granddad drove a cab, my nana took in washing for better-off people. The family didn't have much money. My mum told me as a baby she slept in a clothes drawer because they couldn't afford a cot.

'That was cruel,' I said. 'Wasn't it really dark and scary?'

'They didn't close the drawer once I was in it, you idiot,' she laughed.

Bombed in the Blitz, evacuated to six different places, schooling disrupted, she nonetheless made it to university, at a time when only a tiny fraction of the population had that immense privilege. And of that tiny fraction, an even tinier fraction were women. And of that even tinier fraction, a yet tinier fraction had grown up on a council estate. My mum's two sisters and brother all got to university, too. Some achievement, that, back in the fifties. The tragedy is, I'm not sure it would – or could, though it certainly damn well should – happen now.

Such stunning social mobility meant, as the sixties dawned,

that those four siblings' children – my cousins, near enough every one of them in attendance to hear these words, my brother, me – could all enjoy childhoods of more ease, choice and comfort than our parents could ever have imagined.

I sometimes tell my own kids, comparing their current rich range of options with my own narrower one in the seventies, they don't know how lucky they are. The truth is, however, that compared with the one before, it was actually my generation who didn't know how lucky we were.

30 January 2016

OK, eulogy to my mum, recently deceased, part two. Here we go.

Sorry to bang on. Profuse apologies. I am, rest assured, fully aware that such self-obsession has no place in what purports to be an upbeat, lightweight, entertaining, diversionary column. A lapse. Not to mention an abuse of privilege. Not to mention a contravention of all manner of codes of conduct, staff handbooks and proclamations on media ethics.

But hey, so what? Sometimes you have to be guided by a moral authority far higher than mere etiquette. Besides, if you're lucky enough to have access to a national newspaper and your mum dies, and you don't then exploit that access to pay tribute as best you can, then what sort of son or daughter are you?

In any case, following my initial efforts last week, I've been touched – gratified, indeed overwhelmed, thank you, one and all – by the number of people contacting me with condolences, sympathies, shared experiences, and so forth. Some readers, I estimate, can bear a further instalment.

Or are at any rate willing to indulge it.

Such musings are, after all, the stuff of life. Or, rather, death. And for those still young enough or fortunate enough not yet to have been scarred by the soul-hollowing brutality of bereavement, I say may that moment be as far away as possible and, meanwhile, listen up.

On the day of the funeral, the cortège due to depart the house at 10.45, the service scheduled for 11 a.m., the committal at 12, post-match tea and buns at 1 p.m., I judged it about right if I got my arse into gear at 8 a.m. Which I did. Levered myself reluctantly out of bed, made some tea, attempted – with no audible results – to rouse both my children and my cousin, trudged back upstairs to my wife.

Legs wobbly, heart pounding, head throbbing, throwing my full length on both the bed and her mercy, I told Nicola – not for the first time, and surely not for the last – that I found myself in a state and needed her help.

'What's wrong?' she asked.

'I've got to make this speech and I'm not sure what I should say,' I wailed.

The context being that, as a dutiful son, I had intended to get my eulogy written, refined and rehearsed the previous evening. At the latest. And yet, I had, as a grieving son not minded to do much of anything, failed to complete this task, preferring instead to sit up yakking with my cousin George. That'd be the same cousin George who, as of this next morning, was snoring away, oblivious to my urgings to get himself the hell up.

Incidentally, while I know scores of women and at least a dozen gay guys every bit as skilled in the art of hardcore gossip as me, cousin George is the only straight bloke able to rival myself in this regard. It's frankly extraordinary we're both heterosexual.

Nicola – so often the way – assumed control. She told Sam to make his dad a cup of heavily sugared tea. She told Rachel to make her dad several slices of heavily buttered toast. She told George to assist his cousin in his hour of need by assuming a position not only conscious, but also vertical. And then, turning to her jittery, overwrought, bordering on losing the plot husband, Nicola told him what to say.

I had, I explained, already nailed the biographical, if you will, public elements of what I wanted to say. That, however, was the easy bit. What had eluded me thus far, I told my wife, was a suitable homage to my mum's personal qualities. Qualities that (while undeniably considerable) were, ahem, not always, in the case of some specific individuals, female in-laws most prominently, directed in an entirely benevolent fashion.

If you get my meaning. Which many daughters-in-law instantly will. My wife for one, after forty years' acquaintance with her once and future mother-in-law, certainly appreciates the distinction.

And yet, to her immense and everlasting credit, Nicola dismissed her own not entirely happy relationship with her mother-in-law and instead reminded me how she had first been to our family home as a fourteen-year-old schoolfriend in 1978. How, in what had been a vastly different era, a much colder, more uptight, less accepting time, our house had been a friendly, welcoming, tolerant place, full of fun and chat and debate among all manner of visitors.

'And that was down to your mum,' said Nicola. 'You didn't necessarily notice it, because you were used to it. But it was unusual at the time. That's what people will remember and value. That's what you should say.'

So that's what I did say. And going by the smiles and nods of recognition, Nicola was spot on. Funny how you never really appreciate the very things that are right in front of your face.

What a woman.

13 February 2016

And so it begins. Starting tomorrow and running through to the end of March with my son's birthday, I'm facing six significant family occasions in six weeks. After Valentine's – Romeo Bob swarming up to the bedroom window, red rose clutched between his teeth – comes Mother's Day, my daughter's birthday, my wife's birthday, Easter and, finally, Sam's celebration. With our wedding anniversary to follow, by way of an epilogue, one month later.

It's a big ask for a boy, right?

And what this boy is looking at, I calculate, is, first off, five lots of presents. That's not five presents, total, but five sets of multiple presents. All wrapped up nice and neat – and we all know how much middle-aged men love spending their leisure time wrapping presents, don't we? Scrabbling to locate the free end of the Sellotape, scratching apart half a roll into thin pitiful shreds, finally securing half a dozen usable strips, only to watch in pleading, swearing anguish as they each furl suicidally in on themselves one by one, the folds of the packaging paper springing slowly open, you back precisely where you started. Great fun.

I'd better not forget an Easter egg for Nicola, either. She sorts the kids out, but likes me to procure hers. Creme Egg was always her favourite, but Cadbury recently ballsed up the recipe, she informs me, so I'll have to use my initiative instead. Not a position in which a chap likes to find himself, as regards wife, gifts for the buying of.

Then I shall have to attend, and in some cases organize, a minimum of four, more likely five, meals out. Maybe even six, unless I can scupper the other three's annual attempt to have Easter Sunday lunch in a restaurant rather than at home.

In addition, starting tomorrow morning – or maybe this

afternoon to be on the safe side – I need to sort out two lots of flowers for Nicola. Not roses, carnations or tulips, mind, something more imaginative. And 'imaginative' is – as with 'initiative', 'inspiration', 'spontaneity' and (the horror!) 'Surprise me' – not a word you want to hear in this context. I should also supervise the children's efforts to supply flowers, cards and a trinket or token or two for their mother, both on Mother's Day and on her birthday.

It's a whirlwind of table reservations, florists, stationers, bookshops, clothes shops, chocolate shops and infuriating pointless shops that sell gift cards, cushions and candles. A late-winter meets early-spring slog of booking, buying, phoning, wrapping and, worst by a long way, choosing. Every year, I'm frankly surprised I find time to slump in front of any Six Nations games at all. Let alone pretty much all of them. Anthems and analysis included.

Of course, at almost nineteen and almost seventeen, Sam and Rachel don't really require me any longer to chivvy them to do right by their mum. Certainly my daughter doesn't, and neither docs my son – apart from when he's completely forgotten, as teenage boys are inclined to do. Still, old habits die hard. I can't deny I have yet fully to adjust my parental technique – insofar as I have anything as exalted as a parental technique – to the emerging reality of my children having almost become adults.

My wife has made the transition – women seem (generalizing wildly) to have a better instinct for these things. We fathers, I find, often struggle to progress beyond a fixed picture of our offspring as helpless innocent creatures for ever aged about six. Our own role in this unchanging tableau is twofold: teach the little blighters what's what in the world; destroy anyone or anything posing so much as the merest threat to those same blighters' wellbeing. I think most dads will recognize that as a fair summary.

Trouble is, chaps, they grow up. So eventually we have to move on from this mindset. Or, at least, refine it. The first part, anyway (the second stays pure and true) – and I'm not sure how to make the change. My wife, nonetheless, says I must, so I'll probably find a way.

Never mind 'probably', try 'definitely'. Why? Because the other night both children called me out (although not in so many words) on my didactic tendencies, the way (they said) I dominate conversations with a recitation of facts they don't know, personal experiences they haven't had, moral instruction they don't relish and opinions they don't always share. Opinions that, they both said, I deem to be irrefutable.

The complaint related specifically to my alleged hijacking of any family discussion of current affairs, politics, international relations or historical events.

'You just behave as if what you say matters more than what we say,' was how Rachel put it.

'It does,' I replied.

'That was not,' my wife told me much later, after the smoke had cleared, 'the most helpful response you might have made.'

19 March 2016

Last weekend found my wife and me staying at a place called North Cadbury Court, an Elizabethan country house in Somerset, hired by a friend for her birthday get-together. Nicola and I were billeted in a cosy room right up in the eaves affording, as the venue brochure may well put it, a stunning vista of the estate's lawn, parkland and lake and, beyond them, the patchwork fields and peculiar plateaued hills rolling away south towards Dorset. All very nice.

If you could see it, that is. Which I could, despite the presence of a handsome parapet wall running across half the height of the window. Nicola, standing a crucial nine inches shorter than her husband, had to balance on the radiator to appreciate the view.

'Shall I see if we can borrow a stepladder?' I suggested.

'Very funny,' she replied, levering up the sash window and climbing out on to the roof.

'I can't help thinking,' I said, peering gingerly over the edge, 'of Nigel Pargetter plummeting to his death in *The Archers*.'

'Lower Loxley Hall doesn't have a parapet wall,' said Nicola.

'How do you know?'

'Wouldn't have fallen off if it did, would he?'

Excellent point.

Back on terra firma, we took a stroll down to the lake.

'See this terraced bit here,' I said, as we reached the boundary between the lawn and the park, 'is it what people call a ha-ha?'

'No,' said Nicola, 'a ha-ha has an inclined ditch below a vertical drop. The ground here is flat.'

'In that case then,' I continued slyly, 'is it a *trompe l'oeil*?'

'No, it's not that either,' Nicola explained patiently. '*Trompe l'oeil* means "to deceive the eye", and this, er, doesn't deceive anything. Nor try to.'

My inability to impress my wife never ceases to amaze me.

Just past the not a ha-ha that wasn't a *trompe* blinking *l'oeil* either, we began to come across a lot of golf balls lying half-hidden in the damp grass – golf balls which, it being in my nature, I started to collect up. Golf balls that, it being in her nature, Nicola was both keen and able to locate way before I did. She directed operations; I stuffed the muddy wet spheres into my coat pocket, eventually retrieving seventeen to return to the Big House. Nicola had spotted all but three of them, including one I'd been treading on at the time.

As we explored further, it turned out the house was superbly stocked with diverting entertainments. I played table tennis, twice – and lost twice – against a fellow guest in our party, wives dutifully watching on. This chap and I then teamed up against two others for a frame of snooker, there being a full-sized table available. Thanks in large part to my struggle to effect even the slightest acquaintance between cue ball and target ball, we lost.

Or maybe we shook hands on the draw, honours roughly even after an hour of mounting fouls. Biggest break: eight. Shockingly hard game, is snooker – the distances involved truly are considerable.

The venue also boasted a swimming pool, albeit a small one, ten metres at most.

'Sport Relief Swimathon soon,' I said to Nicola. 'I'd better get a few lengths in.'

I did twenty, which equates to one tenth of the yardage I'm required to complete in today's event.

'Nothing to worry about,' I assured my wife, in response to the extreme scepticism emanating from the recumbent figure in the jacuzzi. 'It's best to be tapering off my training at this stage anyhow.'

'What training would that be?' she asked.

And so, finally, the following morning, night-time revelry and generous cooked breakfast slowing your columnist's ascent to little more than a crawl, we returned once more to the roof. Not, however, to the gully outside our room this time, but to a magnificent Astroturfed dais mounted above the centre of the house, the better to facilitate the absolute genius pastime of whacking golf balls out across the wide green expanses fifty feet below. Hence our ball haul the previous day.

Ushering Nicola to one side, I gripped a seven iron and warned her to watch out for my swing.

'I've done this before,' I told her, smashing the club down to make only the most marginal contact with the ball, sufficient for it to dribble forward three feet off the platform and roll into a gutter.

'And I've never done this before,' said Nicola, before curving a perfect pitch a hundred yards into the park.

Beginner's luck? No chance. We hit another dozen balls each: my best just about inched past her worst.

A mile or two away, perched on an outcrop across the A303, we could admire the remains of Cadbury Castle, an Iron Age fort formerly called Camalet and said, like everywhere else in Somerset, to be the site of King Arthur's legendary court. No one's going to be offering me first dibs on yanking Excalibur out of the stone, are they?

18 June 2016

One of my wife's many (numerous? countless? endless?) gripes (suggestions? pointers? helpful tips?) about my behaviour concerns the fact that I swear way too much. In front of the children, the mother-in-law, the vicar too, in all likelihood, if we ever came across a vicar.

'Hey,' I always claim, 'I'm one of those creative types. I've got long hair, stubble and everything, the full package. Swearing is what we do. We get a pass. It's like rock stars being allowed to take drugs and shag around.'

And guess what? While Nicola isn't even slightly convinced, let alone impressed, by this admittedly flimsy argument, I have noticed that Potty-Mouthed Bob, unlike my many other incarnations, does get something of an easy ride. I guess when set against the prevalence of other, far deadlier sins – pride, envy, wrath, gluttony, greed, sloth, lust, pretty much the full set as it goes, not to mention dishonesty, incompetence, flatulence – profanity has to shuffle respectfully to the back of the queue.

Besides, although it was a long time ago, Nicola did work in the City for ten years. There are just as many expletives per capita chucked around in the Square Mile as there are in what used to be Fleet Street, that's for damn sure. Probably more.

And anyway, let's not forget, Nicola knows as well as any intelligent person that swearing is a whole lotta fun, pure and simple. And funny. If only, I often say, I were allowed to swear, freely and outrageously, in this very column, then it'd be twice as moderately amusing as it already is.

Be that as it may, the salient point (there is one, I promise, it'll arrive any minute, bear with me) is we are, as a family, a bit beyond paying any penance for swearing. That particular ship has sailed. Fact is, Chez Crampo, the occasional half-hearted crackdown notwithstanding, most reasonable observers would be shocked by the language routinely employed. It wouldn't be out of place in a barracks. Or a locker room. Or a gutter, frankly.

I offer no justification. I don't defend it.

I can't pretend I'm proud of it. I accept that this state of affairs represents a resounding parental – or rather, paternal, Nicola has tried her best – failure. But hey, it is what it is. Apologies all round. Gotta pick your battles, right? And pick them not only as a parent, but also as a child. Which is to say, in terms of mitigating their father's excesses, my offspring recognize that the use of a swear jar, by way of deterring the deployment of foul and abusive language, is a non-starter. Ain't gonna happen. No way, no how. Waste of time.

This particular realization, however, has not lessened the appeal of monetary forfeit in general. Both sense an opportunity for financial gain. Both also sense an opportunity to mock, satirize, undermine, denigrate and otherwise disrespect their dear old dad, an opportunity they have obviously grasped with both hands.

And thus – with, I have to say, eager assistance from their mother – Sam and Rachel have studied their father's most frequent utterances and created a jar into which I must put a whole pound sterling each time a designated phrase escapes my mouth. The jars are all lined up, neatly labelled in my daughter's admirably tidy handwriting, on a shelf in the kitchen. They're all filling up nicely.

I'm not clear as to where the money is eventually likely to go. Sam says charity. Rachel says clothes. For her, that is.

The first jar is labelled 'But I've barely eaten all day'. This is my excuse when I get busted rummaging around in the fridge at 11 p.m. The second jar says 'Me legs have gone', while the third says 'I just need a little lie-down'. One or other or both of these is apparently what I say when I come in from seeing Sapan, my personal trainer, or football, or the lido, or walking to the shops, after any form of exercise at all, basically.

The fourth, fifth and sixth jars relate to when I'm working at home. They say, respectively, 'I'm on a deadline', 'No, seriously, I'm really up against it' and 'Christ, can't I just have two minutes to finish this?' The seventh jar is for when they've just made themselves something to eat and are hoping to whisk it away to their bedrooms to scoff it in privacy and peace. This jar says 'I'll just have a little bite of that before you disappear, if I may'.

The final jar simply says 'Phoaaargh!' This refers to the random noises I make performing even the most minor physical action – sitting down, standing up, entering a room, etc.

Cheeky rascals, eh? They've only gone and rumbled me.

And now Nicola is threatening to add a whole new series of extra jars to cover the separate catchphrases and clichés I reserve for her benefit.

2 July 2016

'So that's that,' I said to my wife last Friday morning at 6.30 a.m., having just woken to the big news of the EU Referendum result, 'you're going to have to give up your job.'

'Eh?' said Nicola. 'What are you talking about?'

'Wife,' I replied, 'my decision is final. Don't worry your pretty little head about it. Not only should you leave work, but Rachel must leave school straight away. Educating girls only makes them less appealing to a potential suitor, and I don't want to see any daughter of mine on the shelf.'

'Are you feeling all right?'

'Never better, wife,' I said. 'As you know, I pride myself on staying in touch with the national mood. Moreover, as a respected commentator, it is my duty to reflect the cultural consensus. I have therefore decided that we as a family should revert to life as it was lived before jolly old England got itself tangled up with all these ghastly foreign types.'

'And this means I can't go out to work and Rachel can't go to university?'

'Indeed it does, wife,' I intoned. 'Although as you know, I am neither an unreasonable nor an old-fashioned man. Should you wish to seek out some suitable task to fund your chosen – and, may I say, charming – feminine fripperies, that is acceptable. Provided,' I added, 'my tea is on the table when I come home. As for Rachel, she needs to find herself a nice husband and settle down.'

Thus did I repair to the bathroom for my daily shave. It would not do, after all, to encounter the bank manager – or, God forbid (hah hah, I am not an unhumorous man), the vicar – while resembling a vagrant.

The following day I informed Nicola that she ought to purchase some new bed linen. Scratchy, uncomfortable, synthetic, obviously. 'None of that weird Nordic duvet nonsense!' I said.

I also regrettably had to let go our long-standing cleaner. 'Sorry, Svetlana,' I said, 'but you are Ukrainian after all. Now do one!'

After which I went for my fortnightly short back and sides. A few stray hairs subsequently irritating my neck, I concluded that Alessandro, the owner, is of an, ahem, Latin (and also, I suspect, possibly homosexualist) persuasion. And yet as my weekly bath night falls tomorrow, I chose to endure the discomfort.

The next day, knotting my tie prior to attending church, I further informed my wife that I would prefer if, on our return, the Sunday roast had been blasted to within an inch of total carbonization. 'Well done is how we like the beef of old England,' is how I put it – rather sonorously, even if I may say so – 'and well done is how we Cramptons shall henceforth enjoy our meat.

'And be sure to leave the veg in the pressure cooker for a minimum of four hours,' I added as an afterthought.

And then, dammit, with just ten minutes to spare before the service started, the bloody Rover wouldn't start. Buying British can be such a trial . . .

You get the idea.

I was eleven when we held the last referendum forty-one years ago. I remember it all too well. Shops didn't open on a Sunday. Divorced mothers were fallen women. The boss was respectfully addressed as Mr So-and-So (never Mrs, nor Miss, nor – heaven forfend – Ms), mostly because the boss wasn't ever female, and partly because Ms was a term considered about as alien as the pizza, curry, muesli and other assorted new-fangled foreign muck then just starting to emerge on the high street.

General Franco was running Spain. Apartheid was going strong in South Africa. Hardly anyone, do-gooders apart, minded too much – after all that Mandela chap was a trouble-maker, wasn't he, good job he was safely locked up. David Bowie looked like a right dodgy bender. Feminism and environmentalism were strictly for loony lefties. Racist gags were all the rage on telly. Jimmy Savile, Rolf Harris, Cyril Smith and Stuart Hall were much-loved national treasures. When any of the two and a bit telly channels were actually broadcasting, at any rate.

These icons notwithstanding, as a rule, if you had a regional accent and you wanted to make your way in the media, politics, the civil service, finance, medicine, science, the law, business, the army or even, in some cases, sport, with aspirations to reach a national level of recognition, then you got rid of that accent, pronto. Otherwise, well, I know this northern fellow seems awfully bright, but he doesn't sound quite right, does he? I say we stick with Piers. He's a good chap.

What else? Oh yeah: kill a fox, ban women from the club, beat up a queer, frame a Paddy, grope a dolly bird, swill six pints and drive home, laugh at the disabled guy, bully the weird kid . . .

And so on and so forth. Turn the clock back to 1975? No, ta.

6 August 2016

Restored, revived, rejuvenated and rebronzified following our customary back-end-of-July fortnight in south-west France, here I am swinging once again into the Beta Male saddle. Feels good, this saddle, I must say. The worn leather, the stirrups, the rhythmic friction of the, er, pommel whatsit, mounting up is nothing less than a major case of oo-er missus.

Ahem.

I can't deny I needed a break from the rigours of columnar labour. When he toils away hacking at the sociocultural linguistic coalface, week in, week out, hewing and hauling mildly amusing, occasionally diverting observational nuggets to the surface for the entertainment of strangers, a man must sometimes award himself a rest.

That said, dedicated to bringing the news to the nation as I am, even as I lay on my lounger in jolly old Lot-et-Garonne, or stood around bored witless while my wife perused the local

markets, or stuffed my face in a series of sun-dappled squares, I
kept half an eye on the job. Mais oui and bien blinking sûr I did!
When you've found your vocation in life – mine being to bear
witness in a shockingly self-indulgent fashion to the minutiae of
my own existence – you're never truly off duty. Oh do please
shut up and get on with it, Robert.

There are five dining options in our local town – six if you
count the newly opened Bar des Arcades, but we're withholding
judgement on this addition for the moment. Four of the established five are distressingly French – two in the sense of enticing
tourists with rich French food, which my kids (and indeed,
sadly, my own digestive system) don't much like, and two in the
sense of ostentatiously not catering to tourists and therefore
being exclusively full of palpably hostile French people. Bottom
line: we go for restaurant number five . . .

. . . Which serves a mixture of classic regional cuisine and
contemporary international scoff. Magret de canard and cheese-
burgers, basically. Something for everyone, there. The clientele
is pretty much half French and half foreign. Foreign, in these
parts, being roughly equally divided between Brits, Dutch and
Scandis.

Our favoured place also does pancakes. The presence of
which on the menu allows me to ask the children, night after
night after night, regular as clockwork, if perhaps they fancy
taking a crêpe? A géant crêpe, ideally. To which they dutifully
say yes. To which I say they really ought to have had one before
we came out to eat. Witty, eh? I then amuse myself by asking the
waiter for a 'bum and raisin ice cream, s'il vous plaît'.

Can't beat the English abroad, eh?

Never mind that, though. I'm fully aware that all any regular
reader wants to know is whether I had any further hilarious
Gallic-based motoring mishaps in the Volvo. Right?

For the uninitiated, I should explain that for fifty weeks of the year I am a designated non-driver, my wife having decided long ago that I wasn't to be trusted behind a wheel in London. For the other two weeks, however, in France, I am allowed, under sufferance, to potter about in the twenty-year-old banger that used to belong to my mum and dad.

Three years ago, attempting to navigate my way – against Nicola's firm advice – along a bumpy, overgrown, deeply rutted forest track, I only went and got the blasted vehicle stuck. Had to be towed out by the neighbouring farmer. Nicola not happy.

I wrote a piece about it. And ever since, whenever I bump into a reader, this Volvo-in-the-forest column is all they want to talk about. Pretty much defines my career, that article.

No such drama this time, I'm afraid. Truth is, over two weeks I put fully three hundred miles on that baby – an average of more than twenty-one miles a day – without so much as a scrape. I did reversing, parking, hill starts, all sorts. One morning I went all the way to Issigeac. And back. And even with my son in the passenger seat urging me to let rip, take the racing line, overtake slow-moving farm machinery on blind corners and generally trying to be a bad influence, the journey passed off safely and securely.

Apologies. Contrary to popular opinion, this is journalism, not fiction. I cannot tell a lie.

If it's any consolation, whenever she was present in the car (and often afterwards, by way of an evaluation, or beforehand, by way of a briefing), Nicola relentlessly slagged off every last aspect of my performance. Speed, gear selection, sitting position, wiper usage, poor maintenance of windscreen squirters . . . nothing was immune. It didn't help that I wound her up by insisting on doing doughnuts in the yard each time we went out.

Not that I can do proper doughnuts, obviously. I just circle the car moderately fast on full lock shouting, 'Yee-haw, I'm in

The Dukes of Hazzard!' Which is amusing to me. If not anyone else.

10 September 2016

Once in a while, not often, I find myself thinking about my happy family, and my nice house, and my interesting job, and I start wondering if this whole Beta Male business is entirely fair. And then I think of all the things I'm no good at and all the skills I don't have and all the subjects I don't know about. It's quite a long list. Quite a profound list, too. Take music, for instance. Not only can I not hit two consecutive correct notes in a song, or extract two consecutive correct notes from any instrument, I don't fully understand what the word 'note' actually means. I don't really understand the difference, in the musical context, between the words 'note', 'tone', 'key', 'tune', 'melody', 'beat', 'pitch' and 'rhythm'. I've had it explained to me, and I've looked up the definitions, but I have no feel or intuition or intelligence regarding the distinctions.

Thus, while I can appreciate lots of forms of music, if I hadn't been told, not only would I not know why Mozart was any better than a band in the pub, I wouldn't necessarily know even that he was any better. I fundamentally don't understand what's going on.

The same goes for art. Perspective, I can get that – making things look further away by drawing them smaller, right? But when photographer friends start going on about composition, while I might understand what they're talking about in relation to a specific image, I can't then generalize what they say and apply it to another image. Same goes for something called 'use of colour'.

I'm not being deliberately philistine here – I rather like a lot of modern art; I go to galleries; I have been known to read occasional works of art history – I'm just being honest about the way I see the world. At exhibitions, I often find the biographical details and historical context of the artist's life more interesting than the actual work.

It's a bit embarrassing really, supposedly being a creative person and yet having no feel for either music or painting.

Nor acting, truth be told. When Gene Wilder died the other day, and all the obits on the telly were showing clips of *Willy Wonka and the Chocolate Factory* and *Blazing Saddles* and the critics were raving about how great Wilder had been, I was prepared to accept their verdict, but I couldn't understand how they'd arrived at it.

Even closer to home, I have no flair for foreign languages and (whisper it) have never fully got to grips with grammar and syntax and whatnot in my native tongue. Some people remark – in a nice way – on the simplicity of the language in this column. That's partly a matter of style, for sure, but also a matter of not having the confidence to use longer, more complicated words.

Further from my comfort zone, obviously, I find myself further adrift. I parted company with maths and the trickier sciences when I was about fourteen and it started going all x and y and particles instead of one and two and cutting open dead frogs. I still try to read the odd science book, but I struggle, even with the pop stuff. And besides, the idea that space and time can theoretically bend or run backwards is such obvious nonsense I can't take a lot of what I read seriously.

At university, they had to lay on extra classes to get me through the economics component of my degree.

As for more practical skills, again, as with music, it's not just about not having the skill, it's also about not having any appreciation of what it might take to acquire that skill. Again, this problem manifests as a struggle with the relevant words.

With cars, for example, I wrestle with nearside and offside, while torque and understeer remain a mystery to me.

I'm not exaggerating a lack of mechanical knowledge the better to come over all sensitive and intellectual. I hold practical know-how in high regard. I just don't possess it.

Even in sport, which I do know something about, I don't really understand what pundits mean by positional sense in football or reverse swing in cricket. And obviously the laws of rugby are as big a puzzle to me as they are to everyone else.

My recent enjoyment of a history of Trafalgar was marred by a failure to grasp the terminology of sailing. I know the jib (or boom?) swings around and clouts people overboard, but as for larboard and leeward and the rest, I have to really concentrate. Diagrams help. But I still fundamentally can't get my head around how a sailing ship can move even when the wind isn't directly behind it. Or why it floats, come to that.

All in all, you'd have to say getting tagged with a letter as early in the alphabet as beta is actually pretty generous.

Acknowledgements

It's almost sixteen years since I started writing Beta Male in *The Times Magazine*. In that time, I've been lucky to have worked under three superb editors, the first being Gill Morgan, who initially commissioned the column, largely because (she swiftly admitted) she'd come up with the title and was so pleased with it she needed someone to provide the accompanying copy.

That's how we roll – not always, but often – in the wonderful wacky world of journalism.

When Gill left the paper in 2009, Louise France took her place and proved an equally generous patron. When Louise stepped aside, Nicola Jeal has in recent years fulfilled the role of the woman who tells me what to do. At work, anyway. The other Nicola (see dedication) bosses my domestic life. Although each Nicola, given their nature, essays frequent raids on to the other's territory.

Suffice to say, without Gill, Louise and Nicola, Beta Male would not exist. I am enormously grateful to the three of them.

As I am to the many other colleagues with whom it's been my pleasure to collaborate. I am in their debt. All of them, without exception, have improved my efforts, whether via their diligent revision of my grammar or their inspired suggestions regarding content, style, tone, rhythm, and so forth. Chris, Amanda, Kevin, Emma, another Chris, Christian, Claire, Nigel, Simon,

James, Lorraine, Lisa, Colette, Louise, Grace, Tony . . . I'm sorry if I've forgotten anyone, there may well ought to be another Chris in the mix . . . you've done me proud. Thank you.

My fellow *Times* writers – in particular Alan Franks, Hilary Rose and Ben Machell – have over the years also been hugely helpful, even if they didn't necessarily know they were being so at the time. Which is to say, their chat, gossip and observations have provided me with a wealth of material. In the best traditions of the British press, I have gleefully and greedily stolen their jokes, insights, anecdotes and ideas. Cheers, guys!

I'd also like to thank my agent Mark Lucas and my publishers Larry Finlay and Bill Scott-Kerr, primarily for their patience, given this book has taken fully nineteen years to deliver. And it isn't even the same book they originally commissioned, way back in 1998. While the reading public still awaits the arrival of that volume, the completion of this one owes an enormous debt to the guidance, talent and acumen of my editor Andrea Henry.

My wife Nicola and my children Sam and Rachel (in addition to many other relatives, friends and colleagues too numerous to mention) have, over many years, also been wonderfully supportive. Other than when they haven't been, of course.